About the Author

Elmer L. Towns has become a recognized authority in the study of church growth. An earlier book, THE TEN LARGEST SUNDAY SCHOOLS, which went through six printings on its way to becoming a best seller, launched him into a vital interest in what makes a church grow. His sermon on the subject has been preached in over 300 churches all across America. Dr. Towns is the Vice President and Academic Dean of Lynchburg Baptist College in Lynchburg, Virginia, an aggressive school which trains pastors and workers to go out and become leaders in growing local churches.

AMERICA'S FASTEST GROWING CHURCHES

AMERICA'S FASTEST GROWING CHURCHES

Why 10 Sunday Schools Are Growing Fast

by

ELMER L. TOWNS

January, 1972

impact
books
Nashville, Tennessee

Dedicated to

The greatest Sunday School authorities
in
the United States
Dr. Beauchamp Vick, because at one time he pastored
the largest Sunday School in America, Temple Baptist
Church, Detroit, Michigan. Also because he was president
of Baptist Bible College, Springfield, Missouri. This
school and its heritage was responsible for pastors of 23
of the 75 largest Sunday Schools, according to the 1970
listing in *Christian Life* Magazine.
And
Dr. Dallas Billington, because he founded and pastors the
largest Sunday School in America, Akron (Ohio) Baptist
Temple.

Introduction

Three years ago, I wrote the book *The Ten Largest Sunday Schools,* which went through six printings and appeared on the list of 10 best sellers in the *Christian Bookseller* magazine. The story of the 10 largest Sunday Schools evolved into a sermon which I have preached over 300 times since beginning the original research.

Many friends have jokingly said to me, "Why don't you write a book on the 10 smallest Sunday Schools?" At first I laughed off their remarks, but I heard the phrase "10 smallest" so often that an attempt was made in *Christian Life* Magazine to write a series on 10 small, but outstanding, Sunday Schools. The articles failed to gain reader interest, and the series was aborted. People are not interested in small Sunday Schools, but they are interested in growing Sunday Schools because growth reflects life.

From this background has grown this book, *America's Fastest Growing Churches.* Many people were impressed with the larger Sunday Schools in America, first by their novelty, and second by the assurance that masses respond to the teaching of the Word of God. However, the principles used by the 10 largest were not applicable to many small Sunday Schools still struggling to break the mold of the "one-room Sunday School mentality."

This book is written to show how 10 churches are growing *today,* just as the first book was written to show how 10 Sunday Schools did it in the past. Readers may not agree with the principles used by these 10 churches, but they cannot deny the fact of their growth. These 10 churches are growing and reaching the masses in our modern age, when most mainline denominational Sunday Schools are declining in attendance.

There is no easy analysis for declining attendance. Some have gone down in attendance because of creeping liberalism. When a humanitarian message is substituted for the gospel, apathy sets in. Lack of vision kills other churches. Churches stop growing when they cease to provide expanded facilities and expanded staff. Also, the employment of wrong principles and methods kills the church. A prime illustration of this is the old wives' tale that "quality leads to quantity"—i.e., the good church will be a growing church. However, there is no cause and effect relationship between quality and quantity. I have seen many outstanding churches that have not grown in the last 20 years. By the same token, I know of some churches which thrive on gimmicks and grow on promotion, yet the results are disastrous because the Word of God is not rightly taught.

When listing the causes for church decline, we cannot overlook sin. The minister who runs off with the deacon's wife, or the treasurer who absconds with the finances can stunt the growth of the church. Also, subtle sins eat away the heart of the church. When the standards of Sunday School workers are broadened and separation from sin is minimized, God takes the spiritual power away from the teacher. Sin ultimately takes away a Sunday School teacher's incentive to evangelize a neighborhood.

Perhaps the greatest reason for decline in Sunday School attendance is its subtle shift in the past few years from evangelism to education. The Southern Baptists built the largest denomination in America on the motto "The Sunday School is the evangelistic arm of the church." In the past 15 years we have seen the Sunday School movement reach a high in attendance and begin its gradual decline. During this time, we have also seen it shift from an evangelistic instrument in the hand of God to a sophisticated "Christian Romper Room."

Edification is absolutely necessary, but in the list of God's priority, evangelism comes first. The Sunday School teacher, armed with a mandate from God to lead every child in the community to Christ, will produce a growing class. At the same time, the class whose goal is to "mature the whole man in Christ" loses some of its spiritual intensity and drive. The 10 churches in this book place evangelism primary in purpose, hence they are growing. Their methods may differ, but their mandate is unmistakable: They are to "Go into all the world and preach the gospel to every creature" (Mark 16:15).

This volume tells the growth of 10 fast growing churches in America. I am not sure these churches are the *fastest* growing in the nation. In fact, no one knows which churches are the fastest growing. When analyzing growth, two methods are used: first, growth is measured by percent; and second, growth can be computed by rate over base. In the first case there are many churches growing from

50 to 100 in attendance, which is an increase of 100 percent. But another school grows from 500 to 550, the same rate over base increase, but a much smaller percentage growth. At the same time, a third church grows from 1800 to 2400, a healthy increase of 600 rate over base, but low statistical gains. What is the fastest growth?

The basis of determining growth for this book is both percentage and rate over base. A church had to be considered growing faster by percent and rate over base, than those of comparable size, to qualify for this book.

Also, quality became a factor in choosing 10 churches for this volume. In my previous book, I had no choice but to include the 10 largest Sunday Schools. The choice for this second volume was not as confining, since no one is sure of the exact fastest growing churches. So I included 10 churches that not only could be a challenge by their expansion, but also be an example by clear use of biblical principles and obvious employment of quality biblical teaching.

This volume, as the first, measures size and growth by actual Sunday School attendance. Some may attempt to determine size by Sunday School enrollment, but such a survey would reveal "paper growth" of expanding rolls. But this does not reflect vitality or actual accomplishments. Also, church membership does not reflect the size of a church. Since most churches do not take accurate attendance at morning worship services, this comparison could not be made. Therefore, the best criterion to determine size and growth is Sunday School attendance.

Robert Raikes began the Sunday School in 1780, and since the early days, numerical attendance has been used to reflect the strength of the movement. Therefore, Sunday School attendance is the basis of comparison. The next question to face is, "What is a Sunday School?" This question will be more prominent in the next 10 years. Even though some may attempt to make the modern Sunday School a "religious Sesame Street," the definition of Sunday School reflected in the movement begun by Raikes is still valid. 1. The Sunday School involves factual instruction in the Word of God, not employment of the catechism used predominantly in religious education during Raikes' day. 2. The Sunday School employs laymen to teach and administer the program; the clergy teach religious education, as was predominant in Raikes' day. 3. The Sunday School centers on the children of the streets, not the children of church members, as in religious education of Raikes' day. As a matter of fact, many clergymen fought the Sunday School, refusing the ruffians access to the church. 4. Finally, the purpose of Sunday School was evangelistic, to bring pupils to Christ. Religious education during Raikes' day centered on edification. The Sunday Schools which will thrive in this decade will be those that remain true to the original purpose of the Sunday School, which reflects the aim of the New Testament church.

After carefully studying Sunday School growth for several years I have concluded that most Christian educators are wrong about several factors believed to cause growth. First, many Southern Baptists believe "The laws of Sunday School growth" published in *The Pull of the People,* by J. N. Barnette, caused them to become the largest Protestant denomination in America. I do not agree. Too many schools have organized according to these laws, yet became stagnant. The laws were not causal, but Sunday School growth is the result of the strong evangelistic thrust of Southern Baptist churches. The laws of growth were used to organize and consolidate the gains from evangelistic outreach. The lack of growth in the contemporary Southern Baptist statistics stems from less emphasis on evangelism today than in the past.

Many leaders in the National Sunday School Association believe that Sunday School growth will come from a relevant ministry organized to meet the needs of the individual. Maybe the answer depends on what the needs are. Meeting needs can produce self-centered Christians, resulting in a humanistic program, centering on the pupil. These Sunday Schools do not grow. If needs are viewed through the eyes of God, where the pupil is seen as a sinner needing salvation and spiritual growth, then the Sunday School will expand.

Programs, methods and organization are not causal factors for growing New Testament churches. As a matter of fact, organization that leads to institutionalization will harm growth (see chapter 11). The chapter on "The Sociological Cycle of Church Growth" attempts to analyze the vitality of a church in its growth stages. Also, the chapter attempts to set forth factors that lead to deterioration or attendance decline.

Great leaders build great churches. The spiritually gifted pastor who determines to capture a city for Christ has the potential to build a great church, and he usually does it through the Sunday School. Chapter 12 analyzes the natural gifts of charisma and how the Holy Spirit can use a man to build a work for God. This chapter does not deal with charisma as defined in the Pentecostal churches. The term "charisma" relates to sociology.

Some will criticize including only Baptist churches in this book. Some denominational churches are growing, but usually, more Baptist churches are growing and more Baptist churches are large.

(Eighty-four of the 100 largest Sunday schools in *Christian Life's* 1971 listing were found in Baptist churches.)

Some will criticize the fact that 8 of the churches in this book are listed in the yearbook of the Baptist Bible Fellowship, Springfield, Missouri. This is the fastest growing organized body in America ("The Fastest Growing Sunday Schools in the U.S." September, 1968, *Christian Life*). Also, as I travel the country, I find Baptist Bible Fellowship churches more anxious to grow and, in fact, I find more of them registering numerical growth. This movement has lessons that should be shared with other churches. Their success should be an encouragement and stimulus to all Bible-believing churches.

These 10 churches were chosen because they reflect the biblical definition of a church. "A church is a group of baptized believers in whom Christ dwells, under the discipline of the Word of God, organized for evangelism, education, worship, fellowship, and the administration of the ordinances." Many religious groups meeting on Sunday morning do not qualify to use the New Testament term "church." Our decade will see theological debate over the doctrine of ecclesiology. "What is a church, its composition, nature and purpose?" The "Jesus People" on one extreme deny it by their practice. Interdenominational advocates deny its priority by their claim that the church has failed, thus justifying their existence. Anti-establishment sentiment seems to be growing and, with it, anti-local-church feelings. These 10 churches have an expressed priority to organize themselves according to the requirment of the Word of God.

I have been in each of these 10 churches, examining them as closely as possible. I used 3 questionnaires and held in-depth interviews with the pastor and staff. Each chapter has been submitted to the pastor so he could verify the facts, evaluate the story for a true representation, and eliminate any embarassing inclusions.

I have tried to remain positive in reporting the facts of this book. We have too much negative witch-hunting in today's journalism. My commitment is to evangelize the lost, and I question if this can be done through constant criticism. These 10 churches have faults, as do all churches. But their strengths outweigh any criticism, and we can all learn from them. Therefore, I write as I do.

If all churches were growing as these, and if all churches were teaching the Bible as these, we might have the revival in America that is possible through the power of the Holy Spirit.

Sincerely yours in Christ,
ELMER L. TOWNS

Table of Contents

13

Chapter 1

How to Get Started Right

Calvary Heights Baptist Temple

St. Louis, Missouri

Rev. Carl Baugh and his wife pulled a Chevy automobile loaded with suitcases, the kids, and the family puppy into St. Louis, Missouri, the last Friday of August, 1969. Baugh had a vision of starting the largest Baptist church in St. Louis and reaching the city for Jesus Christ. Late Friday afternoon was not an ideal time to make contacts, but moving with definite strategy, Baugh implemented his predetermined plan. First, he located a plot of ground—5.2 acres at the intersection of Interstate I-244 and the Page Avenue Expressway—and made verbal commitment for the property. Two hours later he had arranged to rent the North Junior High School in Creve Coeur, Missouri.

Twenty-seven persons attended the Sunday School the following Sunday when Calvary Heights Baptist Temple opened its doors in the temporary quarters of the rented public school. An option was quickly signed on the acreage. A $23,000 down payment was needed within 90 days on the total price of $90,000.

The Bible Baptist Church of Savannah, Georgia, had pledged financial support to the salary of Baugh and paid the expenses for moving the pastor from Florida to St. Louis. This was a bold new venture of faith in building a self-supporting Baptist church from a single supporting "mother church." The Reverend Cecil Hodges, pastor of the Savannah church, explained, "We took the St. Louis project as a challenge from God because we trusted Carl Baugh and knew his ability to start a church."

14

Nine families committed themselves to the vision, and on Sunday, November 23, 1969, Rev. Cecil Hodges of the Savannah church presided and organizational services were held. The church was constituted three months after its first meeting and the congregation immediately extended a call to the Reverend Carl Baugh to remain as pastor, adding to his title "founder."

Before the Sunday School opened in St. Louis, Baugh went on record as setting a goal of 100 pupils within the first three months, 300 within the first year, at which time a Sunday School wing of the edifice would be built. Baugh further extended his vision and stated he expected 500 pupils within three years and 700 at the end of the fourth year. Finally, Baugh climaxed his projection by stating he expected 1,000 in Sunday School within six years.

Christian Life Magazine, impressed with the integrity of Baugh, committed itself to a plan of "church watching" over the next three years to see if Baugh would reach his goal. Robert Walker, editor, stated, "Often we write about churches who have reached a goal, but we would like to follow the St. Louis church so our readers may be encouraged as they see a church unfolding before their eyes." *Christian Life* Magazine went on to state, "Foolish or visionary, only time will tell. But Baugh does have precise goals and plans." Most magazines report success stories after they have been accomplished; however, *Christian Life* Magazine intends to give periodic growth reports of this infant Sunday School. The magazine went on to state, "Why choose Calvary Heights Baptist Temple in St. Louis? For one reason: Carl Baugh has been used of God to pastor two other growing churches. If he can build growing Sunday Schools in other cities, he will probably do so again."

Carl Baugh had been pastor for six years of Edgewood Baptist Church in Rock Island, Illinois, during which time the Sunday School attendance grew to 500. Baugh moved to Tampa, Florida, and led West Gate Baptist Church to a height of 702 in Sunday School. The membership grew by 265 additions in his last year there; altogether 370 conversions were listed that year. Mayor Greco of Tampa invited Baugh to visit his office anytime and explain the unparalleled rapid growth of the Florida church. Baugh left West Gate Church in Florida, successful by all standards, because of his growing burden to go as a missionary to St. Louis. When his wife developed an allergy to salt water and had to move from the ocean climate, Baugh felt this was God's seal of approval on his direction to St. Louis.

Even though Baugh was visionary before the founding of the St. Louis church, he felt success was not automatically guaranteed in

The first service was held in early fall, 1969.

St. Louis but stated, "The past 15 years have evidenced great Sunday Schools in our movement (Baptist Bible Fellowship), progressively making great spiritual strides while employing New Testament methods of personal contact."

Reasons Why the St. Louis Work Would Prosper

Baugh wrote a prospectus giving five reasons why he felt the St. Louis church would prosper. The following list is adapted from his manuscript written before the church was founded.

1. *A Burden from God.*—Baugh was reared in Springfield, Missouri, and had often heard of the need of a great evangelistic church in St. Louis. Each year the burden grew heavier, until he was constrained to begin the church. According to Baugh, "A passing fancy with the city or temporal enticement did not prompt a move." (Baugh took a drastic cut in salary.) Years of constant direction from the Lord prepared Baugh's heart for coming to St. Louis. He states, "Since God is directing, He will prosper the work. God's callings are His enablings."

Baugh indicates there is a sense in which a God-called minister has a burden for every field in the world. He states, "I have flown into sprawling metropolitan areas across America and have visited hamlets on foreign soil. Rarely have I ever seen great masses of people without realizing that before me lies a mission field and that each soul will face God in eternity." Baugh indicated this general burden for reaching lost people accompanied his call into the ministry. In the second pace, Baugh indicated a definite, permanent burden for St. Louis came when he realized there was not a church effectively reaching the entire city. He asked himself the question, "Will I be successful in building a vital city-wide ministry?" As he looked into his human limitations he expressed doubt. But Baugh declared that by faith and determination he was going to reach the city.

2. *The New Testament Methods Employed.*—Baugh believes that most secular and denominational ministries are attempting to de-emphasize the individual through mass conformity. In opposition to this practice, the New Testament accentuates the value of the individual for whom Christ died. "We exist to reach people for Jesus Christ," stated Baugh. Jesus used and recommended personal encounter, as did Paul. Baugh plans to build his work on personal encounter called soul winning. This will be accomplished by house-to-house visitation. He feels people are still complimented when you care enough to visit their home, personally representing Jesus Christ.

In stating the purpose, Baugh wrote, "Our purpose is to present the ministry of the local church and not simply to erect an edifice with its organizations and committees. But we intend to provide the institution that was founded by Jesus Christ, which is composed of baptized believers from all walks of life who have come into a personal encounter with a living, resurrected Christ. Baugh is uncompromising in his desire to build a New Testament local church.

3. *The Location of Church Property.*—Baugh believes the location will help insure success at the new work. According to him, 150,000 cars pass the location every 24 hours on the expressways. Baugh told the infant congregation that as Jesus instructed lights to shine and said that a city on a hill cannot be hidden, so their new property on a hill will also reflect the message because it is within sight of over 4,000 new homes. The State Department of Transportation estimates that between three to five million people pass the site every year. In addition to the immediate location of the bypass, the church has access to 15 miles of scattered new subdivisions. A survey in consultation with a real estate company substantiated Baugh's analysis that the spot was ideal for building a local church. Dr. Charles Billington, co-pastor of Akron Baptist Temple (largest Sunday School in America), stated, "For starting a church, this is

the most ideal spot of any I have seen in America." As Baugh stood on the grass-covered hill looking down the expressway he stated, "The fields are white unto harvest."

4. *The Spirit of Success.*—Baugh built the church on the old formula "Nothing succeeds like success." Personal contact in the home normally guarantees that there will be response to the claims of Christ at the time of public invitation. The altar call is strategic in building a growing Sunday School. Baugh believes that if he is faithful as a soul winner, when the new Christians come down the aisle to openly profess Jesus Christ, their open confession will motivate the congregation. This public image of response is contagious. Baugh indicates, "We encourage people to take a public stand for Christ; this in turn encourages others with whom we have not had time to deal personally." From the very beginning, Baugh never entertained a doubt that souls would be saved.

5. *Growth of the Work.*—Baugh began knocking on doors inviting people to Jesus Christ. A 29-year-old blind man was led to Jesus Christ in the home. Another family had several children, and they indicated a desire to ride the Sunday School bus. Within three months attendance had passed the 100 mark. Several Christian families, expressing a desire to leave their "dead" church, united with Calvary Heights Baptist Temple. One Sunday the Edmond Sansovini family, returning home from church, saw the temporary sign on the five acres and noted the cars parked in front of North Junior High School. That evening they returned and visited the small congregation. Sansovini, successful by the world's standards, was executive vice-president of the luxurious Chase Park Plaza Hotel located on Forest Park in downtown St. Louis. Sansovini, a former Roman Catholic, had been saved for ten years. When he met the vision and optimism of Carl Baugh, their spirits were immediately welded together. Sansovini used his expertise in public relations to give the struggling congregation city-wide coverage. The *St. Louis Post-Dispatch* carried a front-page article on the Calvary Heights Baptist Temple and an additional article on its rapid growth. Attendance campaigns were planned, and attendance reached over 200 on special occasions.

During the summer of 1970 the local press announced that a $30 million shopping center was to be built across the freeway from the church location. Thousands of additional people would be passing the site every month. The value of the church property doubled overnight. The bank of St. Louis attempted to buy one acre for $100,000 and when the church refused, raised the offer to $150,000.

Pastor Carl Baugh

At the close of the first service, Pastor led the group to the hill of the future property and claimed it for God. The church now owns ten of those acres.

After one year, the congregation that began with an empty bank account had a net worth of over $1,100,000.

Sansovini became so immersed in the work of the church that when offer of a $30,000 raise came, transferring him to Miami, he refused because he felt God wanted him to remain in St. Louis and help build the Calvary Heights Baptist Temple. Other associates were added, even though a salary could not be given. The Reverend Gary Rimer was called as associate pastor, Ralph Green assumed the position of minister of music and the Reverend Richard McKirihan became minister of youth.

First Anniversary

A dilapidated nursing home with a four-car garage was situated on the five acres, but had not been used for a number of years. Vandals had taken their toll and weeds had grown over the property. The congregation rolled up its sleeves and went to work. The partitions were torn out of the four-car garage, making it one large room capable of seating 200. Walls were painted, acoustical tile installed on the ceilings, and plumbing renovated. Space heaters were installed in the corners, a platform was built, and new tile floors gave the place a "like-new" appearance. During August, 1970, Sunday School attendance dropped appreciably as members and pastors spent their time in repair work, rather than visiting. But everything had to be in order.

The author (Dr. Elmer Towns) was the speaker on the first anniversary, September 20, 1970. One hundred and seventy-six attended Sunday School (not the highest attendance) and over 250 came for the church service. Three people responded to the invitation, reminding the whole congregation that the church was still in the soul-saving business.

Not only was the refurbished nursing home dedicated, but the first anniversary also featured the ground-breaking for a 400-seat auditorium to cost $100,000. Immediately after the morning service, the congregation walked to the top of the hill overlooking the expressways. In four directions, the observer could see more than 4,000 homes. Then, I had the privilege of turning the first shovel of sod, commenting that, "This broken ground symbolizes the fact that we plan to *plow* the hearts of the community and sow the Word of God." Baugh turned the next shovelful of sod and stated, "As I plant this shovel, let it be known that I am planting my life in St. Louis." Every staff member and deacon was then given opportunity to turn a shovelful of sod and give a testimony. Then Baugh turned to the congregation and announced, "This church does not belong only to the leaders, but to us all." He handed the shovel to a nine-year-old boy who in turn took his scoop and simply said, "I love Jesus." Just as Baugh believes it's every member's job to build the church, every person present took part in turning the sod. After 200 members had dug a large hole, the contractor jokingly said, "Pastor Baugh is practical; we've got a start on the project for tomorrow morning."

A. J. Cervantes, mayor of St. Louis, sent a congratulatory telegram: "September 20 will be a historic day, not only for your church, but for the greater St. Louis area. The eyes of St. Louis are upon you and your church."

The new 400-seat building was occupied February 7, 1971. Most pastors might take such opportunity of great accomplishment to bask in the sunlight of success—but not Baugh. On the walls of the brick and glass foyer, he hung the artist's plans and architect's prospectus for a 3,000-seat auditorium.

How to Start a New Church

Carl Baugh is considered successful in planting a new church. Several ministers have requested an interview with him, looking for principles of starting New Testament churches. The following list was written by Baugh before he began the St. Louis work.

1. *Pastoral Direction.*—Baugh believes that New Testament evangelism has been successful when a God-called man with a message and vision threw his entire life into the task of reaching lost people with the gospel. Baugh points out that dedicated men have always determined the direction of history. He believes that the minister should give direction to the local church. This does not mean that co-workers and officers are eliminated or negated. Instead, laymen can have a greater personal ministry because the pastor gives definite direction to the growth of the church. Then layworkers can involve themselves in planned action, making the most of their time and gifts. Thus, the personal ministry of officers and workers becomes enlarged to greater capacity. Baugh deeply believes that, even though the pastor is the leader of the congregation, the final decisions are made by congregational vote.

Baugh has publicly stated that a young man who is afraid to lead and make decisions can never establish a church. He reminded a young student from Baptist Bible College that Satan hates the local church and is opposed to the establishment of a local church. Therefore committee action or natural evolvement will not bring a church into existence. Baugh indicated a man must, with spiritual courage, carve out of a rock a church that will bring glory to Jesus Christ.

2. *Personal Contact.*—Baugh began at once to lay plans to visit every home in the immediate area. He wanted to give a personal invitation to attend the services of the church, but he realized that "enlistment evangelism" alone would not be successful. His house-to-house visitation carried a soul-winning emphasis. "Does anyone in this family know Jesus Christ?" Baugh often asked. As he left a home he reminded them, "We preach the old-fashioned gospel. A — person or family can be changed by the power of the gospel."

3. *Bus Ministry.*—At first, Baugh rented bus services to reach children for the Sunday School. Ed Sansovini donated the first church bus and shortly thereafter three buses were in operation, bringing people to Sunday School. His entire thrust begins by picking up children for Sunday School, then reaching into the home to win parents to Jesus Christ.

4. *Training of Central Workers.*—Baugh realized he could not perform every ministry in the church by himself. Therefore, he felt immediate necessity to train a corp of workers who would be loyal to the local church. A 6:00 P.M. Bible Institute was inaugurated on Sunday evenings before the evening service for training. Workers were taught Bible knowledge and soul-winning techniques. In the early days of the church, the evening service was turned into a class on prophecy, with Baugh using a large chart to teach the signs of the end of the age. Prayer meeting also constituted a time of training his staff to reach the neighborhood. Baugh believed that, in the final analysis, every meeting of the church should train laymen to be better workers for Jesus Christ.

5. *Bible-preaching Curriculum.*—One of the basic foundations of the new church was a belief in the authority of the Word of God. Baugh believes that the human heart is hungry and nothing satisfies it like knowledge of the Word of God. The teaching and preaching services of the church are designed to give exposure to the Word of God because, as Baugh stated, "God always uses the Scripture to convict the soul of sin and implant eternal life."

6. *A Warm, Vital Song Service.*—The services at Calvary Heights Baptist Temple were never designed with ritual or liturgy in mind. Baugh believes that gospel songs warm the heart of the common man. He was overheard telling his song leader, "Our music is not designed to create a ritual service, but gospel music communicates

The new 3,000-seat auditorium in the planning stages

the message to the human heart." Baugh believes that, since the common man heard Jesus gladly, he could reach the common man today through gospel songs. He went on to state, "After the heart of a man is warmed with gospel music, the preaching of the message falls on fruitful soil."

7. *Enlarged Public Ministry.*—Baugh explained this point by stating, "We are attempting to reach the community by every means possible." Sansovini prepares newspaper releases and advertising. A church paper was instituted which Baugh distributes weekly. Special campaigns are planned to give each member motivation to reach his neighbors. Baugh indicates that he instructs his people to use a campaign properly, so visitors may be brought to the church.

The challenge to Carl Baugh in Calvary Heights Baptist Temple is not unusual. There are hundreds of cities in the United States that have no aggressive evangelistic church. The fields are white unto harvest and the laborers are few. God has planted Carl Baugh in St. Louis to reach that city. Whether he does, only time will tell. However, if past success is indicative of future growth, Calvary Heights Baptist Temple should become a large, aggressive evangelistic church.

Chapter 2

Capturing a Town for Christ
Thomas Road Baptist Church
Lynchburg, Virginia

Thomas Road Baptist Church, the fastest growing church in America, is built on the principle of *saturation*—reaching every available person, by every available means, at every available time. The human architect of this super-aggressive church is Jerry Falwell, a man with perhaps more personal magnetism (charisma, Chapter 12) than any other minister in America. This chapter is divided into two parts: first, The Improbable Man in the Unlikely Circumstances, and, second, Saturation Evangelism.

The Improbable Man in the Unlikely Circumstances

Jerry Falwell, the improbable man in the unlikely circumstances, built one of the largest churches in America in sixteen years. The Thomas Road Baptist Church was begun in June, 1956, when 35 adults and their children gathered for the first meeting in the Mountain View Elementary School in Lynchburg, Virginia, a school Jerry Falwell had attended as a boy. It is unlikely that any of them in their fondest dreams, ever contemplated the phenomenal growth and ministry over the next sixteen years, reaching an average attendance of over 5,000 and diversifying its outreach to the whole world with the gospel.

Jerry Falwell, the son of a rich man, attempted to build a church in Lynchburg, Virginia, an unlikely place. Lynchburg was Falwell's home town, sophisticated by Southern standards. The city's church background was dignified by church standards. Besides, many would think, a home town boy could not build a large church in Lynchburg because the Scriptures teach, "A prophet is not without honor, save in his own country." Yet, the tentacles of the gospel reaching out from Lynchburg to the whole world begin in the heart of Jerry Falwell. His influence as a pastor, educator, administrator and author make him a candidate for the position "the twentieth-century Spurgeon."

Jerry Falwell is evangelism through the Thomas Road Baptist Church, a gigantic congregation where 50 to 100 respond weekly to the invitation and receive Christ. Jerry Falwell is evangelism through the Old Time Gospel Hour, broadcasting the gospel weekly through the electronic miracle of television over 140 stations. Jerry Falwell is camp evangelism through Treasure Island, where over 2,000 children come free for a week every summer, many receiving Jesus Christ. Jerry Falwell is evangelism through Elim Home where men under the curse of alcoholism come free of charge to receive spiritual therapy and renewal. Jerry Falwell is evangelism through Hope Aglow Ministries where the gospel is preached to convicts in prison throughout the Eastern coast. Jerry Falwell is evangelism through the Lynchburg Christian Schools, giving quality Christian education to children and teenagers in their formative years. Jerry Falwell is evangelism through the Lynchburg Baptist College, training and motivating young men to build churches throughout America, similar to the Thomas Road Baptist Church. Jerry Falwell is evangelism through the printed page, the Old Time Gospel Hour press distributing five million brochures and pamphlets last year, and *Word of Life,* a monthly newspaper reaching 80,000 homes. Jerry Falwell is evangelism through pastors' conferences, stimulating pastors to build super-aggressive local churches similar to the Lynchburg congregation.

When he was a young teenager, Falwell's mother would leave the radio tuned to Charles Fuller, "The Old Fashioned Revival Hour," on Sunday morning, knowing full well that Jerry would not get out of bed to turn off the program. The seeds of the gospel were planted in his mind as a young man. During his sophomore year at Lynchburg College, Jerry visited the Park Avenue Baptist Church in Lynchburg. He was impressed with the sermon and seriously considered going forward during the invitation, obviously under conviction. During the week, at study in his pre-mechanical engineering course, Falwell recognized that the revival style of preaching by Reverend Donnelson at Park Avenue was like what he had heard over the radio. The following Sunday evening, Jerry took his buddy, Jim Moon, to the church with him. The building was packed, with over 300 people attending the service that cold winter evening. The ushers put the two young men on the front row.

Falwell eyed an auburn-haired girl playing the organ. "I'm going to get a date with her," he told Jim Moon. Moon picked out Macel Pate at the piano. (Both boys married the opposite choice they made that night. Jim married Delores Clark, the organist and Jerry married Macel Pate, who has been the only pianist at the Thomas Road Baptist Church.) Jim Moon, lifelong friend of Falwell, is the co-pastor at the church and teacher of the second largest Sunday School class.

Jerry came to church that evening with the intention of going forward, but he lacked courage. An elderly white-haired gentleman put his hand on Falwell's shoulder, and said, "I'll go with you." Garland Carey knelt at the altar with Falwell and led him to Jesus Christ. No one spoke to Moon, he just followed and was also converted. The example of Garland Carey speaking to Jerry Falwell continues in the Thomas Road Baptist Church to this day. During every invitation Christians are seen speaking to the unsaved. Even teenagers can be seen reaching over pews with open Bibles to witness to other young people, inviting them to go forward. Seldom does an individual come down the aisle alone. There is someone walking with him. "I'll go with you" is the common invitation to those attending the service.

The Thomas Road Baptist Church cannot be correctly analyzed apart from understanding Jerry Falwell. He is the leader of one of the greatest churches in America. He has been used of God to lead scores of lost people to Jesus Christ. Robert Walker, editor of *Christian Life* Magazine, presented a plaque to Falwell which stated: "America's Fastest Growing Sunday School, the Thomas Road Baptist Church, Lynchburg, Virginia. Sunday School attendance increased by 1471 per week from a previous average of 3386 in 1970 to 4857 in 1971, as listed in *Christian Life* Magazine. Presented to Dr. Jerry Falwell, pastor, September 1971." In response, Falwell said, "In honoring me, you have honored all of the workers of the Thomas Road Baptist Church, for without them we could not exist." Even in spite of Falwell's humble reply, every church worker knew his labor would not produce the present spectacular results without the leadership of Jerry Falwell. Therefore, the following conclusions are offered as insight into the heart of Jerry Falwell to help outsiders understand how he has built such a fast-growing church.

1. *A commitment to the ministry.*—Nothing stands in the way of Falwell's desire to build a great church. He works 52 weeks a year

Pupils sing the songs of Sunday School.

Dr. Jerry Falwell

without vacation, managing to sandwich in one day or so a month for a physical repréi. This author has seen Falwell minister and preach all Saturday, then drive his Buick back to Lynchburg, arriving Sunday morning at 6:00 A.M. Falwell stated, "It's amazing how a Pepsi can revive a man," then proceeded to preach Sunday morning, visit in the afternoon, and preach again Sunday evening. Finally, he remarked on Sunday evening that he was tired. Also, this author has seen Falwell sit in a motel room answering mail from 11:00 P.M. to 1:00 A.M., and finally open a Bible and pore over its contents for the next hour before going to bed.

Falwell's commitment to the work grows out of a driving conviction that people are lost and going to hell. Last summer, a middle-aged gentleman in the cardiac section of the local hospital called for Falwell. The nurse on duty stood in the door and would not let him in the area. After a few minutes of "verbal fencing," Falwell bluntly stated, "If you don't move, I'm going to walk past you because that man needs spiritual help and he has requested that I visit him." The supervisor of nurses finally arbitrated the argument and Falwell witnessed to the man and led him to Jesus Christ.

Falwell's deep commitment to the ministry is not measured by the size of a crowd. One afternoon he spoke to the Michigan Sunday School Convention in Cobo Hall, Detroit, Michigan, that seated 16,000. The following night he ministered in a small country church to less than 100 present.

During a Sunday morning invitation, Falwell directed the author to a man in the audience. The pastor had witnessed to the man the previous week but was not able to lead him to Christ. "Go get him to come forward and receive Jesus Christ," said Falwell. The man did. Falwell returned home from a speaking engagement one night at 2:00 A.M. and in the morning made a call on a family that had just lost a teenage daughter. Time and physical limitations do not keep him from ministering the Word of God.

During December, 1971, Falwell promoted a "My Heart's Desire" campaign. He had every person in the church write the name of one person for whom he would pray and work to get saved. Thousands of cards were turned in. Viola Pillow turned in the name of her boss, and two weeks before "My Heart's Desire" campaign actually began, her boss walked forward to receive Christ as Saviour. She expressed deep appreciation for Falwell's helping her have more concern to reach people. Those who know Falwell intimately, realize he will spend any effort, money, or program to reach people with the gospel.

2. *A faith in God's provision.*—Most preachers interpret "God's provision" as a supply of money. Falwell interprets "God's provision" to apply to power to lead people to Jesus Christ. He believes the enabling hand of God must be operative in the soul winner's life to lead people to Jesus Christ. The lights in Falwell's office were on late one evening and a member of the church who was visiting dropped in to see him.

"I can't seem to lead anyone to Christ," said the discouraged layman.

"How many did you expect to reach this evening?" asked the pastor.

"You can't expect somebody to get saved every time," was the excuse.

"That's why you can't win any," reasoned the wise pastor. Falwell expects God to work in the heart of every person when the gospel is preached. His faith gets results. He sees sinners get saved every time he preaches.

Falwell also believes God will provide the finances. On Christmas Sunday, 1971, he announced to the congregation, "Pray with me for a quarter of a million dollars needed for television outreach." Half of the congregation felt he was visionary, the other half knew he would get the money because Falwell doesn't step out on faith but what God answers. Monday morning, he had a check for $250,000.

Missionary Don Stone had been called home from Taiwan because of the sickness of one of his children. Stone needed $2,200 for plane fare back to the mission field. Falwell shared the need of the $2,200 with the congregation and challenged them, "I'll give the first $100; are there 21 other men who will give a hundred dollars each?" Men jumped to their feet all over the congregation. Within 90 seconds the money was raised.

The Reverend J. O. Grooms, director of soul winning, testified in his first week at Thomas Road Baptist Church, "When Jerry said he needed $150,000 to meet the bills that week, I knew this church was on its last leg." He wanted to pack up and go home. However, Grooms testified that the money came in by Friday.

3. *Sensitivity to people.*—Many have commented that the Thomas Road Baptist Church is people. Another went so far as to say, "Everything Jerry Falwell touches turns to people." However, to Jerry Falwell, people are not digits on an IBM card. He has a deep compassion for the 11,000-member congregation and can call almost all of them by name. The author questioned the customers at a local restaurant; all knew Jerry Falwell, but less than 25 percent could name the mayor. After a church service, he has time to speak to a

The Sunday morning service at Thomas Road Baptist Church

millionaire who wants to give a large gift, as well as counsel the teenager who has a pressing problem. All the children in the church call their pastor "Jerry," even though the dignified members of the congregation attempt to elevate his position. When the children see him, they still sing out, "Hi Jerry!" After a crowded Sunday morning service, Falwell held a little child in his arms and states, "If this little girl is not claimed in five minutes, she's mine." His love for all is apparent. Even though he walks onto the parking lot in a suit, he will stop to throw a football with the fellows and, according to their testimony, he can still throw a pass 70 yards in the air.

Seldom does Jerry Falwell go into the home of a needy widow without asking to see her Bible. He leaves a twenty-dollar bill in it for necessities. Alan Roberts, a student at Lynchburg Baptist College broke his leg and was facing financial difficulties. During a pastoral call, Falwell left a handful of large bills on the night table as he walked out. According to one businessman in the church, "Who knows the many thousands of dollars he has distributed out of his pocket in an unpretentious manner around this city?"

Falwell loves the sinner but hates the sin. This is characterized by his personal leadership against a proposed city ordinance for liquor by the drink. Yet, his deep compassion is reflected in the ministry of Elim Home for the forgotten man of society who struggles with alcoholism. Also, the jail ministry is an extension of his care of men behind bars.

4. *The bright future of soul winning.*—One of the elements of a charismatic leader is the fact he has never failed, at least outwardly. The hand of God has been upon Jerry Falwell to guide him in building a great church. If he has made mistakes in leading the church, they are not evident to the observer. There has never been a hint of a church split. The numerical and financial goals that he sets are reached. The congregation is optimistic that the future is bright and God is going to use their pastor to make a serious impact on the United States. As a result, individual members give more money and spend more time carrying out the work of the gospel than in the average church. Falwell believes he will average 10,000 in Sunday School; therefore, he has committed himself to build more buildings, promote new programs, hire new personnel and to contract more television stations. Should God use Falwell to reach America, it will truly be "the improbable man from unlikely circumstances."

Saturation—Capturing a Town for God*

The secret to the phenomenal growth of the Thomas Road Baptist Church is found in the blueprint for evangelism called "saturation evangelism." Falwell explains his concept, "Saturation is preaching the gospel to every available person at every available time by every available means." The young preacher points to the experience of the early Christians in Jerusalem, who saturated the city with the gospel. The disciples were arrested and brought before the Sanhedrin, and charged, "Ye have filled Jerusalem with your doctrine" (Acts 5:28). This insignificant verse is the key to the ministry of Jerry Falwell. He states, "We want to fill Lynchburg with the gospel." Therefore, he takes the gospel to all people by all means: radio, TV, newspapers, Sunday School busing, the alcoholic ministry, telephoning, jail ministry, organized visitation, brochures, mailing, etc. Falwell indicates, "I want to saturate the community and to saturate the conscience of every individual. He believes that every man at some time in his life comes to the end of his self-reliance and turns to God. The young pastor states, "When a man seeks God, the Thomas Road Baptist Church will be there with the gospel, and we can help that man find God." G. D. Smith was called to the emergency room of Lynchburg General Hospital; he found the mangled body of his son on the operating table. His son had crashed his

---

*A complete study of saturation evangelism at The Thomas Road Baptist Church is found in the book *Church Aflame,* by Jerry Falwell and Elmer Towns (Nashville: Impact Books, 1971).

motorcycle head-on into an automobile on the interstate. Smith paced the dimly lit halls of the hospital, praying, "O God! . . ." but the prayers bounced off the walls. He promised God to repent, but he had broken many other promises made to God. Smith just could not pray. He was the owner of G. D. Smith Lumber Company and the Virginia Appalachian Lumber Corporation, but was now faced with a problem that money could not solve. Finally, Smith accepted God's Son and salvation. He remembered the pastor of the Thomas Road Baptist Church visiting him. Also, he had watched the church service over TV and received the church paper, *Word of Life*. Smith visited the church the following Sunday and is now one of the faithful members who was reached through total saturation of the community.

Falwell explains his evangelistic program as (1) Contact, (2) continuous contact, and (3) a consciousness of no limitations. Falwell believes the church should not be limited because of poor location, poor building or what is felt to be a limited population. He states, "I found in Lynchburg, Virginia, a city of 53,000 people, that there is no limitation of what can be done for God." Falwell gave an example: "When the church started 16 years ago, we thought that 500 would make a large church, but when we reached 500, we found ourselves reaching for 1,000, then 2,000, next 3,000 and finally 5,000." Then he went on to state, "I honestly believe we can average over 10,000 each Sunday in Thomas Road Baptist Church." When the possibility of over-saturation was pointed out to Falwell, because one of every ten people in the city attended his church, he stated, "We can grow because there are many lost people in Lynchburg."

Falwell believes the population explosion is an ultimate challenge to the church. There are four billion persons in the world, and experts in demographics predict that by the year 2000 the population will more than double. Falwell indicates that the Great Commission is a command to get the gospel to every person in the world. He indicates, "God never commands us to do anything but what He also enables us to do it." He believes that nothing will take the place of teaching and preaching the Word of God from house to house. But at the same time, he feels we can never expect to reach the world by these conventional methods alone. He states, "Saturation evangelism is demanded for several reasons. First, the population explosion demands it. Primitive methods of evangelism will not suffice. Second, the imminent return of Jesus Christ commands that we reach every man with the gospel—soon. And third, people are dying every day." Jerry Falwell believes we will stand accountable at the judgment seat of Christ for our failure to utilize every available means to reach "every creature."

One event in the emergency room of the local hospital transformed Falwell's attitude toward ministry *now*. He had been called by an accident victim who had heard Falwell preach the gospel over radio. "I'm not ready to meet God," the suffering man whispered. Falwell dealt with the man concerning his soul, for he was obviously under conviction.

"Please step out of the way for a few minutes," the doctor asked Falwell. The bleeding had not stopped. From the other side of the room, Falwell watched—the man died. "I will never let anyone interfere with soul winning again," stated the determined preacher.

Even late in his ministry he had not forgotten the lesson. Last summer, a large mutual fund company had been offered free to the Old Time Gospel Hour. Falwell was to meet with the board of directors including two U. S. congressmen, the president of a bank and the former president of the Security and Exchange Commission. Falwell was witnessing to the young stock clerk who had heard the Old Time Gospel Hour over TV and wanted to make a decision. The board of directors asked Falwell to come in. Even though they were offering him the company, and the combined influence of their position should have impressed Falwell, he kept them waiting while he witnessed to the young clerk.

Saturation evangelism takes many forms. At the Thomas Road Baptist Church it takes the following avenues:

1. *Telephone evangelism.*—In preparation for a large day, Falwell asked 109 people to come forward during prayer meeting. He gave each of them one page from the telephone book (Lynchburg has 109 pages in the phone book). Each one was supplied with the mimeographed greetings to use in asking people to come to Sunday School. The instructions read: "Hello, I'm Mrs. Jones from the Thomas Road Baptist Church. My pastor, Jerry Falwell, asked me to phone you to ask you to come to our services tomorrow. Dr. Falwell will be speaking on the subject, 'Will we know one another in heaven?' He felt you might have some interest in this message and wants you to be his personal guest for his class in the morning." The only exceptions were businesses and other obvious numbers that should not be called. Falwell's Sunday School class averages 2,000. He maintains personal contact through 100 group captains, each having between 30 and 100 people to follow up. Each week, group captains phone those who are absent from Sunday School.

2. *Sunday School bus evangelism.*—The church has two full-time bus directors, the Reverend Jim Vineyard and Carrol Ferguson, and two full-time mechanics to keep the 80-plus fleet of buses in operating condition. Under Vineyard's leadership the number of bus riders grew from 800 in April, 1971, to 1700 in November of that year. Five buses reach into Roanoke, 50 miles away, to bring people to Sunday School. On a recent large day, 450 people rode the buses from Bedford, 25 miles away.

3. *Cassette evangelism.*—All the services at the Thomas Road Baptist Church are recorded on tape and made available to shut-ins in convalescent homes, servicemen, college students, and members who desire to purchase them from the office.

4. *Radio evangelism.*—Because of the influence of the Old Fashioned Revival Hour and Dr. Charles E. Fuller, Jerry Falwell had a deep conviction that his new church should be on radio. Therefore, in 1956 he purchased a half-hour daily broadcast over WBRG and began reaching the city through this medium. For a number of years, Falwell drove to the radio station and made the broadcast live each morning at 6:30. Later, broadcast facilities were constructed in his office. Now, according to surveys, it is the most listened-to program on any station in Lynchburg during that time slot. Falwell does not preach to his audience, but rather "chats" with the city. He feels people do not become weary of a conversational approach over a long period of time. This broadcast is taped and distributed to over 26 other stations.

5. *Television evangelism.*—Falwell believes that, without question, the most effective medium for reaching people is television. No matter how poor a family may be, there is very likely a television set in every home. When the church was approximately one year old, Falwell approached the television station concerning a half-hour program. They had no videotape facilities, therefore he produced a live telecast every Sunday afternoon at 5:30. In 1967 black-and-white television cameras and equipment were made available to the church and they began producing the morning service. Later, he began to make the program available to other stations in the general area of Virginia. Today, the Old Time Gospel Hour is seen over 120 stations throughout the U. S. and Canada, costing approximately $25,000 dollars a week to keep the program on the air. Last year the program was switched to color when a half million dollars was invested in new color equipment. Falwell is careful not to have a "produced program." Rather, the cameras look in on the morning service and catch God at work as the Scriptures are preached. Many religious

programmings are adapted to the TV camera, but Falwell believes the TV camera should adapt to what God is doing in the church.

6. *Printing evangelism.*—Falwell believes printing is an inexpensive means of getting the gospel out. Paper is an inexpensive item. He points out that every church should have an offset press. A printing press can be obtained for a reasonable price. If a church has little finances it should start with a mimeograph. He feels that every church should have a newspaper for continuous contact with homes in the area. He goes on to state that most pastors could never reach every home in the neighborhood every week, but the church can go into thousands of homes through the printed page. Everyone who visits the Thomas Road Baptist Church is placed on the mailing list. Over the years, this has proven to be the greatest prospect file for the church. Visitors receive the *Word of Life* newspaper permanently until they request that their name be taken off the list. Falwell states, "People will realize the church has not forgotten them and is showing a continued interest in them." In addition to this, sermons and Sunday School lessons are printed and sent out to those on the mailing list.

The printing ministry has grown from a small beginning to an extensive outreach. At first, a secretary did the necessary printing. First one printer, then another, and finally three are necessary to print the five million items produced in the shop each year. Some complain the church sends out too much literature. Falwell confesses, "If we're only getting a small percentage of people to read our literature, we are making a terrific impact." He believes printing is one of the main reasons why there are so many visitors and guests coming into the church, aside from TV, radio, the visitation program, the alcoholic ministry and Treasure Island Youth Camp.

7. *Promotion evangelism.*—The church uses campaigns and Sunday School contests to reach people. Falwell announced to his teachers, "We've got to get over these silly ideas that it is carnal to use promotion to win people to Christ." He went on to state that if more people are reached with the gospel, then more will be won to Christ. Falwell indicated, "K-Mart, Kroger and A&P are all in the promotion business and they don't feel they are wasting money by running full-page advertisements." People may criticize Falwell's promotion but he states, "If promotion is wrong, secular organizations have some inefficient public relations people working in their organizations. But that is not the case. They build new buildings; people are going to purchase in their stores. If it will work for them, why not for the Lord?" Falwell follows the statement made by Dr. Jack

Hyles, "Most preachers will do anything scriptural to get people to the house of God, but I will go a step further. I will do anything that is not against Scripture to get people to the house of God."

8. *Camping evangelism.*—Each summer over 1,500 campers come from ghettos, tenant farms and the exclusive areas of Lynchburg to Treasure Island Youth Camp. All come free, and last summer over 300 found Christ. The strength of the ministry is in Bible teaching, evangelism and close association with the local church, Thomas Road Baptist Church.

For several years, Falwell had been praying about and looking for a suitable piece of property on which to establish a youth camp. A friend was taking him on a boat ride up the James River one afternoon when they passed the YMCA island. This is a 35-acre island located near the elite section of Lynchburg. There was a beautiful and very large home on the island, and a bridge that connected it with the city. The man-made canal was on the city side of the island, while the main body of the river flowed by on the Amherst County side. The island immediately captured Falwell's attention. He was even more fascinated with its beauty and its perfect location for a youth camp ministry. They circled the island several times. As they made the last circle, Falwell bowed his head and claimed this island for the Lord, by faith. Although the friend assured him the island was not for sale and that the land was priceless, Falwell believed that God would enable the church to procure it. Later that day, he visited the owner and was told that it was not for sale. The man's wife disagreed with him and showed an interest. Several days passed, and Falwell went back again. Both husband and wife were now interested. They suggested he make an offer for the island. He did, and they accepted.

There are many young people in the ministry today because of Treasure Island Youth Camp. There are young people today who are becoming useful citizens and servants of the Lord in various places because of this outreach.

9. *Deaf evangelism.*—The Thomas Road Baptist Church has the only complete ministry to the deaf in Central Virginia, providing free transportation and an interpreter for every service.

10. *Educational evangelism.*—Two schools operate in the facilities of Thomas Road Baptist Church under the charter of Lynchburg Christian Schools, of which Falwell is president. The Lynchburg Christian Academy has over 600 students in kindergarten through grade 12, receiving a superior academic education in a Christian environment. The Lynchburg Baptist College began operation with 241 full- and part-time students in the fall of 1971. (The author is

Aerial view of Thomas Road Baptist Church

co-founder and academic dean of the college.) Falwell believes that
within the next ten years, over 100 men can be prepared to go out
and build churches comparable to Thomas Road Baptist Church.

11. *Alcoholic evangelism.*—Twelve years ago, Falwell established
Elim Home under the direction of Mr. and Mrs. Ray Horsley. Lo-
cated in Amherst County, the dormitories sleep 18 men and the
Horsleys give constant spiritual care to the men who come for help.
Restored men now live normal lives, thanks to the transforming
power of the gospel. Some men high in the business field and others
who are laborers thank God for the life-changing experience at Elim
Home.

12. *Prison evangelism.*—The Reverend Ed Martin is an associate
pastor at the church and a director of Hope Aglow Mission, an organized ministry to reach into the penal institutions of America with
the gospel. Martin has visited prisons in 41 states to preach, counsel,
and follow up those who need the gospel.

Conclusion

The Thomas Road Baptist Church is making more effective use
of mass media than perhaps any other church in America. In a nation that has spawned the electronic generation, perhaps we catch
some insight into the reason for its outreach. But media alone will
not create a strong, growing New Testament church. The message
must be biblical, finances must be collected, buildings must be built
and Christians must be spiritually fed. Growth is seen in a church
that "puts it all together." Jerry Falwell is God's man who has simply claimed by faith the promises of the Bible. He has experienced
answers to prayer. God has built a great church because God can
work through the life of Jerry Falwell.

Chapter 3

The Heart of a Pastor

The United Baptist Church

San Jose, California

The United Baptist Church, San Jose, California, is an energetic, dynamic church, growing because of aggressive evangelism, described as having "electricity-like outreach." Since great churches are a reflection of gifted men, the reader cannot understand the United Baptist Church without understanding its pastor, the Reverend Larry Chappell. When he came in September 1966, 15 people greeted him at his first prayer meeting, and the following Sunday 126 were present for Sunday School. Since that time the congregation has reached a high attendance of 2,315. Attendance is averaging 1,298 during the fall, 1971. The United Baptist Church has a leader who has banded together his laymen with a vision of reaching not only San Jose, but the Santa Clara Valley. Chappell has made no apology for his goal, to build the largest Sunday School in the world through evangelism by reaching lost men and women and discipling them in a New Testament church.

The church is located in an area once called the Hamilton Range, the hazy blue Santa Cruz Mountains in the background. The once-lush orchards are continually giving way to expanding subdivisions. Some call the former "garden of Eden" an ever-expanding concrete expressway. United Baptist Church is built on a Western motif, each classroom opening onto a walkway or second-floor balcony.

But a church is more than buildings—it is people. The swings and playground equipment used for weekday school activities are filled with children before Sunday School begins. Visitors are ushered to the registration tables in the patios. Ushers are located at strategic spots to help children get to classes. The people at United Baptist Church seem happy and expectant; they enjoy coming to church. There is a driving inner compulsion among the lay leaders of the church. Church is more than enjoyment, it is a way of life, for each staff member and lay-worker shares the vision of reaching lost people for Jesus Christ.

Joel Potter, a policeman on the force in San Jose, was saved and baptized at United Baptist Church, as was his wife. He is now an active deacon in the church and a great soul winner. On one occasion this last summer, during the church visitation program, he led 13 people to Jesus Christ. Larry Harper accepted Jesus Christ a little over two years ago and is now bus director at the United Baptist Church and a young people's Sunday School teacher. Ben Smith, also saved and baptized in United Baptist Church, is mechanic for the bus fleet. For over two years, he has invested his Saturdays in working without pay to keep the 20 buses on the road. There have been times when he worked all night on the buses just to keep them rolling on Sunday. John Hamilton was an accountant for General Electric. He stated, "I have been a Christian for 20 years, and have never been in a church that did not preach the gospel; but I have never been as excited as I am about the ministry here at United Baptist Church." Hamilton took a 30 percent cut in salary to leave General Electric and come to work full-time for United Baptist Church as business administrator. Ed Railey takes care of the sound system in the church. At one time he managed a radio station and is now actively engaged in the Lord's work helping keep the gospel on the radio through the United Baptist Church and the tape ministry.

These men are only reflective of the growing band of dedicated lay-workers assembled at United Baptist Church. United Baptist Church has great laymen because the leader, Larry Chappell, has the magnetism that draws men into the service of the Lord. Of course, the power of the Holy Spirit draws these men into the work of the local church, but God always uses an instrument to accomplish His purpose on earth. God's instrument in San Jose is Larry Chappell to reach men for Christ and then inspire them to the ministry that they are now doing. The people feel Pastor Chappell is the best preacher in the world. Mrs. Pat Carr testifies that when her family was looking for a church to attend, "We were told over and over again that all Larry Chappell preached was salvation and there was no deep Bible teaching. However, my heart now thrills to the messages he preaches. They are simple enough that my Junior High students

Students preparing to leave Sunday School

enjoy his preaching—yet deep enough that I have learned more about Bible truth in the last four years than I did in the 15 years I attended another church. Whether Sunday morning, Sunday evening or Wednesday evening, we hear pure Bible exposition."

But preaching alone does not build a church; leadership begins with example. Chappell is a leader when it comes to personal evangelism. He has never asked his people to make soul-winning calls that he was not willing to make himself. Many American preachers exhort laymen to soul winning, yet the congregation seldom responds. The people of United Baptist Church are soul winners because their pastor is engaged daily in reaching the unsaved.

Chappell's willingness to do even the simple jobs motivates his men to extra dedication. One layman testified, "On several occasions I have seen him put on a pair of overalls and do a job that needs to be done." Another layman testified, "On one occasion this past summer, he was out driving a tractor along the back, leveling the terrace for landscaping." On another occasion, the man ordinarily gasing the buses was sick. Dick Seaton, then assistant pastor (he has now returned) saw Pastor Chappell driving a bus to fill it with gas and check the oil.

The young pastor indicates, "When going to college, I went all-out to win souls. I remember at the age of 18, writing to my parents that I was going to spend my life doing what I loved most—winning souls." Today, Chappell writes, "The direction is now the same, only more intense. I now have my direction confirmed by God's plan—the church. If, my life is aimed at winning souls, I want to be successful at that job. The reason is simple, God wants His people to be progressive, positive, and successful. God is positive, and from my study, I learn that He has been successful in every task He has undertaken. Since God is not programmed to fail, why should I?"

A young preacher may question Chappell's desire to be successful. To this he responds, "If I am to be a soul winner, what is the measuring rod for success? Some might say quality of converts; I agree. Quality must precede quantity, for without quality, quantity cannot become a reality. Therefore, I must spend time with God and have a quality life according to God's laws. I want to reproduce after my kind. Therefore, I want to have a quality life so the people of my church will have quality lives. Also, remember, the goal of my life is to be successful at seeing people saved; therefore, I must produce quality converts in order to multiply my soul-winning ministry through others. For this, God has a plan: win them, baptize them, and teach them. I pursue this with all of my might. Following this reasoning, I must conclude that quality is not the goal—quality is a means to an end. The purpose of a Christian is to reach and win as many people to Christ as possible."

Chappell reflected on his desire to build a large church, "If a man devotes his life to being a fruit harvester, his success is not measured by the quality of the fruit, but the quantity he amasses. This illustration has obvious weaknesses, but the truth is, God has called us as laborers in His harvest. I want to reach as many people as possible through God's plan—the church. Therefore, my success is measured primarily by the number of souls won to Christ and enlisted for service in the church. I am pressed by a driving burden to reach as many people as possible." When someone asked, "Why?" Chappell simply says, "My friend, I want a large church because I don't want your husband, wife, children, in-laws, mother, dad, neighbor, friends, or acquaintances to go to hell. Therefore, I must carry my burden and yours too."

On several occasions Chappell has been accused of being egotistical because he wants to build a large church. He notes that these critics do not understand his motives, and his rebuttal is projectionism: "Those who make this cry are usually little men, failures, with egos that need desperately to be boosted. They project their selfish motives onto me. I do not work for a large church, I work to win as many people to Jesus Christ as possible. The large church is not my aim. The large church is the product of my goal, reaching people with the gospel."

Larry Chappell was converted at age 13 at an American Sunday School Union camp at Cortez, Colorado. His first eight grades were in a one-room, one-teacher school, that was also used for church on Sunday. During his early teen years the small group of worshippers were organized into a Baptist church. Chappell later attended Pillsbury Baptist College, Owatana, Minnesota, and then pastored a small church in California, before coming to San Jose. Reverend Jack Baskin, of the Foreign Mission Board of Baptist Bible Fellowship, invited Larry Chappell to visit a ministers' fellowship at the First Baptist Church, Costa Mesa, California. "I was floored at what I heard at the ministers' meeting," said Chappell. "Each pastor expected to build a great church, win souls to Jesus Christ and reach cities." His wife, Maxine, indicated, "He spilled excitement for weeks after coming back from Costa Mesa." She went on to observe, "Larry was a new man, as though he had been in the presence of God." After this event, the United Baptist Church drifted away from the Conservative Baptist Church of America into the Independent Baptist orbit.

Chappell is an evangelistic expository preacher, covering the Scripture verse by verse. He indicates, "Sunday morning I preach to the lost; Sunday evening I preach to Christians, attempting to meet the needs of my people." Chappell does not allow anyone to fill his pulpit for Sunday morning. Even the great R. G. Lee came and sat in the front row. Chappell has a deep conviction that "his people bring guests to hear him preach." There may be better preachers than Chappell, but a visitor does not come to hear great preaching; he will judge the church by the pastor. "If they are converted under my ministry, they will continue," feels Chappell. He has found by previous experience that members do not work as hard to bring guests when he is out of the pulpit.

Jim Schaller, chairman of the deacon board, indicated that, "Chappell has wisdom beyond his years." When speaking of the pastor's leadership, he indicated, "Chappell is not a dictator; our church is a democracy. In a dictatorship the people must follow the leader. We *want* to follow Chappell." Schaller continued, "Chappell leads by love and wisdom." Schaller indicates, "I will do anything he asks, because he is God's man to reach this community." In a day when many fundamentalist preachers are autocratic, Chappell still says "Yes, sir" to other gentlemen.

Chappell does not introduce a guest speaker to his people but rather introduces his people to the guest speaker. To the author he said, "I would like you to meet the greatest church in the world. I plan to spend my life here." Marion Tirri, the first person Chappell won to the Lord in the home in San Jose, is still in the church, faithfully serving the Lord, and is one of the best soul winners in United Baptist Church.

Chappell testified, "God called me to lead His church. My faith has grown each year to expect more from God. First I expected 200, then 500. Breaking the mental barrier of 1,000 was a crisis; now I believe the sky is the limit." Since Chappell believes it is the preacher's fault if the church does not grow, he feels lack of growth at United Baptist Church will be his fault.

The Church

In 1940 a small mission Sunday School established by the American Sunday School Union was organized into the Evergreen Baptist Church in the fruit orchards of the Santa Clara Valley. Not far away stood another small, struggling work, the Tropicana Baptist Church. Because of the small size of both congregations, the two were combined into the United Baptist Church in 1960, with

Pastor Larry Chappell

twelve charter members who worshipped in a refurbished horse barn. Two years later a prefab church was purchased and United Baptist Church continued to struggle.

When Pastor Chappell came to the church, it was a member of the Conservative Baptist Convention, but Chappell has led them out of that relationship, stating, "I didn't want a national committee determining the position of my church."

Upon his arrival, Chappell began to take personal responsibility for the direction of the church. His first task was to pull leadership responsibility into the pastor's office and take direction of the business management. John Hamilton, the Programs Coordinator for the church, was an accountant for General Electric, and replied that he "thought centralization of authority was great; if we were going to accomplish growth we needed a central head." Next Chappell did away with the office of Sunday School Superintendent and took that responsibility to himself. No standing committees were reappointed for the following year. Chappell indicated that if committees were needed, they would be appointed by the pastor in consultation with the deacons and be dissolved after their work was accomplished. The aim of Chappell's reorganization was to convert the Sunday School from the traditional mold into an aggressive evangelistic instrument that God could use to reach the entire Santa Clara Valley with the gospel.

During the reorganization, seven bank accounts for Sunday School, general, missions, special accounts, etc., were abolished and a centralized budget was instituted with a cost-fund accounting system. Hamilton coordinates the finances with a vice-president from a local bank, keeping the church operating on a sound financial footing, acting as comptroller, purchasing agent, and superintendent of buildings and grounds. Chappell indicated, "John Hamilton took the responsibility of details off me so I can attend to the ministry." Each Saturday afternoon, Chappell sees a financial statement so that he knows exactly how much money is needed on Sunday.

The church auditorium is simple: folding chairs, asphalt tile floors, and no air conditioning. There is no liturgy or ritual to aid in the worship service. The preaching of the Word of God is what attracts people and keeps them coming, according to Pastor Chappell.

When church is over and the benediction is pronounced, a bell is rung to inform the children's churches of the benediction. Kids tear out of the classrooms, happy as children leaving public school for home. They run, play and yell in the schoolyard and race for the best seats on their bus. The patio in front of the church is full of people, and Chappell knows that the warm evangelistic thrust brings the crowds to church.

Those who visit the church reflect every walk of life. Women are seen in house dresses and fashionable dressmaker suits. Some men have dungarees and white tee shirts; others, white shirts and ties.

The church is one of the best-integrated in America, with no problems among the races because San Jose is a well-integrated neighborhood. About 125 black children attend the Sunday School (this count was made by the author and was not available from the church). When Chappell was asked how many blacks attended his church he replied, "We don't have any blacks—all we have are Baptists." The black children are in the church by design, because the Sunday School bus goes into their neighborhood. A Spanish-speaking class was just instituted in Sunday School. When asked about racial problems, a layman answered, "Blacks give us problems just as whites, but we treat them all fairly and that's why they continue to bring their friends."

John Hamilton circulates among the classes on a Sunday morning, administering the school—making sure children are in the classrooms. He saw six black high schoolers get off the bus and start walking up the road. Hamilton intercepted them and indicated that if they ride the bus they have to stay for Sunday School. The black teenagers took the admonition well, knowing that black and white are treated equally by the staff.

Two little black boys walk up to a fence and look into a neighboring yard at a dirty-faced, barefoot girl playing on a tricycle. "Ask your mommy if you can come to Sunday School." A teacher came over to get the two second-grade boys for class. They explained, "We gotta git dis girl to come."

Growth

Growth is characteristic of United Baptist Church. It was stated, "If anything, we are successful at packing people into buildings." Last Easter, a mother who was a first-time visitor, brought two children and looked into one of the classrooms. Seeing the room so packed, she said to an usher, "I wouldn't want my children in that classroom—it's too filled." As she walked to the parking lot, the usher went to help her get her children in the car, and she said, "You don't need more people, you need more buildings."

When Chappell was asked why so many people come to his church, he simply said, "We have an aggressive program." San Jose is one of the fastest growing cities in American. However, Chappell comments, "People don't come to our church—we have to go after them."

The church has built three buildings and remodeled another in the past four years and, according to Chappell, "Each time we get a building completed, we have outgrown it before we move in." Chappell believes that if a church is doing God's work, growth is the natural outcome. He went on to state, "There is no such thing as a good *little* church. If it is good, it will grow and become large." He went on to comment, "Quality and quantity cannot be separated. If a church has quality teaching, it will grow into a large quantity." He continued his argument: "Some pastors deceive themselves thinking that even if they are small, they have a quality ministry, and that's not true." He concluded, "Large churches must have quality or the masses will not come." Chappell deeply believes the standard he has set for himself: "If the hand of God is on a church, people will become converted, then baptized, and become a part of numerical results of growth."

Chappell believes in statistics: "Figures help us know how well we are doing in the ministry." As an illustration, 85 percent of the present adult members were saved in United Baptist Church; very few church members transfer into the church.

Chappell preaches growth to his people all the time. He has constantly said, "We are not going to be a small church." As a result, some members left because they saw no end to the growing process or constructing new buildings. He indicated that on several occasions he thought the attendance would level off at 200, 400, or 500. When preaching growth, Chappell does not set attendance goals such as 4,000 or 6,000. "Unrealistic figures scare people." However, he has said United Baptist Church will become the largest in the world. He has a five-year plan to reach 3,500 by 1974.

Chappell clarified his concept of numerical growth, "If a church emphasizes soul winning, numerical growth will take care of itself." Some of the members who have left complain that the church is in one continuous revival meeting and the people have no time for themselves. Chappell replied, "We are organized to reach people and will bear down. Just as long as lost people in San Jose are going to hell, we will try to reach them."

There have been Christians visiting from other churches who have admitted they did not want to become a part of this church. They simply did not want to work as hard as the other members. Chappell is clear: "People know they are not going to be spoon fed, but will have to work. United Baptist Church is a place for people to serve, support and go reach the lost." This is by no means a museum for old saints but a workshop right in front of the doorway to hell.

When attendance had leveled off at 500, Chappell brought a recommendation to the church to purchase eight used school buses from Perrysville, Indiana, for $7,000. The bills in the church were mounting and some of the individuals doubted the wisdom of in-curring a $7,000 debt. Chappell challenged the folks to "go and soul-win, and new converts would pay for the buses. These buses will help us reach 1,000 in Sunday School." The vote was unanimous, and by the following fall attendance had reached 1,000, vindicating Chappell's decision.

Chappell indicates Sunday School busing is not a principle, but a tool. He feels the principle is evangelizing and reaching as many as possible; the tool is the bus. Every captain visits on Saturday and during the week.

Recently, Louise Seaton visited all day on Saturday for a special day (Seaton Sunday—Dick Seaton was soon to return to serve there). That Sunday Mrs. Seaton had 253 on her bus. She had three buses and made two trips with one bus. Her bus area covered only 20 blocks. On the same day, Terry Thompson and Sid Cleveland had 232 on their buses. Seven buses on that Sunday went over 100 and two went over 200.

Commitment calling is the plan used for Sunday School busing at San Jose. The captain visits on his route and asks each home he visits, "How many can we expect to ride the bus tomorrow?" After a person rides the bus to Sunday School, the captain goes back to every home, every week. "Can we count on your children riding the bus tomorrow?" he asks. This way, he knows the living conditions as well as the pupils. The purpose of commitment calling, visiting the riders every week, is to reach the parents for Christ. The largest attendance was reached when 1,833 rode the 18 buses on one day. The church averages between 40 and 50 riders per bus, each week. One of the staff members meets every bus and greets the children as they arrive. The bus is logged in at the time of arrival and attendance count is taken. Approximately 10 percent of the bus riders are adults. Unlike many other churches with a bus ministry, over half of the bus workers visit for riders in areas with $30,000 homes and above. Thirteen of the buses are used for Sunday School classrooms.

Chappell employs the "high-attendance day" philosophy to motivate his people. "We previously held a campaign to break 1,000 on a one-time basis to convince our people we could do it. After that, we felt we could average 1,000 pupils on a continuing basis." Chappell went on to explain, "I expected that we would drop back to our previous level after the high-day promotion, but we haven't done so." Usually the church retains a high percentage of those who attend. The church has doubled its Sunday School attendance every two years. In 1969, during the fall campaign a high attendance of 1,256 was reached. In the spring of 1970, 1,358 was achieved; and in the fall of 1970, 1,666 was reached. Then in the spring of 1971, 1,773 was recorded.

Now people expect to be in a continual building program. The young minister announced, "It's not *if* we are going to build a new building, but *when*; not *if* we are going to buy property across the street or next door, but *when*." Chappell went on to say, "We must keep the mental attitude of the people on a positive note, expecting growth. We *are* moving ahead, the question of *when* is a matter of timing."

The Reverend C. W. Fisk, who worked in both First Baptist Church, Hammond, Indiana, and United Baptist Church, indicated one advantage of working in San Jose is that more baptized converts stay in attendance than converts did at the First Baptist Church of Hammond. The adult department has been the fastest growing in the Sunday School.

When a person comes forward during the invitation, he is taken into a side room to be counseled by a soul winner. At this time he is led to Jesus Christ, then presented to the church as a candidate for baptism. If the person is coming forward as a public profession of faith, he is baptized immediately. When young children come forward, a permission slip is sent home with the child, seeking the parents' approval for baptism. Chappell indicates, "We baptize children, but only through a follow-up ministry." The children in grade six and down are not in the auditorium for the Sunday morning service, therefore not as many of them come forward for baptism. However, after visiting and counseling with the parents, Chappell believes that children should be baptized if they have received Jesus Christ and understand what they are doing. He answers his critics, "To discourage a child against baptism is to encourage him to disobey God. I won't take that responsibility." He goes on to state, "When we baptize a 10-year-old, we are fulfilling biblical priorities."

Chappell baptizes adults immediately after conversion, which may mean the following Sunday. There are many families—father and mother—who are won to Christ through the Sunday School busing ministry. Chappell brings both father and mother into the baptistry and baptizes the mother first. He announces, "Upon your profession of faith in Jesus Christ, I baptize you in the name of the Father, Son and Holy Spirit." When the person is brought up from the water, a chorus of *amens* greets him from the congregation echoing their approval. Chappell indicates one of the advantages of immediate baptism is that the corporate expectation of a congregation is transferred to the new believer, that he is expected to fulfill New Testament obligations upon him.

Organization

Chappell points out the following organizational principles that guided him in the early days of the church. (1) "We began baptizing immediately after conversion." This is biblical and it helps to hold in the church those who are saved. (2) "I needed help in the ministry." Chappell told the infant congregation that a bus and then a secretary were needed, in that order. The first bus was purchased in April, 1967. (3) Promotions and advertisements would be used to attract people to hear the gospel. The church uses newspapers, direct mailings, flyers, special days, radio, and contests. Chappell believes in spending little actual time in Sunday School on promotion but investing the time teaching the Word of God. He stated, "I never believed promotion would work as effectively as it has. One out of three who came to Sunday School through promotions has gotten saved." (4) Chappell instituted a weekly teachers' meeting where he keeps the spirit of his people revived to expect great things from God. (5) Chappell constructed a flow chart of responsibility and reorganized the organizational authority of the church. Delegation of authority is the key to Chappell's ministry. He has indicated, "A pastor will multiply his own ministry by extending it through other

Special-Emphasis Sunday

people." He went on to indicate, "The ministry should never be centered in gimmicks or promotion, but in the hearts of the preacher and the people."

When Chappell first came, the church did not have an established Sunday School enrollment as most schools. Hamilton indicated, "We grew so fast that enrollment got awkward. As a result, the only records we keep are church membership. When people attend our church they are put on a permanent mailing list, but we do not have Sunday School books with enrollment. Also, names are kept in prospect and contact visitation files so individuals that quit attending can be followed up." Today the church has a full-time record co-ordinator who administers the Sunday School enrollment records.

The lay leadership of the church is young; so are the full-time staff members. Chappell indicated he prayed and asked God for certain types of men, who were young and aggressive leaders who could be trained and inspired to reach the city of San Jose. A survey of the adults of the congregation reveals that almost every man does something for God. Chappell indicates that a trained layman with proper direction is a powerful instrument in the hands of God. He also points out, "We don't want a lot of activity and committee work out of our men, rather we want scriptural results. Laymen will work ten times as hard to get souls saved as they will to sit on committees or to fulfill Christian busy-work."

Chappell has the philosophy that if he treats a man as a man, he will do a man's job. If he treats a man like a kid, he will do a kid's job. He said, "Every man in my church can do what I can do; I consider no one a threat to my leadership because this is God's church and God is the leader."

Chappell made 114 visitation calls in one day; however, now he phones before making the visit so that his time is not wasted driving all over the valley. Everyone on the church staff is required to visit. The secretaries are given half-days off for calling on the unsaved. The staff at United Baptist Schools, located in the church, must attend visitation on Thursday evenings.

The workers are organized into pairs and sent out visiting Thursday night and Friday morning. This does not involve the 40 workers who visit on Saturday and during the week. Each pair of visitors are given four cards or assignments which they are to return to the church after making the visit.

In April 1971, Chappell called his staff together for an executive session. The previous Sunday 1,773 had been in Sunday School and there was absolutely no space for expansion. The city would not allow the church to construct a new building because no space was available to expand parking. Chappell announced, "We are not going to let circumstances keep us from growing." At that time the church had six adult classes. He announced that by combining all of the adults into one auditorium Bible class, four rooms would be released for space to teach children. (The auditorium was the only space for expansion.) Some of the staff members presently teaching adult classes wanted to keep their ministry of teaching, but they realized the perplexity. Each staff member then expressed willingness to give up his class to provide extra space for children's classes.

Tithing is expected of all of the members. Hamilton, who keeps the book, indicates that some of the members give 20 percent or more of their income to the church. When asked how this is possible he indicated, "People are willing to give money to see the unsaved converted."

Chappell was asked to answer a number of criticisms that have been leveled at his work.

Emphasis on numbers. Chappell answered that criticism with a question: "Do you think that a 12 year-old boy has a soul, and do you think that soul can be saved?" He went on to state that if you feel a boy has a soul, he is going to reach as many people as possible, which implies numbers, because all those who are un-converted will go to hell.

Being called a dictator. Chappell indicated that he does not answer that charge. "God has called me to lead this church." If the people like my leadership they can follow; if not, they can go elsewhere. People are not forced to attend the United Baptist Church. He went on to indicate, "Those who accuse me of being a dictator are *outside* of the church; you won't find my people accusing me of being a dictator."

Baptizing children. The young pastor laughed at this criticism, indicating he baptizes almost as many adults as children. He went on to indicate that if he discouraged children from being baptized he would encourage them to disobey God. He says, "Believers' baptism is scriptural; therefore every person who can believe in Jesus Christ should be baptized."

Bribing members to bring visitors. Chappell indicates that if it is carnal to bride people to do right, then why does God hold out the incentive of rewards to motivate Christians to serve Him? Chappell went on to indicate that he is trying to motivate people to do that which is biblical.

Proselyting. Pastor Chappell indicates that every visit he makes into a home is for the purpose of soul winning. He does not believe in "enlistment evangelism" as taught by the Southern Baptists. He indicated that most Christians in evangelical churches dry up on the vine because they are not winning souls to Christ. A church can be fundamental in doctrine, but dead in methodology, causing Christians to backslide. Therefore, Chappell says, "I will proselyte every church in town to get Christians to win the lost to Jesus Christ, because our church is carrying out the Great Commission and most others in town are not." Chappell indicated that the United Baptist Church does not have many friends because of this position, but he is not there to make friends but to evangelize San Jose.

Conclusion

Dr. Jack Hyles had preached at United Baptist Church and Chappell took him to the airport. As Hyles was leaving the automobile, he bent over, looked Chappell in the eyes, and stated, "You've got the greatest potential to build the largest Sunday School in the world, if you keep your heart right and stay clean." Chappell thrives on such challenges. He just might build the largest Sunday School in the world.

Chapter 4

Evangelism, Militancy, and Method

Indianapolis Baptist Temple

Indianapolis, Indiana

Indianapolis Baptist Temple's dynamic leader, Dr. Greg Dixon, was prepared by God for his life of local church evangelism. Born in Wichita, Kansas, Greg was left fatherless when he was only three. Because of the deep days of the Depression, his mother had to leave him in various foster homes—until Phase I of God's plan for him began the following year. Greg's mother one day led him into a barber and beauty shop, where she parked him in the men's section and went to have her hair fixed.

A one-legged barber named "Luke" (W. O. Lucas) asked the boy, "Where do you live?" The four-year-old snapped back, "I don't like where I live; the woman drinks beer." Luke replied with equal vigor, "Come live with me." When his mother returned, Luke said to the young mother, "I'll keep your boy." He sent Greg and his mother to 1433 Mosley Street with the instructions, "Tell Mrs. Lucas this boy will live with us."

Greg's mother walked out of the barber shop clutching the young hand, turned left, walked three blocks and climbed to the porch. When the lady of the house came to the door, the mother said, "Luke said you'd take care of my boy." The two ladies talked. Greg remembers going to sleep in a big overstuffed chair, but waking up the following morning in a bed. "Mr. and Mrs. Lucas were wonderful Christians," Greg testifies. "While I was with them I got Sunday School pins for regular attendance." His mother remarried when he was eight, and Greg returned to live with her and his stepfather.

Phase II in the providence of God occurred when Greg was a rowdy 14-year-old. He knocked a fat boy off a bicycle and cursed him. "I'll tell my Mommy," the fat boy cried, running home to his mother.

Sassy Greg ran up on the porch and told the lady, "Your son's a sissy!" The lady was the wife of Dr. Art Wilson, now pastor of the Wichita Baptist Tabernacle, who would serve three times as president of the Baptist Bible Fellowship, then a B.B.F. missionary to Mexico City. She responded to the smart aleck by inviting him to a tent meeting. Young Greg lied, "I'll try to go," not intending to keep his promise. The next day Mom Lucas phoned and invited Greg to the same tent meeting. "Yes, ma'm, I'll go," was his response. Mom and Dad Lucas picked him up that evening, and on entering the tent, Greg saw the fat boy in the aisle. Greg doubled up his fist and threatened, "I'll get you after the meeting." The evangelist that evening was the fat boy's father.

The meeting resembled the typical American tent revival. Sawdust was scattered on the floors, boards had been nailed into benches, and naked light bulbs hung from the tent poles. Greg recalls the topic of the sermon 25 years later: "Will We Have a Third World War with Russia?" He went forward at the invitation. After the meeting he stood at the altar and the fat boy, Ray Wilson, was the first to shake Greg's hand. "I'm sure glad you got saved." Greg and Ray have been friends ever since, and the Indianapolis Baptist Temple supports Ray as a missionary in Mexico City to this day.

Phase III in the life of Greg Dixon happens in the summer of 1969, when he came extremely close to death through a condition later diagnosed as hemorrhaging from the colon. He had six major operations in one year, three within 12 days at Mayo Clinic, Rochester, Minnesota. Through congestive heart failure, he was clinically dead for three minutes—but God. News of the crisis was flashed to Indianapolis Baptist Temple and 300 people gathered at the church and prayed all night. Today, when he preaches on sin to his people, he reminds them that they prayed for his life, so they should rejoice in his rebuke. Dixon looks to Scripture as the purpose for God's sparing his life, "To abide in the flesh is more needful for you" (Phil. 1:24).

He indicates the deep waters have made him a better preacher and pastor. "I used to wonder if what I said to others in sorrow and grief would be sufficient for me. It was." He goes on to indicate, "I didn't hear voices or see light when I was near heaven. The Word of God was all I needed. If I had my work to do over again, I would work harder at training individuals in soul winning."

A small incident reflects the intense competitive nature of Dixon. He discussed a revival meeting with the deacons at the Indianapolis Baptist Temple. They were debating whether to get a small or a large tent. After several minutes of discussion, the deacons answered, "If we had an outstanding evangelist we should get a large tent, but since our pastor's going to preach, let's get a small tent." Dixon went home crushed that his people had such little confidence in him. During the night, his depression turned to righteous anger. He couldn't sleep. The following morning he ordered a tent twice the size as the largest discussed by the deacons. God blessed the meeting. The tent was crowded out and over 100 came forward, most of them for salvation. Today, many key workers in the Indianapolis Baptist Temple look back to that revival as the time they met Christ.

History of the Church

In the winter of 1949, Rev. and Mrs. George Young came to Indianapolis from Bedford, Indiana, with a desire to organize a fundamental Baptist church. The first Sunday in town they visited a large church on the near north side. As they sat in the services, the Lord convicted them that they should have their own services the following Sunday. January 7, 1950, following a week of services, Rev. Young started a church in the dance pavilion of Longacre Park. Twelve persons were present in that first service. Among them were Mr. and Mrs. Elston Beal and their son Joe, who are still in Indianapolis Baptist Temple.

The church was organized March 23, 1950 with 17 members. A week later the church moved to 3333 Madison Avenue and continued their ministry until moving to the present location in 1953. Three acres of land were purchased from George Buscher, and the first building was erected by volunteer labor. In 1956, the Reverend Bernie Rogers was called to candidate as pastor for the small flock, but he wrote a letter indicating God was not calling him to Indianapolis and recommended a young man named Greg Dixon as pastor. Indianapolis Baptist Temple had 149 in attendance when Dixon preached his first sermon on the last Sunday of June, 1956. In the eyes of some he looked too young to pastor a church, yet while a student at the Baptist Bible College, Springfield, Missouri, Dixon pastored the Temple Baptist Church in Marshfield, Missouri and had built the small congregation from 30 in attendance to over 100.

God used Greg Dixon to build Indianapolis Baptist Temple into one of the fastest growing churches in America. Three years ago the church averaged 1784; this year 2553 attended the church each Sunday, including two Sundays with attendance of 4700 and 5800,

A portion of 40 buses and drivers

Dr. Greg Dixon

respectively. On February 21, a record attendance was set with 5,893 in Sunday School. It caused such a stir in the city that the next morning the *Indianapolis Star* carried an article headlined "Church Causes Devil of a Traffic Jam." On September 26 they came back with an attendance of 4,752, and on October 10 they broke an all-time record for White Castle Hamburger sales (3000) when they took over 1600 children to an air show on Sunday afternoon, provided by Col. Clare McCoombs and his son from Grand Rapids, Michigan. Nearly 40 buses and attending cars provided quite a sight as they proceeded the 10 miles to an airport owned by a member of the Temple. The two million-dollar buildings attest to the fact that a church can be built on soul winning, prayer, and Bible preaching. Thirty-eight Sunday School buses operate each week. A large deaf ministry and the other aspects make the Indianapolis Baptist Temple a great New Testament church.

Militancy

Dixon believes that, since Christians are in the Lord's army, militancy is one of the foundation stones in building a great New Testament church. He feels that militancy is an outgrowth of the deep conviction that sin both destroys and damns a life. "Even though we crusade against sin, our ministry is not a social action," states Dixon. "Our militancy is tied to soul winning." Dixon feels that militancy is usually the first element to slip when a church begins to go liberal: The pastor worries about embarrassing businessmen or politicians; then he begins to change his attack on sin; and, finally, he changes the message of the gospel. The people of Indianapolis Baptist Temple take on the rebuke of a militant church.

When Dixon was asked why he uses militancy, he replied, "It's not what militancy will do for my church, it is a matter of what is right." He goes on to state that, "The influence of Christianity at the foundation of our country gave us the freedom to preach." He indicates that the church must be more than "pro-Jesus, we must be anti-sin." The church must preserve our heritage of liberty, which is the by-product of the gospel. "If the church does not uphold the heritage of the United States, who will?" asks Dixon.

Dixon believes that the large, dynamic church has the authority (voting power) of the people. However, politicians are listening to the wrong preachers. Liberal politicans and liberal preachers are setting the policy, but they are not influencing their people, nor do they have the ear of the masses. Fundamentalists should stand up and be counted on issues of morality because their people listen to them. Because of this, Dixon directs sermons and press releases against public sins. He writes to key people in the government. Recently, he helped get an antismut bill passed in the city council. Mayor Lugar had challenged Dixon, "You preachers are not doing the job, or we politicians would not have the problem of pornography." Today, Indianapolis has one of the strictest laws against pornography for a large city. Over 1,000 people from the Indianapolis Baptist Temple crowded into the committee room when the bill came before the city council recently. Dixon commented, "Twenty churches of 100 each would not have made the impact that our church of 5,000 made."

Dixon indicates that people will respond to a church that is right on biblical separation. He explained, "I want to be as narrow as the Bible, but not more strict that the Bible." By this he means he is separate from sin but not from the sinner.

Militancy has its cost. During one campaign when Dixon was speaking out against the revolutionaries in the civil rights movement, the militants were upset because they thought Dixon's criticism over the radio would hurt their fund-raising efforts to get more radicals to Washington, D.C., and the phone rang at 3:00 A.M. The voice at the other end whispered, "Reverend, we're going to bomb your house tonight." Dixon didn't know what to do. He was concerned for the safety of his wife and children who were asleep, and yet he had the deep confidence that God was on his side and his cause was right. He indicated he would not leave nor run as a coward. "I lay and prayed all night. Every car that passed, I wondered if this was it." The morning light revealed that the threat was harmless, but Dixon had been through the valley of the shadow of death. However, the threat did not muzzle his sermon the following Sunday.

Militancy leads to social action because it speaks out against sin. Dixon laughs at most social action taken by liberal churches. He states, "Social action without the right motivation simply salves the conscience of the unsaved." Dixon went on to report, "We have more blacks coming to our church on accident than do the liberal churches on purpose." At a recent showing of a 16mm film on the Indianapolis Baptist Temple, Dixon was indicating that he thought very few black children came to the church; however, in every department shown, there were a number of black students. Most come through the bus ministry because of the placement of government housing projects in formerly all-white neighborhoods.

Why a Large Church?

1. *A Large Church Gives the Best Service to People.*—Dixon be-

lieves that the large church can better care for the needs of his people than the small church. He notes that after a church reaches 300 in Sunday School, one man cannot pastor all of the people, so he needs to build a staff to minister to all people in every point of need. Recently, a lady in an Indianapolis hospital commented, "Oh, it's so wonderful to have *all* these fine pastors." Dixon pointed out that most people have only one pastor, but the members of his church have seven. The enlarged staff gives Dixon more time to counsel and minister to the flock. He stated, "I give more time to counseling individuals with 5,000 members than I did when I had only 200 in Sunday School." He goes on to explain that he can concentrate more on the needs of individuals with a staff than he could without a staff.

2. *The Large Church Can Attract the Attention and Reach the Masses.*—Dixon pointed out that most small churches have small vision, hence a small outreach into the city. However, the large church usually plans to reach the entire city. He pointed out that his recent campaign with Bob Harrington drew larger crowds than a city-wide campaign sponsored by many churches. Also, there were more decisions for Christ at the altar. Because his people know that converts will be followed up and become a part of the local church, they work harder than those working in city-wide revivals with many cooperating churches. In addition to city-wide campaigns, the large

Signs marking the entrance to the Baptist Temple

church can evangelize the city through Sunday School buses, television broadcasts, and organized visitation.

3. *The Large Church Encourages Christians.*—Dixon believes that many Christians are discouraged in their small church with mediocre Sunday School teaching and a mediocre musical program. Since small churches have inadequate budgets and a small pool from which to draw talent, their programs are usually second-rate, even though the people are sincere in serving Christ. However, the large church usually attracts the best of music, Bible teachers, and administrators, and the larger budget enables them to have the best in building facilities. Recently, Mr. James Barth, a former deacon from a small fundamentalist church who is now a member of the Indianapolis Baptist Temple, commented to Dr. Dixon on his way out, "The thing I like most about the Indianapolis Baptist Temple is that I always leave with the victory." Also, Dixon believes that the large, successful church is an encouragement to struggling churches, and the other churches in Indianapolis benefit from his ideas, encouragement, and the evangelistic seed sown in the hearts of the unsaved. Dixon indicated, "Many souls led to the Lord by our personal workers end up in other churches in Indianapolis." Pastors in other churches indicate that, because evangelism works for the Indianapolis Baptist Temple, they realize that it will work for them. Dixon indicated, "I sometimes have six or seven visiting pastors in our services."

4. *The Large Church Gives People Respect for Sound Doctrine.*— Recently, the editor of the *Indianapolis Star* indicated, "Greg Dixon proves God is not dead, but alive." To this, Dixon replied, "A large church demonstrates, not proves, the truth of the Scripture." By this he explained that, when the Scriptures are correctly preached, a number of people will become converted, hence adding to the growth of the church (Acts 6:1,7).

Dixon believes that the large churches will lift the image of fundamentalism. He said, "Too many people think of us as fanatical hillbillys, and when they see the response of the neighborhood, the city at large will respect us."

Dixon feels there are some disadvantages to being large, the first being greater responsibility. "When I was running 300 in Sunday School, I was the underdog and could say anything I pleased; now I am the largest in the city and have a greater responsibility. I speak for the other fundamentalist pastors. I don't mean to assume responsibility for them, except that the politicians judge most fundamentalist churches in Indianapolis by what I say."

Dixon also feels there is some jealousy on the part of some because he is large. Dixon went to hear the famous liberal minister Dr.

E. Stanley Jones. The local pastor introduced Dixon to Dr. Jones stating, "Rev. Dixon is pastor of the largest church in the city." To this Dr. Jones replied, "Do you have a donkey for the children to ride?" and walked away without offering to shake hands. Dixon's reply to this is that a true liberal will never respect fundamentalism. He went on to say, "I wish I had thought to reply, 'No, but I need a jackass for next Sunday and you'll do.' "

Sunday School Busing

Dixon believes that Sunday School busing is the most effective medium for reaching the unsaved today, more effective than any other principle that can be used by a local church. He indicated that, "The children of this generation are wiser than the children of light." And the unsaved have used busing to bring people to the public schools and shopping centers, yet most church people jeer at those who use it in the church. There are six reasons why Dixon has used Sunday School busing in his church.

1. *Availability.*—He indicates that the public schools first used buses in the rural schools and now to establish racial equality in the neighborhoods (which he opposes). Because of public school busing, the vehicles are available to churches on a purchase basis or can be rented from public transportation.

2. *Cost.*—Dixon believes Sunday School busing is one of the most inexpensive mediums of reaching people in the church. He indicated that the money invested in Sunday School busing brought in more individuals than money invested in newspaper advertising, radio, television, or mailing ministry. Of course, he uses all of these media to bring in the masses to Sunday School, but the Sunday School bus program accounts for more visitors each Sunday than any technique of advertising.

3. *People Are Oriented to Riding Buses.*—Dixon indicates the common man rides buses to school and to work, and few people have any reservation about riding a bus to Sunday School.

4. *An Outlet for Christian Service.*—The Sunday School busing ministry provides many avenues of service for Christians. A new Christian can drive a bus the Sunday after he is saved, whereas he must be trained before he can teach Sunday School or serve in other capacities in the church.

5. *Reaching the Neighborhood.*—Dixon indicates that Sunday School busing puts the "go" in the gospel. It is a means of reaching large masses of people by going to their door, first presenting Christ, and then offering them free transportation to Sunday School.

6. *Certain Segments of Society Have No Transportation.*—Those

living in ghettos, housing projects, and the inner city area do not have transportation. Dixon makes no apology for reaching the poor, while at the same time he has many rich in his church. He stated, "Sunday School busing of the poor does something to the heart of the church—it keeps away sophistication that destroys older churches." He indicated that true worship is obedience, not liturgy or ritual. "Everything we do is worship to God, even when our first bus driver leaves on Sunday morning to go pick up children—that's worship." Dixon continued, "False worship is 'having the form of godliness but denying the power thereof.' False worship has no concern for the masses who are dying and going to hell." Dixon remembers that when he came to Indianapolis, an older pastor gave him the wrong advice, that is to conduct worship in the morning and hold evangelistic services in the evening. To this he replied, "If a church service is not evangelistic, it's not worship. How can I worship God without proclaiming Him to those who are lost?"

Dixon indicated, "Don't take the worst members and put them on the bus route. Use your best members on your bus routes. They are like the Green Beret or Marine Corps. They hit the enemy first and hit hardest; therefore, they must be a disciplined corps." The Indianapolis Baptist Temple has 38 buses and the fifth largest Sunday School bus ministry in the nation. The drivers come from all walks of life: one driver is a carpenter, and one woman rides her bus in a mink coat.

Dixon calls his Sunday School buses "rolling billboards." He indicates that they are great advertising for the church. A deaf couple could not find the church and could not communicate with service station attendants but when they saw a bus from the church, followed it, attended the church, and got saved that day. Dixon indicates, "When I go into a town and see a number of Sunday School buses parked on the church parking lot, I know that is a good church; you never find liberals with Sunday School buses."

Dixon indicated some will resent the bus kids coming into the church. But when the people see a bus kid get saved, then see him go to Baptist Bible College and eventually stand as the class speaker, then they know the Sunday School bus ministry is worthwhile. Dixon is proud of the 36 young people from Indianapolis Baptist Temple who have gone into full-time Christian service, many of them reached by the Sunday School bus ministry.

Dr. John Rawlings, in Cincinnati, put a Santa Claus suit on every bus driver and had one of the largest attendances on the buses, resulting in one of the largest crowds on Christmas when attendance usually dropped. Dixon believes in one-man-ship, so he put Santa

Claus suits on his bus drivers every Sunday in December and broke a month-long record. He believes that 38 men showing up in Santa suits goes farther to dispel the Santa myth than preaching a sermon, and yet brings hundreds of children into Sunday School to hear the true meaning of Christmas. However, bus drivers who were in the choir were not allowed to wear their Santa Claus suits into the choir because a film was being made for the telecast.

A prominent minister's wife was visiting in a nursing home and saw a handbill from the Indianapolis Baptist Temple advertising goldfish. She turned to her husband, "Honey, you won't believe this," and made fun of the handbill. Linda Dennis, a new convert and a member of the church, came into the lobby and suggested that the minister's wife could have as many of the handbills as she wanted. She felt that surely á minister's wife would be interested in evangelizing the children for the Sunday School.

Finances

The success of a great church is dependent upon its financial program. Greg Dixon indicated the following principles are used by him at the Indianapolis Baptist Temple.

1. *Get a Lot of Money and Spend a Lot of Money.*— This may sound rather trivial but Dixon believes that you cannot reach people without money and the only way to get money is from Christians. He has constantly said, "A minister cannot be timid about going after finances." Whereas most ministers feel guilty about asking for money, Dixon feels he is never getting enough money from his people. He simply stated, "When a man begins giving money, God will bless him financially and prosper his life." He goes on to indicate, "I've seen too many of my people who began in a state of poverty and advanced to riches because they have sacrificed for God." In retrospect, Dixon said, "My only regret over the years is that I didn't challenge my people to give more money to God."

Dixon indicated there are several principles necessary in raising and spending finances. He indicated this is one of the primary concerns of the pastor because a great church cannot be built without money. The first principle is get as much money as possible and spend as much money as possible. He went on to indicate, "We do not have any money in the bank and we are always running close in the general fund."

2. *Go Fishing for Money.*—Dixon points to the illustration of the Temple tax. When the disciple Peter needed money, Jesus directed him to go fishing. Peter found the coin in the fish's mouth. Dixon indicates, "Soul winning is the key to finances in any local church."

A pastor should win lost people to Christ and teach them to tithe to the church. He believes that people want to invest in a church that is growing and going for God. If souls were not being saved weekly in the Indianapolis Baptist Temple, people would give grudgingly. But since the aisles are filled with the lost each week, Dixon indicates his people give gladly.

3. *Large Churches Need to Diversify Their Income.*—Over the years, Dixon has never taken pledges; he has only preached tithing. However, he feels that any large church must now examine bequests, annuities and life loans. Even though he realizes the small church cannot do it, the large church must explain to the congregation the scriptural use of wills and deferred giving. Recently the Baptist Temple added a full-time staff member, the Reverend Don Price, to head up their stewardship program.

When asked if the Indianapolis Baptist Temple has any financial crises, Dixon answered, "Yes, every week." To this he confesses a conservative stand in doctrine and politics, yet he is liberal in finances. He comments, "I believe in deficit spending." The Indianapolis Baptist Temple would not have expanded if Dixon had not launched out by faith and *risk*. Yet each time, God supplied. Today the church property is worth over $2 million as a testimony to the faithfulness of God.

Advice to Pastors

Each week, several pastors visit the services of the Indianapolis Baptist Temple. These men question Dixon concerning his phenomenal growth. The following advice is given to young pastors who want to build a large church. First, he states the beginning work must have a good location. He believes that a church should not start in a poor geographical location with the idea of moving later to a better one. A new church should be located on a main expressway, with at least five acres of ground and property available for future expansion. Dixon indicates that land is more important than the people at this point. Today, the automobile and Sunday School busing can overcome the site location. Also, Dixon believes a church should be started in the suburbs with the intent of reaching the inner city through Sunday School busing.

A second area of advice Dixon gives to young pastors concerns emphasis. "Concentrate on adults," he advises young pastors. Some pastors give the impression that only children can be saved. The young preacher who wants to build a permanent work must reach adults who pay for the work, spiritually undergird the work through prayer, give leadership to the work, and help in reaching children.

The third area of advice has to do with a balanced ministry. This spiritual balance concerns itself with the nursery, busing, financial debt, buildings and administration. Dixon warns, "Don't go to seed on any tangent." The pastor must give oversight to the total growth and ministry of the church. Also, *balance* concerns the type of ministry a young minister should have. Dixon encourages a young pastor to spend time feeding the flock and exhorting the flock, as well as reaching the lost. He amplified, "A balanced ministry emphasizes both *holding* and *building* the congregation."

Another area of balance included finances. At the beginning a young church should give some finances to foreign missions, but this area of giving must be kept in line with the building fund, and reserving enough money to employ staff members to reach lost people. However, the Baptist Temple is one of the leading missionary churches in America, and their budget will approach $90,000 for foreign missions this year.

Sunday School Campaigns

Dixon believes balance applies to Sunday School campaigns. A church can have too many campaigns and wear the people out physically. Also, some churches never have a campaign and as a result never make a concerted effort to reach people in the community and bring them under the hearing of the gospel.

Dixon plans approximately 20 weeks of Sunday School campaigns out of the 52-week year, 10 weeks in the spring and 10 weeks in the fall. During some of these campaigns, he "pulls out all the advertising stops" and promotes to get people to hear the gospel. Recently the adult class was divided in two, and there was great competition between the teams. During Sunday School announcement time, the rear doors swung open and six pallbearers came in with a casket, followed by women in veils, all mourning. The big gray casket was rolled down the aisle to the front of the auditorium. A hush fell over the assemblage as one team began a funeral service for the other—the predicted losers. Within a few minutes all were laughing at the skit to motivate the teams to action.

Many people accuse Dixon of being a dicator, to which he replies, "On Wednesday prayer meeting and visitation I wish I were a dictator." He indicated if he were a tyrant or had absolute control over his people, everyone would tithe, everyone would visit, and everyone would be in prayer meeting.

Cautions

Dixon gives one caution to pastors concerning campaigns and ad-

Dept. 6 (six-year-olds), Mrs. Thelma Vandervort, Supt.

vertisement. "First," he said, "don't advertise your inexpensive handouts in the newspaper. People who read the newspaper don't come to Sunday School to get a free McDonald's hamburger." Dixon suggests that the young pastor advertise his campaigns through handbills distributed along the bus route and by direct mailing to those who ride the bus. He has given out baseballs, bats, snow cones, cotton candy, goldfish, and kites with his picture and the motto "Flying high with Jesus."

"Jesus walked on the water to get people to listen to Him, and He miraculously fed 5,000," reported Dixon. "Since I can't do that, I'll give away soft drinks and preach to those who come."

"A young pastor must spend time counseling individuals as well as preaching to the multitude," stated Dixon, continuing on his theme of balance. Finally, he emphasized a balanced ministry to both children and adults. Most neo-evangelicals spend the majority of their time on adults, fundamentalists spend more time on children. A New Testament balanced ministry emphasizes both.

Another area of advice Dixon gives to young preachers concerns itself with precedent. He stated, "A church must be careful what they begin. The foundation in church-planting is essential." By this, he pointed out that "once a church takes the form and strikes a direction, it is hard to change." He amplified, "A church will financially maintain a pastor at the standard of living when the ministry is begun." He points out, "Many deacons promise a pastor will receive more money if he will sacrifice at the beginning." Dixon does not believe this is so, although when he came to Indianapolis he lived for a few weeks in a one-room shack with no running water.

Image is another area of concern to a young pastor. An "image" is the sum total impression received by those on the outside of a church. Dixon believes a pastor can control the kind of image the people have of the local church. He pointed out that President John Kennedy controlled the image people thought of him and his administration. Dixon went on to indicate, "I care what people think about me, because I care what they think of Jesus Christ." When it comes to image-making, Dixon indicates, "There is no room for hypocrisy. The people know when you're fudging." Dixon pointed out that putting politicians into the pulpit or running cheap contests will ruin a church. But, in contrast, bringing an outstanding man to preach in a small church will help its image. Dixon indicated, "It did something for my people when they realized that Dr. G. B. Vick would come and preach in my church." He advises young pastors to invite outstanding men to the pulpit, even if the honorarium must be more than usual, simply because outstanding men accomplish outstanding results." Dixon also has invited the governor of the state, and the mayor of the city to participate in his programs.

Greg Dixon was motivated to build a large church at the Baptist Bible College, Springfield, Missouri, where he graduated in the first graduating class in 1953. Dixon indicated that the total school, rather than one particular professor, made an impression on him: "It was the spirit of being around the men who built great churches that changed my life." He went on to point out Proverbs 13:20 as his guide: "He that worketh with wise men shall be wise." Dixon built his church on the principle that "like produces like." He stated, "Indianapolis Baptist Temple has grown because I had the pastors of large churches come and preach in my pulpit. When I am in other towns, I always visit the largest church and talk with its pastor to determine what has made it grow."

Dixon indicated five men made the greatest impact on his life. First, Dr. Art Wilson, pastor of the Wichita Baptist Tabernacle for 27 years, who led him to Chirst. Second was Dr. Bill Dowell, pastor of High Street Baptist Church, Springfield, Missouri, when Dixon was a student at Baptist Bible College. Dixon said, "He gave me, as a young student at college, a passion to build a great church. I determined to reach a city for Christ just as Dr. Dowell had done."

The third influence on his life came from Dr. G. Beauchamp Vick, pastor of Temple Baptist Church, Detroit, Michigan, and president of Baptist Bible College. "Dr. Vick gave me the principles by which to build a church and a desire for order and organization in my life." Another man who made a great impact on Dixon was Dr. John Rawlings, pastor at Landmark Baptist Temple, Cincinnati, Ohio. "He gave me many practical suggestions that worked." Dixon confessed that Indianapolis Baptist Temple is more like Dr. Rawlings' church in Cincinnati than any other church. Dr. Rawlings was willing to come and preach when the Indianapolis Baptist Temple was small." On many occasions the older pastor took time to talk with Dixon, a young preacher, and tell him how to build a church.

The final man who influenced him was Dr. Noel Smith, editor of the *Baptist Bible Tribune* and Dixon's theology professor at BBC. He gave him the philosophical foundation for his theological beliefs.

Television

Indianapolis Baptist Temple went on television four years after Dixon came, when the Sunday School was running 400 in attendance. There was a simple half-hour program on Saturday nights, but its prime time captured a large viewing audience in Indianapolis. Today the church has a half-hour Sunday morning program on

Interior of auditorium that seats 3,000.

Channel 4, one of the largest independent stations in the United States. Dixon indicated television did several things for the church. First, it gave an image of growth and expansion—the city knew that the church was going forward. Second, the Indianapolis Baptist Temple and Dixon became household words among Christians. Since he was the first to go on television, many Christians prayed for him and supported his broadcast. Dixon became the standard-bearer for all fundamentalists who felt the evil influence of television could be blunted by a gospel testimony. Visitors brought to the church because of television became a third advantage. Dixon realizes that most were not saved through television, but were brought to hear the gospel where they could respond. The fourth advantage of television was the open door of outreach. When soul winners went visiting in the neighborhood, the unsaved identified with the TV program. The seed of the Word of God had been sowed in many hearts long before the church workers visited the home.

Recently, the Baptist Bible College honored Greg Dixon with an honorary Doctor of Divinity degree for building an outstanding church. Dixon replied, "Everything I've got is due to my people. I owe everything to them. This honor for me is an honor for them."

Dixon said that the Indianapolis Baptist Temple has grown primarily because of lay members who were willing to cooperate with him in soul winning, such as Paul Boyll, a treasury agent who built an adult class from 6 to nearly 200 per Sunday. Other volunteer workers such as John Biggers, Carl Glascock, Teddy Henderson, Marshall Mitchell, Sam Sylvest and John Vandervort, who are members of the Hundred Club (meaning they have brought more than 100 in one Sunday on their bus routes). Marshall Mitchell holds the record with 163 on one Sunday.

And then, there is C. Fred Johnson (whose insurance agency continues to lead the nation in sales) who gives two to three days per week in soul winning and acting in an advisory capacity to Dixon and the church in their financial decisions. Dixon and the entire congregation is indebted to W. E. Hawkins of Church Builders of America, whose sacrifice and wisdom has provided the space to keep up with the Temple's phenomenal growth. Through the years, he made it possible for nearly 100,000 square feet of buildings to be erected at far below the normal contract prices. And yet the progress would have been impossible without a faithful paid staff which includes such tireless workers as Mary Sue Kennedy, secretary; Jerry Medley, music and Sunday School Coordinator, who now has the responsibility of putting the Baptist Temple Sunday School in the Top 10; and David Bowell whose hard work and intelligence put together in three months the Indianapolis Baptist High School with an enrollment of over 200.

The outstanding converts in his church made Dixon realize he can reach anyone for Christ. He won his stepfather to the Lord after praying for him for 15 years. Therefore Dixon believes he can build the largest Sunday School in America. He can if his physical health remains strong. Dixon has set an immediate goal both for his Sunday School and for himself. He is confident his church will be listed in the 10 largest Sunday Schools in the near future. Some people might think this is selfish motivation. He replied, "I don't care what people say about my motives. I plan to win as many lost people as possible while God gives me strength. I don't have time to worry about motives. God will deal with that at the judgment seat."

Conclusion

Mr. and Mrs. Lucas are now dead. To this day, Dixon has a deep love for the one-legged barber who changed his life. Luke's favorite song was, "I will meet you in the morning, just inside the Eastern Gate." Dixon choked up and cried when he told this reporter, "I expect that he will be the first to meet me, when I come through."

Chapter 5

A Leader and His Church

First Baptist Church

West Hollywood, Florida

"Let's paint the church in one day," challenged Pastor Verle Ackerman to the congregation of over 2,000 at the First Baptist Church, West Hollywood, Florida. The following Saturday morning, over 250 devoted laymen appeared after breakfast with scaffold, brushes, rollers and buckets, each ready to paint. Anyone who has supervised a work crew knows the gigantic task of directing 250 dedicated, but untrained, laborers. Pastor Ackerman had previously assigned one man as supervisor for each of the many walls surrounding the church building. He told each supervisor, "Don't pick up a brush; don't go for paint: just keep everyone happy by keeping them working." Shoppers stood in the adjacent shopping center staring at people swarming over the church like bees—some on ladders, others on scaffolds, others reaching over the roof—painting the church. The casual observer might have thought chaos ruled the day, while those on the work crews knew exactly what they were doing. Two coats were applied in half a day. Mrs. D. Candia, an Italian lady, prepared a spaghetti feed for all of the helpers. The efficient and effective leadership of Verle Ackerman reflected in the employment of a multitude of lay workers illustrates the reason for numerical growth at First Baptist Church, West Hollywood.

When Ackerman came as pastor, May 1, 1967, there were 506 in Sunday School that week. The churches on the east coast of Florida were suffering their usual slump during the month of May. Ackerman courageously attacked the problem by calling for a Saturday

Pastor Verle Ackerman

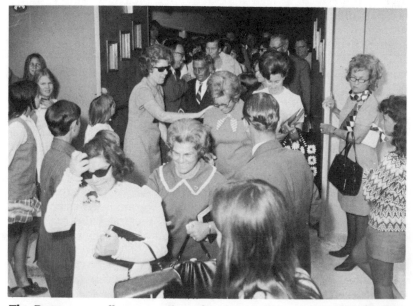

The Pastor personally meets all as they leave after services. The church is known for the warmth of its congregation as they greet all visitors.

visitation. Many thought the new pastor was visionary, but over 100 came for visitation. Then, over 100 new visitors attended Sunday School the following day. On face value, Ackerman's leadership looks automatic; however, he contacted 10 men of the church, asking each one to be responsible to bring 10 to the Saturday morning visitation.

Visitors driving off U.S. 441 and Taft streets onto the church parking lot are greeted by the friendliest ushers in the world. As a car with visitors is directed to a parking spot, an usher opens the door, greets them and shakes hands with each new arrival. The usher directs them to the church building. Another usher stationed outside the main doors of the church meets them and shakes their hands. Ackerman has stationed an usher at every door and stairwell throughout the church, with the primary assignment to shake hands with every person he sees. Mrs. Maynard, church hostess, greets the elderly ladies by a friendly, warm embrace. Many believe this is one of the friendliest churchs in America, yet Ackerman believes that friendliness is not automatic: "We have to work at being friendly." He got the idea of having ushers open the car door when he visited an east Texas church and noted many early arrivers parking in a bank parking lot. He had to ask if it were permissible to park there. Then Ackerman got lost delivering his children to Sunday School in the different buildings. At that point, he determined to be friendly and meet every visitor coming to his church.

People are stationed at sections of the auditorium, with the duty to shake hands with everyone in their area. Ackerman rotates these hosts so their greetings will not become mechanical. Also, during every service, Ackerman has the folks stand and shake hands during the singing of a hymn. Immediately after the benediction he asks that they once again meet their visitors and shake their hand.

Pastoral Leadership

The First Baptist Church is an aggressive church because the pastor is a strong, positive leader. He sets the example in every phase of the ministry. Ackerman believes the Lord gave him charge of this flock. He states that in "raising sheep" he must not drive them, for sheep will follow a leader. Ackerman is a shepherd, and perhaps his leadership is no more evident than in his soul-winning ability. It is difficult for the unsaved to say no to Verle Ackerman. He approaches soul winning with the attitude that everybody wants to go to heaven and the Bible tells them how they can know for sure they are going to heaven. When Ackerman concludes his presentation of the plan of salvation, he never asks, "Would you like to be saved tonight?" or "Would you like to ask Jesus Christ to come into your heart tonight?" He always concludes, "Mr. Jones, I am sure you want to go to heaven, and I don't think that God made any mistake in leading me here tonight. Let's get on our knees right here and I will pray with you, and you ask the Lord to come into your heart so you can know for sure that you will go to heaven." At this point, the person either has to say, "I don't want to go to heaven" or offer some other excuse. It is not easy to say no to Verle Ackerman. He leads people to Jesus Christ, then leads them into the local church and, finally, leads them into reaching others for Jesus Christ. To Ackerman, the Christian life is simply obedience to the Word of God. He states, "I simply believe the Bible and teach it."

Mrs. Shirley Peoples remarked, "The more I get involved in this church, the more I want to do for God and I can't help but be a soul winner because of the pastor's leadership." Mrs. Helen Crebiston remarked, "Pastor Ackerman has a highly infectious disease called "Go get 'em," with which he infects us all. This disease causes all of us to pray more, read our Bibles, teach Sunday School classes, drive our buses, and do many other things to spread God's Word. The only known cure for this disease is called *backsliding*." She goes on to indicate Ackerman is a born leader.

The Reverend Bill Rogers, assistant pastor, indicates that, while living in Miami, Florida, and working in the secular world, he felt the Lord must be blessing him financially so he could give to the church. One Sunday he observed the senior high department teacher who was, in his words, "unprepared to teach and had no concept of how to deal with the needs." After much prayer, he brought the situation to the attention of Verle Ackerman and the following evening the pastor called on him and said, "Okay, you have opened your mouth, now I'm going to let you put your foot in it. I want you to teach the senior high school department next week." Ackerman went on to assure Rogers that he could teach and he would help him study the lesson. Young Rogers began teaching in the book of Romans and Ackerman supplied several books to help in his study. Rogers indicated, "I had never taught a class before in my life and the thought was frightening, but it was impossible to say no to Verle Ackerman." After teaching the class for six months, Mr. and Mrs. Rogers took the pastor and his wife out to dinner. Before the meal was over, Ackerman looked straight at him and said, "Are you happy in your job?" For the first time, Rogers analyzed himself and within six months surrendered himself for the ministry. Today as assistant to Verle Ackerman, he testifies, "If the pastor had not buttonholed me, I would still be in the business world trying to convince myself that God wanted me to make money."

Mrs. Arthur Mayo indicates her pastor is a good leader because, "He insists upon discipline and order in the Lord's house, tactfully and firmly; yet with Christlike kindness and love." Andrew Stevenson, a bus driver commented on the pastor's leadership, "I never have to look back to see the pastor's leadership; I always look forward because he is out front leading, not behind pushing."

The pastor, Ackerman, acts in accordance with the strong convictions of what is right. He has an unswerving allegiance to the Word of God. A man who came to know the Lord wanted to serve God, but Ackerman showed his hesitation because of the man's long hair and unkempt appearance. The next week the man showed up, and the pastor did not recognize him. He had short hair, his moustache was shaved off, and he was neatly dressed in a suit. Pastor Ackerman let him begin driving a Sunday School bus and later promoted him to teach a Sunday School class. Phyllis O'Malley comments on the biblical base of the church and states the church is growing because, "God promised to bless His Word, and it is taught and preached plain and straight every Sunday from the Bible."

Ackerman indicates he tries to know his people personally. Every Sunday he shakes hands with the majority of those attending church. He goes through the church auditorium meeting the visitors and his members. He stated, "I can lead people I am in contact with."

Verle Ackerman is a natural organizer and administrator. He loves to organize everything he touches. One of his personal rules is, "Whatever I organize, I see that it functions." Sarah Maynard comments on his leadership ability, "He is a good leader because there is no job that he asks you to do that he hasn't already done himself." Ackerman indicates, "I never criticize anyone publicly. I try to compliment my workers. We try to leave a meeting with a positive atmosphere." He went on to indicate that people work harder from positive motivations rather than negative criticism.

Ackerman directs the finances of the church. He indicated, "I must know where the money is going, to properly lead the church." He initials every bill and always knows what is being purchased. Once a month he meets with the finance committee composed of trustees and deacons. They receive a *printed forecast* which lists every bill that is to be paid in the next month. This list is read to the men and if there is any question, it is answered at that point. Also listed are the monthly payments, weekly accounts and salaries. Ackerman indicates, "I can purchase anything I want, but I must give an account to the finance committee." A layman signs all the checks of

The Messengers Quartet, Jacksonville, Florida, was one of the highlights of "Break the Record Day"

the church, even though Ackerman gives direction to the finances. The pastor indicated the church has a yearly budget based on last year's budget with a margin for this year's growth. The congregation approves their yearly budget. Financial details are not brought to the congregation except major items. Last year, the church gave over $50,000 to foreign missions and had a total budget of $330,000.

Ackerman indicates a fondness for taking a dead organization and building life into it. When asked how he does it, he follows four simple steps. (1) Giving the people a deep spiritual direction. (2) Creating an organization that functions. (3) Showing a deep love for each person in the organization. (4) Being enthusiastic in all that is done.

When Ackerman came to the First Baptist Church, the former pastor, Dr. Bowers, had been sick and the church was going through a period of unrest. The church had dropped in attendance from 800 to 500. The following items were implemented by Ackerman to *revive* the church and get it growing again.

1. *Created esprit de corps among the people.*—The church service needed dressing up, because the services dragged and were unappealing. Ackerman used the motto, "Discover the difference," and realized his church would have to be different. He saw that "visitors needed to be impressed to get them to return to our church." He recruited ushers to meet visitors at the doors and parking lots. Next, he recruited choir members to fill the empty spots in the choir and, finally, he organized his platform staff. His morning service is considered one of the best organized and visitors are impressed with his dignity and orderliness.

2. *Got the Sunday School functioning properly.*—He realized that the students had to have biblical content in Sunday School and began emphasizing Sunday School teaching.

3. *Instituted a visitation program.*—Immediately he organized a weekly visitation program and taught a soul-winning class. Ackerman believes Sunday School bus visitation is the most effective outreach into a community, but the regular organized visitation program is necessary for a growing church. He indicates many families can be reached through soul winners who will not respond to riding a Sunday School bus.

4. *Cleaned up the properties.*—Ackerman indicated that many times fundamentalists have come from the wrong side of the tracks and have given no attention to the building in which they preach the gospel. He began trimming the lawns, painting the buildings and washing the walls. He indicated, "I don't mind things looking worn, but I hate dirt and grime." Ackerman noted that most fundamentalists put all of the emphasis on function, but neglect the form. To him, this is a wrong emphasis. As he stated, "Function without form is void."

5. *Began an advertising campaign.*—Ackerman indicated he needed to get the church before the neighborhood. He began using radio, newspapers, signboards and bus-bench advertisement. In addition to this, he used circulars, sent home flyers from the Sunday School and brochures from the church.

6. *Created a vision of the future.*—Ackerman indicated he "set forth a future plan so his people would have something to look forward to." This vision included expansion in numbers, increase in baptisms, more conversions and financial growth. Finally, he capped off his vision by showing the new buildings that needed to be constructed to carry out expansion. Ackerman constantly remarked to the people that they are building for the future. "I have never set a goal I didn't think we could make and we have never missed a goal," summarized Ackerman. He went on to say there is as much growth

The present church plant is on a main intersection of the city of Hollywood, Florida. A new auditorium seating 3,000 will be constructed this year to the left of the present building.

on the part of his people by setting goals (makes them aspire) as there is in reaching goals (attainment).

7. *Built a youth program.*—Ackerman indicates, "Young people reflect vitality in a church." He said by reaching youth, they can help reach adults, other youth, and even work with children.

Ackerman responded to the question of how he motivates his people: "I eat, sleep and talk First Baptist Church—about anything else, I'm dull." He went on to say, "I include people in what I am doing. They know *what* I am doing and *why* I am doing it."

One of the keys to success is the way Ackerman trains his workers. He uses the following method. (1) A potential teacher observes the class that is to be taught. Ackerman makes sure that they have observed a good class rather than a weak teacher. (2) Methods of teaching are presented at the teachers' meeting. The potential worker observes the use of good methods by Ackerman's teaching style as well as by hearing how these methods should be used. He also discusses such topics as "how to handle discipline problems" and he illustrates different ways of teaching. "We don't have job descriptions for teachers at our church; they just know what to do," answered Ackerman. (3) The potential worker catches the spirit of Sunday School by attending teachers' meetings and hearing the announcements and promotion at the teachers' meeting. He feels the excitement of teaching Sunday School leads to a spiritual burden for pupils. (4) Actual in-service training is used to prepare teachers.

Ackerman has the potential teachers teach a lesson, then he evaluates their effectiveness.

Ackerman is the Sunday School superintendent of the church. He stated, "I run my Sunday School." But, he went on to indicate, "I have superintendents." There is one layman in charge of each department throughout the church. These people are the basis of success in the Sunday School.

Ackerman is a successful leader because of his hard work. His brother, Russell Ackerman, working as Assistant Pastor, stated: "The pastor always does more work in the church than anyone else." He went on to explain, "We know that the pastor will have more people walking down the aisle on Sunday to receive Christ than anyone else, because he is a soul winner." Some might criticize Ackerman for using his family on the church staff. But Ackerman explains, "I always said I wouldn't use my family, but found they are among the hardest workers. I know my brother, and he can do the job." Ackerman handles any potential criticism by never getting together as a family clique. The other staff members note that the dirty jobs are given to Russ for two basic reasons. (1) He needed to learn from the bottom up, and (2) Ackerman needed to know what his brother could do.

Follow-up is an important word in Ackerman's leadership ability. When a job doesn't get done, he wants to know *why*. If the different pastors are not responsible for having anyone forward on a Sunday, Ackerman wants to know *why*. He expects that each pastor will work hard in soul winning and there will be some fruit in the way of conversions at the altar on Sunday morning. One church member described the pastor's leadership ability was inherent in his "commonness"—"He's just like one of us." She went on to say he never seems busy—*too busy to talk to anyone*. Bill Fincher, youth director in the church, indicates, "Leadership is getting things done through people—that's Verle Ackerman."

Each Sunday morning at 9:15 A.M., Ackerman meets with his Sunday School superintendents, the staff, and all the ushers. This group of approximately 30 people meet in the office reception area and Ackerman approaches them with enthusiasm, "Let's have a great day." Ackerman announces the special events of the Sunday, pointing out what features for the next Sunday need to be announced that Sunday, and then emphasizes visitation during the week. The outstanding teachers from last week are announced and then all 30 people get on their knees to pray for a good day. As they leave the room, Ackerman reminds, "Let's keep the children quiet; we have to teach them reverence in the house of God."

The Reverend Bill Rogers indicates Ackerman is a good leader because "He lets you know what he wants and how he wants it done." A mother indicates he is a good teacher because "He pushes—in a nice way."

Every Sunday evening at 5:00 P.M. Pastor Ackerman meets with a different group of church workers. This meeting is to review problems and coordinate the outreach of the church. Future plans and goal setting become a part of this meeting. One week he may meet with children's church workers, the next with the ushers, and when the cycle is finished he begins again meeting with all of his workers.

Development of a Leader

Verle Ackerman indicates that his leadership ability developed over the years by coming in contact with great men of God. Just as heat is transferred to a poker by placing it in the fire, so leadership is developed in a young man by coming in contact with great men who have the flame of evangelism and a burning heart for God. Ackerman indicated seven men made a great impact on his life. First, his father, S. E. Ackerman, was Sunday School superintendent and associate pastor at the Jacksonville (Florida) Baptist Temple. There his father built a Sunday School to over 2,000 in attendance. Verle indicated his father gave him a desire for organization and for enthusiasm to keep a large Sunday School going. At the Bible Baptist Seminary in Ft. Worth, Texas, Ackerman sat in classes under Dr. J. Frank Norris. From this great giant, Ackerman got a vision for soul winning. He indicated Norris was "most like Dr. John Rawlings," pastor of Landmark Baptist Temple of Cincinnati, Ohio. For many years Ackerman worked for Dr. John Rawlings at Central Baptist Church in Tyler, Texas. Ackerman indicated, "John Rawlings taught me how to touch the common man." He indicated a minister should never aspire to greatness but keep common so he can meet the needs of other common men.

Verle Ackerman also worked for Dr. Wendell Zimmerman at the Kansas City Baptist Temple. Zimmerman taught him two things: first, the necessity of preaching the Bible, and second, the effectiveness of Sunday School campaigns. Ackerman feels that the Reverend George Hodges, former pastor of Jacksonville Baptist Temple, had a great impact on his life, teaching him to work hard. The long hours Ackerman invested in the ministry were learned from the example of George Hodges. Next, he pointed to Dr. E. R. Bowers, his predecessor at the West Hollywood Church. Ackerman indicated, "I learned to be positive from Dr. Bowers. He was never pessimistic or defeated." Ackerman continued, "Dr. Bowers gave me confidence that I should never worry about failing but should have an inner knowledge that I could do any job for God." Finally, Ackerman believes the Reverend Al Janney, of the New Testament Baptist Church of Miami, influenced his life. From Janney, Ackerman received a vision of God's provision. The future is always bright. After working with Janney for seven years, Ackerman indicated, "I learned that Janney would let nothing stop him in the work of the Lord." He went on to indicate, "I trust I can have the same type of determination."

At age 42, Ackerman became pastor of the First Baptist Church with no previous experience as pastor. He had spent his life as an associate, serving as the second man in a church. He indicated his relationship with these great men gave him the confidence that he could build a great church. "Since coming to Hollywood, I have never worried about failing." Ackerman went on to say, "I was insecure about my speaking, but I knew I could build a great Sunday School."

Ackerman attended the pastor's conference at the First Baptist Church, Hammond, Indiana, February, 1967. Dr. Jack Hyles challenged him regarding soul winning. God spoke to his heart during that conference and Ackerman told God whatever doors were opened he would go through them and use his capacities to win souls. Three months later he was called to West Hollywood as pastor.

Ackerman's friends were surprised when they heard he had become a pastor. They all thought he was a Sunday School man or music director. Other than conducting Sunday School clinics, he had done very little speaking during the eleven years he worked at the New Testament Baptist Church.

Ackerman was associated with the National Sunday School Association and was co-director for the Miami Sunday School Convention, 1963. He went and took a summer institute at Wheaton College in Christian Education. He indicated, "This opened my eyes to other methods and expanded my vision, but I felt some of these were not New Testament methods of building a church." Later, he slowly drifted away from association with evangelicals. He stated, "Their idea of Sunday School didn't meet my needs." Ackerman continued, "The N.S.S.A. is a liberal education approach to Sunday School. First, they are not church-centered, second, they are not pastor-centered, and, finally, they emphasize human needs rather than communication of biblical content."

Conclusion

First Baptist Church is growing because of the leadership of Verle Ackerman. Mrs. Leo Hohl commented on the causes of his effective leadership: "He is a perfectionist." Everything must be right, from the commitment to teaching the Word of God to the organization. Everything must be right. A favorite and often repeated quotation of Ackerman is "If it's worth doing, it is worth doing right."

The church is growing for several reasons: (1) A soul-winning spirit that is successful; (2) a quality music program that attracts; (3) a friendliness and warmth of people that is not automatic, because the people work at it; (4) the leadership of Verle Ackerman, that is efficient and personable; (5) an organized church that follows the biblical mandate of evangelism; (6) a Sunday School that faithfully teaches the Word of God to every pupil; (7) trained workers who know what to do and follow through on their duties; (8) a genuine excitement over reaching Broward County for Christ; (9) an aggressive advertising program that places the church before the community; (10) an esprit de corps among the people, causing them to clean up their property, attend to details, follow the leadership of the pastor in an aggressive evangelistic program.

Chapter 6

As Spokes in a Wheel
Northside Baptist Church
Charlotte, North Carolina

The 6:00 P.M. news telecast featured a special, "God Is not Dead—He's at Northside." The television screen showed crowds going to Sunday School, Dr. Jack Hudson (pastor) preaching, and the altar filled with people kneeling and receiving Christ. The news commentator indicated the Sunday School had grown from an average of 700 to 2,100 in the last three years. For three successive evenings the five-minute news special showed different facets of Northside Baptist Church, Charlotte, North Carolina. The final excerpt showed hundreds of children getting off Sunday School buses, and the TV announcer concluded, "And people continue to come to Northside."

Many churches desire to grow in attendance, but for some reason do not. The secret of growth at Northside is simple. When the Lord led Dr. Jack Hudson to organize the Northside Baptist Church 17 years ago, he used a plan, of which he states, "I hesitate to mention this plan because it is so simple. Think of a wagon wheel. The hub or center represents the church, the spokes are the various ministries of the church, each one contributing to the over-all growth of the Sunday School." These spokes are visitation, quality education, communication, transportation, a Christian school, Bible training, preaching, cooperation, youth ministry, promotion and adequate personnel. Each spoke represents a section in this chapter. According to Hudson, the spokes have no order of importance, but each spoke de-

Dr. Jack Hudson

Wall-to-wall people! This picture was taken in the present auditorium. Since then two full-length balconies were installed bringing the seating capacity to 1,450.

pends upon the strength of the others, and all are involved in carrying the load. One defective spoke cripples the total operation.

Visitation

Northside Baptist Church has an aggressive evangelistic visitation program patterned after the New Testament model. On Monday night men go visiting, attempting to lead other people to Jesus Christ. Thursday is the regular visitation night, when the whole church is organized for soul winning. Teen-agers participate in this program, especially visiting teen-agers. The ladies of the church meet at 9:00 A.M. Tuesday morning, and visit other ladies who are at home. Also, there is a Saturday afternoon organized visitation program attempting to reach people for Jesus Christ.

Hudson stated, "You cannot build a Sunday School without visitation." He pictures radio, letters, newspapers, and advertising as the air force which softens up the enemy. Next the plodding foot soldier must go in and capture the enemy. Each Sunday School teacher is likened unto the foot soldier, responsible for visitation in his class. The Reverend George Ballard, minister of visitation, heads up and directs the visitation program. He stated, "We try to contact each convert and new member every week to welcome them into the church." Jack Hartman visits the hospital, the convalescent homes, and the shut-ins, and heads up the ministry to the handicapped.

The bus workers are asked to spend three hours every Saturday visiting prospects on their route. These are some of the most faithful visitors for the church; however, they do not have a specified time for visitation, but go out at their own convenience. Usually the bus captain and driver go together. Several of the routes have a man and wife team who visit together effectively.

Quality Education

According to Hudson, visitation is only the beginning; the secret is to keep prospects coming back. He feels quality education draws visitors into regular attendance.

The first step in quality education is a Bible-based curriculum. Hudson stated, "We are living in a highly sophisticated age where people have a good education. The old-fashioned quarterly expertly evaded doctrinal issues, so we write our own, covering a book in the Bible for as many quarters as it takes to complete the study." The Reverend James Corn has been with the church for 16 years and writes the Sunday School lesson for the high school and adult departments. These lessons are printed in booklet form and become commentaries for each quarter.

In the early days of the Sunday School, the Sunday School reflected the Southern Baptist philosophy of education. Dr. Jack Hudson, who came out of a Southern Baptist church, built Sunday School facilities into small cubicles for 10 pupils each. The church has built additional Sunday School facilities seven times in its past 17 years. Each time, Sunday School rooms were made larger, reflecting an evolution in Hudson's concept of teaching. At present most of the Sunday School rooms are large, open rooms, the size of a public schoolroom. The Sunday School has been reorganized into a modified team teaching approach. The Northside Christian School meets in the church facilities. This school with grades K through 12 is one of the reasons why the Sunday School rooms are built according to public-school specifications. There are approximately 30 to 60 pupils in each Sunday School class. Two or more teachers are assigned to each room.

Hudson indicated that the change from small cubicles to open-session teaching did not come easy. Many of the adults, reared in Southern Baptist tradition, were not originally willing to switch to large classes where the master teacher could teach lessons. Hudson recently gathered all adults in the Sunday School together and asked, "How many of you are saved?" Most of the hands went up.

"All right, let's go get boys and girls who are not saved. The very chair you occupy may seat an unsaved boy or girl next week." The pastor pleaded, "We need your seat for children." The response was unanimous; the adults wanted to go to the consolidated class.

Hudson ended with a challenge especially to the ladies: "Bring your husbands with you next week; let them know they will sit with you in Bible class and you can study God's Word together."

When the consolidation took place in Northside's adult department, there were four ladies', three men's and two couples' classes. As a result of consolidation, several benefits accrued: first, Sunday School rooms freed from adult use were made available to children. Second, the adults became enthusiastic when they realized they could reach more children for Jesus Christ. Third, adults were motivated to bring their friends to Sunday School. Wives were motivated to bring their husbands to come and sit with them and study the Word of God together. Fourth, visitors to the church were given opportunity to come into a large class, listen without fear of embarrassment, and learn the Word of God. Hudson believes that many adult men will not attend a small class simply because they might be put on the spot with a question or have to shake hands with men they would rather not meet. In the large class, visitors are not readily identified, yet Hudson believes a warm, friendly atmosphere can be created so they will feel welcome without feeling conspicuous. Finally, the large adult classes utilize the best teachers. The Reverend Steve Byrd, minister of education, indicated that no teachers were put out of a job, but several outstanding teachers were transferred to younger age groups. Byrd indicated, "We challenged these teachers to take large children's classes, knowing this would require more preparation, followup and skill on their part." All of the teachers were relocated into younger age classes. Also, a co-teacher was assigned to every large class. The master teacher leads the lesson, the co-teacher assists.

The children go directly to class without "opening exercises" on

Construction on these new facilities will begin this year. This auditorium will seat 3,000 on the main floor and 2,000 in the balcony.

the departmental level. However, each class has its own opening exercise, which is part of the total teaching time rather than an appendage stuck on before the Bible teaching.

An observer peeking through classrooom doors notices that the Sunday School classes resemble public school classes rather than typical Sunday School classes. Children do not sit in circles but in armchairs used during the week by the Northside Christian Schools. Teachers stand at the front, write on the chalkboard, or sit at the desk. The associates may be working in one corner with slow pupils, or be standing at the door meeting latecomers.

Hudson indicates, "One teacher alone can't take care of fifty pupils, but he can do it with helpers: ushers, secretary and associate teachers." Steve Byrd believes that one large class, with an outstanding teacher complemented by good associates, will accomplish more than several small classes. Hudson wants the same teachers standing at the door each Sunday morning, greeting pupils as they come in. Every student is contacted every week. Some weeks the master teacher takes the initiative, other weeks the associates. One of the advantages of modified team teaching is that the associate is being trained through an apprenticeship with the master teacher.

Communication

Hudson believes that a church must let people know where it is located and what it is doing. This is communication. There are several media of communication used by the Northside Baptist Church.

Radio.—For 12 of the 17 years, Hudson has maintained a radio broadcast to the city of Charlotte. At present, he conducts two daily radio broadcasts, and the Sunday morning services are broadcast on ten stations covering about half of North Carolina. When asked why he uses radio, Hudson replied, "Radio never gets sick, lazy or needs a vacation. People listen to radio in their housecoats, in bed, at the table or while cleaning their home. If I were beginning a church tomorrow, I would try to be on radio the next day."

Newspaper.—The church places 3-column by 6-inch ads in both local papers each week. They are kept interesting and informative. Hudson admonishes, "Avoid 'churchy' ads; rather keep them up-to-date and professional."

Direct Mailing.—Each member of the Sunday School receives a letter from his teacher each week, regardless of the content of the letter. According to Hudson, a weekly mailing tells the pupil, "We care."

Revival Advertisment.—Hudson believes that no church large enough to sponsor a revival should put out less than 3,000 pieces of advertisment. Then he went on to say larger churches should put out at least 10,000 pieces. The Northside Baptist Church usually mails 30,000 post-card-size revival advertisments. Hudson's theory is simple: "If the unsaved do not get to the church for the revival, at least they know where the church is located, and when they have a crisis in their life, they know where to find spiritual help."

Transportation

Hudson maintains America is a mobile nation and the up-to-date church cannot afford to neglect the emphasis that the average American family places upon transportation. Two aspects of transportation are important in church planning.

Parking.—Hudson believes that great churches attract people from long distances. He states, "People will drive as far to church as they drive to buy groceries or to go to work." Therefore, a modern-day church must provide parking if it is to minister to the multitudes. With this thought, the church recently leased two adjacent acres for additional parking, giving a total of seven and one-half acres of parking space.

Busing.—The business community realizes that if it is to sell to the public it must rely on public transportation or provide parking for private vehicles. Most downtown areas that have dried up as far as retail business is concerned, did so because of no public transportation or bus fares were raised so high that the average man cannot afford to ride the bus. The church has been slow to see the value of busing. Hudson agrees that he also has been slow to see the value of Sunday School busing. Approximately four years ago the church had a courtesy bus service that had been in operation for two years with little results from its outreach. The evangelistic bus program was put under the direction of Steve Byrd. He began knocking on doors on the south side of town, because a van-load was coming from that section. He personally helped build the first bus-load, and since then he continues to add buses whenever conditions permit. According to Byrd, beginning a bus route is simple: (1) Get your bus captains and drivers, and (2) get your buses. Then go to work. At present Northside has been curtailing bus activities for lack of Sunday School facilities. Their large blue buses are attractively painted, and recently in *Christian Life* Magazine a picture of the rear of a bus in traffic reflected the sign, "Follow me to Northside."

The bus routes at Northside have a larger ratio than the national average for Sunday School buses. First, the church with 1 to 10 buses averages 36 riders. Churches with 11 or more buses usually average 29 riders per bus. The buses at Northside Baptist Church average 49 riders per Sunday. Also, most Sunday School buses bring in children of primary and junior age, whereas many high schoolers and adults ride the buses at Northside Church, showing an impact on the community. The bus ministry now averages over 700 each Sunday.

A Christian School

The Northside Christian School, organized in 1963, grew out of a deep conviction to obey the Scriptures. Hudson feels that the Lord commands families, "Train up a child in the way he should go." Hudson preaches to his people, "The Federal Government is not responsible to train our children." This year over 700 students are enrolled in the school and most families pay the tuition because they are seeking the best education for their children. The school has attracted some newcomers to the church. However, Principal Paul Montgomery indicates this is not a major source of church growth. Some Christian families being transferred into the city will first look for a Christian school and then a church home. Many of them find both at Northside. Montgomery teaches the College and Career Class in the Sunday School.

Hudson sees two positive impacts on his church because of the school. First, quality Bible teaching five days a week has produced changed lives in students, attracting attention to the church from all walks of life. Many pupils have been led to Christ in the school and others have gained victories over sin. The changed lives of students in turn make an impact on parents and neighbors, attracting them to the Northside Baptist Church.

The second impact the Northside Christian School made on the Sunday School was the size of schoolrooms. It was obvious that the Northside Christian School could not use small Sunday School cubicles, so Hudson visited public schools. He concluded, "If a teacher can instruct 30 pupils during the week, a Sunday School teacher should be able to teach that many or more on Sunday." This insight led him to adopt the modified team teaching approach to Sunday School.

Bible Training

The Northside Bible Institute was organized in 1958 when Hudson realized that some people want more training than can be provided in Sunday School, yet they are not ready to enter a Christian college or Bible school full time. The Institute meets each Tuesday night in the school building. Various subjects are taught on a Bible school level. The Reverend G. Cole is dean of the Institute. The faculty consists of well-trained, dedicated pastors from the area. Hudson indicated, "We do not encourage the students from other churches to become members of Northside; however, many of them wanting a place to serve the Lord do become members."

Promotion

Hudson has often said, "Anything worthwhile is worth promoting." Although many criticize promotion, Hudson compares it to going fishing. He reminds the listener that Jesus called His disciples to be "fishers of men" (Mark 1:17). Hudson likens promotion to the bait, and the gospel to the hook. Bait attracts the fish, but it cannot catch. He asked, "Have you ever tried fishing with nothing but bait? You will attract fish but you won't catch them. If you ever try fishing with just the hook, you'll never catch them. It takes a combination of bait and hook." Hudson indicates he uses promotion to get people to attend Sunday School. Then the teaching of the Bible or the preaching of the gospel in the morning service is the hook that keeps them coming back week after week. The pastor stated, "When I walk to the pulpit, I completely forget about our promotional devices and preach the gospel as though people have come to listen to God." Hudson does not care *why* a man comes to church, only that he is there. Also, he does not use promotion in the morning service but keeps it in the Sunday School hour. He continued, "The way you 'catch' a person is the way you keep him." He went on to indicate that at the Northside Baptist Church they catch people with the hook of the gospel and keep them by preaching the Word of God."

Standing before his teachers, Hudson is the epitome of the true fisherman. He gets up early in the morning, sacrifices sleep and does without breakfast, to reach people for Jesus Christ. Hudson challenges his Sunday School teachers to do more than the weekend fisherman who rises wearily and sits on a wet bank shivering in the cold, just to catch a fish. He exhorted, "We must sacrifice, do without the pleasures of television, even do without meals so we may reach lost people for Jesus Christ."

Hudson also believes, "Do not promote what you cannot produce." He asked the theoretical question, "Suppose Coca Cola spent millions in advertisement and only several hundred dollars on its production plan. In no time, people who are encouraged to buy Coca Cola would become disenchanted if they found the shelves empty." Hudson says simply, "Don't promote what you can't produce." By this he means, do not promote the idea that you are having the greatest revival meeting in your city if you are not.

Four years ago Steve Byrd was given co-responsibility for promotion. This relieved the pastor for other duties. Byrd indicated they have no set number of promotional campaigns per year. "Just when we need it." The church sponsors several special days annually.

Northside claims credit for beginning Transportation Day, now used by many churches. On a designated Sunday, the entire church demonstrates that people still go to Sunday School and do so by driving to Sunday School in a variety of vehicles: antique cars, fire engines, riding lawn mowers, or dump trucks. Last year, a member who is an amateur parachutist, dropped out of a plane onto a nearby driving range, depicting the world's most unique way to go to church. His unfolded parachute displayed a gigantic flag inviting, "Follow me to Northside."

Once a year, Northside Baptist Church has a multi-week campaign. Last fall the Ten Commandments Campaign was held, a favorite of Northside because it was based on the Word of God. A charm bracelet was given to each pupil at the beginning of the campaign. The pastor preached on a Commandment each Sunday and a small charm of that week's Commandment was distributed, so faithful attendance let pupils acquire all ten charms.

Other promotional techniques include Early Bird Sunday (when the city goes on Daylight Saving Time), Twin Sunday, and Youth Sunday. Recently, as Hudson was rummaging around in the church attic, he found the original bell of the old church. He instituted Ring the Bell Sunday. Each Sunday when the attendance remained above 2,000, the church bell was rung. This was especially effective since many Southerners come from rural backgrounds where the church bell invited them to Sunday School.

Byrd indicated gimmicks are not biblical, but Jesus often used external motivation. Christ fed the multitude and told Peter to get a coin out of the fish's mouth; also He healed physical bodies as evidence of His compassion. Byrd formerly had reservations about external motivations until God began to give him ideas for attendance campaigns. When he saw these motivate unsaved people to attend church where they were led to Jesus Christ, he said, "I'll use any means I can to lead people to Christ." Byrd indicated, "I do have reservations about some *gimmicks* used by other churches. A promotional event must be controlled by Scripture and must honor God, otherwise I will not use it."

Dr. Hudson often repeats the statement, "If we make much of Jesus, He will make much of us." This is printed in much of the church's promotional material. Hudson answers, "We use promotions to make much of Jesus."

Byrd used a recent campaign "I Love Jesus Sunday." The bus workers went out visiting on Saturday. They gave each prospective rider a blank application reading, "I love Jesus and will prove I love Him by getting on my Northside bus and going to Sunday School unless something real bad happens that I can't go." No prizes or gimmicks were used. People rode the buses simply because they loved Jesus Christ. According to Byrd, this was one of the best-attended drives in the history of the church. He indicated this type of motivation appeals to the proper incentives, and experience proved that the best way to get people to work in a local church is to appeal to their spiritual motivation.

Last Homecoming Day the church had a record attendance of 3,050. All the teen-agers gathered in the gym for a large combined Sunday School class. The children met out under the trees, where 1,000 folding chairs were waiting. The adults packed into the main sanctuary to hear the pastor preach the Word of God. Following the Sunday morning service, an old-fashioned dinner-on-the-grounds was held. This year the church plans for 5,000 in attendance on Homecoming Day.

Hudson indicated that a church should not plan to bring 1,000 extra visitors without a well-organized program in which attention is given to small details. He advises: (1) Think through every detail; (2) think through the consequences to the people; (3) know what to do when they arrive; (4) have enough help for every aspect of crowd control; and (5) plan every small detail to publicize the event to as many people as possible. Byrd stresses, "Details lead to success." He went on to explain: "Get a lot of workers and make sure they know what to do. Details will make or break you."

Personnel

Hudson stated that every church has every person it needs to do the job God wants it to do at a particular time. However, many churches fail by the wrong choice or management of personnel. He cites the ability of Vince Lombardi to build the world champion Green Bay Packers because he chose his men well. "The church is no different," declares Hudson. "Everything rises or falls on leadership," according to Dr. Lee Roberson, Highland Park Baptist Church of Chattanooga, Tennessee.

Hudson believes you cannot hire people to work for God. You may give them wages for the necessities of life, but if they do not want to serve the Lord more than anything else in life, they will always be hirelings waiting for a more lucrative position in another church. Since outstanding men are hard to find, Hudson feels one answer is fewer teachers with larger classes. He pointed out that fewer than 50 comedians entertain the entire nation on television. From this he drew the conclusion, "Obviously, only the best ones are used because they command the attention of the viewers." Sunday

School teachers are far more important than TV entertainers and are even more difficult to find. Hudson and Byrd carefully choose the Sunday School teachers after prospective teachers complete a questionnaire on the doctrinal beliefs and standards of separation.

Four years ago the Northside Baptist Church had four on its staff: the pastor, secretary, custodian, and the Reverend Hartman, who assisted the pastor in visitation. One of the causes leading to the phenomenal growth has been the addition of eleven full-time staff members.

The leaders feel that their strict standards of separation have produced quality and quantity growth. Teachers are not allowed to smoke, attend movies, mix-swim, or play cards. They indicate this stand each year by a signed statement. However, Hudson says, "Separation is a means, not an end. Many small churches have an aim to be pure, but their whole Christian life is centered around the negative—what they will *not* do." Hudson believes that purity leads to power; therefore, the separated teacher is the useful teacher. He added, "Many small churches are concerned that their teachers do not participate in sin. I am most concerned that my teachers are powerful instruments in the hand of God to transform the lives of their students. Then I know that my teachers are not being troubled by sin."

Preaching

Hudson believes that no matter how well oiled the Sunday School machinery, it is still the preaching of the gospel that builds great churches. He feels that both Sunday School teaching and gospel preaching go hand in hand to build a great church. He feels the message should be warm, down-to-earth "telling like it is," with a definite urgent appeal to be saved *now!*

Youth

Northside Baptist Church has an outstanding youth program. In many cases, a family's choice of a church is based on the program for its young people. This youth program must be enlightening rather than entertaining. Hudson feels that the young people are very knowledgeable and will not attend a church based on gimmicks. They come where the Word of God is taught, where their problems are dealt with and they can be helped to meet the issues of life. Hudson goes on to say, "The church that survives the next 10 years will be the church that gears itself to the youth." The average American youth department numbers 12 percent of Sunday School attendance.

The ratio at Northside is much higher, with 20 percent of the total in a youth department.

Cooperation

Hudson points to the spokes of the wheel; none is more important than the other. If one spoke collapses, the whole wheel is weakened and eventually collapses. He feels very little has ever been accomplished in a New Testament church apart from cooperation. The first church in Acts teaches this: "They were all with one accord in one place" (Acts 2:1). The proper motivation for cooperation is not just making people follow—it's motivating a person to "want to follow." Hudson feels that just as God guides individuals, so He guides churches. And God best guides moving objects.

Conclusion

Hudson and Byrd agree that it is impossible for the Sunday School to "hold on" to their present attendance level. Their program is "geared up to growth." Hudson indicated, "If we tried merely to hold on to our present attendance and not to grow, we would kill motivation and discourage our teachers."

Dr. Jack Hudson has suffered crippling arthritis. One factor in the recent spurt in attendance was his surgery in 1967. Immediately thereafter he resumed a daily radio broadcast on WKTC, which he had conducted for seven years but had dropped due to ill health.

The Sunday morning service is televised on a closed circuit TV network into the six nurseries of the church. Also there are eight TVs in the balcony for those who cannot seee the pulpit. The network is called NBC for "Northside Baptist Church." The gym and other large rooms are wired for TV. During revival meetings and special promotional days, TV sets are installed for the overflow crowd.

The church believes in utilizing outstanding men of God. Just as God blessed His work in biblical times through great men, Dr. Jack Hudson believes in bringing the best speakers in America to his church. Among these have been evangelists Bob Harrington and Freddie Gage; Dr. Lee Roberson; and a perennial favorite, Dr. Lyman Strauss, a Bible conference teacher.

Chapter 7

The Statue of a Man Cast
A Long Shadow Over
The Church

First Baptist Church

Riverdale, Maryland

The continual growth of First Baptist Church, Riverdale, Maryland, is not easy to analyze. The church does not fit the usual mold of other fast-growing churches, yet some of the characteristics are evident. Attendance increase has not come only because of visitation, busing, giving, or from contests. Pastor Herbert Fitzpatrick, pastor, does not offer "give-aways" to coax children to Sunday School, stating, "My church will not be a three-ring circus." A mother walked in to Sunday School and chided her two small children. "Be quiet; God is here. Let us be reverent." Fitzpatrick is an unlikely candidate for one of America's successful preachers, yet he is the cause for the extraordinary growth in the First Baptist Church of Riverdale. Fitzpatrick's preaching is not emotional, but moving. His soul winning is not based on salesmanship, but sincerity. He relates to members, not through counseling techniques but through deep concern. The church is well organized, yet he is not seen as the efficient, hard-driving administrator. He never seems in a hurry. The growth of First Baptist Church of Riverdale is directly accountable to Herbert Fitzpatrick, yet unlike pastors of other large churches, he appears to be shy and retiring. When he is asked to speak at ministers' rallies, he often refuses.

This chapter shows that a leader can attract people without being iron-fisted; a leader can command a following without shouting or using pulpit oratory. Bob Smith, a college student converted at Riverdale, states, "Pastor Fitzpatrick has a quiet way of shouting." Fitzpatrick leads out of deep spiritual commitment. Nelson Keener, a former Mennonite who gave his life to full-time service at Riverdale, stated, "Fitzpatrick is the most humble, unassuming pastor I've known." When asked to comment on his magnetism, Fitzpatrick said, "I don't know that I have magnetism, but people know when you are sincere."

This chapter has two sections. First, the leadership of Herbert Fitzpatrick is examined and, second, the church is seen. First Baptist Church of Riverdale is having an impact on the greater Washington, D. C., area. Some drive thirty miles to attend service. Fitzpatrick hopes to evangelize the entire metropolitan area with the gospel.

The Shadow of a Man on the Church

Fitzpatrick, who speaks with a Virginia accent, reflects his Roanoke background. Even though he was reared in a home of average means, as a boy he was exposed to men of stature. His late cousin was president of Ferrum College, and another cousin is a high-ranking judge in Roanoke. Immediately after Fitzpatrick's salvation, the Reverend E. J. Morris, who led him to the Lord, took Fitzpatrick under his wing to prepare the young man for the ministry. Morris was building the Bible Baptist Church; Fitzpatrick watched him lead the church from a tent meeting to over 200 members. Fitzpatrick indicates, "This was my first introduction to building a church. From the beginning I felt I could also build a church." Fitzpatrick attended Practical Bible Training School in New York for one year and transferred to Bible Baptist seminary in Ft. Worth, Texas. Here he came in contact with Dr. J. Frank Norris, who instilled in him a determination to make something of his life. During Fitzpatrick's school days, he told fellow students, "I feel God has called me to be the pastor of a large Baptist church." Many of his friends reflect back on his school years; most of them thought Fitzpatrick was going to be an average pastor. Today they explain his phenomenal success by his unquestionable commitment to biblical truth, his knowledge of how to build a church, and his unmistakable honesty and sincerity. Fitzpatrick analyzes himself, "By nature, I have always been ambitious; I wanted to be successful at something." He indicated J. Frank Norris instilled a great desire in him through classroom teaching. He recounts how Dr. Norris, called "the old man" in those days, would call off class and preach to students, in his own homespun philosophy telling the class how to build a church. "Just to sit around Norris changed my life," indicated Fitzpatrick.

1. *A hard worker.*—Hard work has made the First Baptist Church in Riverdale successful. Fitzpatrick makes 20 to 25 calls a week, talking to people about Jesus Christ. These evangelistic calls are more

than meeting people at the front door, inviting them to church. Each visit comprises a heart-to-heart appeal to receive Jesus Christ. In addition, Pastor Fitzpatrick makes 20 to 25 hospital calls a week and the staff estimates he has many counseling sessions each week, dealing with in-depth problems of church members. Fitzpatrick indicates he does not visit with the members as most ministers. When members have problems, he suggests they come into the church. If there is a special problem, he visits in the home. When Fitzpatrick first came to the church, he visited the home of every member. Now he uses most of his visitation time in calling on the unsaved. He states, "I am the main soul winner in our church and must set the example so people will follow."

Even though Fitzpatrick believes hard work is the main ingredient in church growth, he comments, "I've seen other pastors work just as hard as I do, yet not succeed." Therefore, he concludes, "Hard work alone does not cause success." He indicated that hard work must follow the biblical pattern of first reaching the unsaved, then training Christians. He constantly maintains that a pastor cannot use good salesmanship to *get* decisions, nor can he use good teaching to *keep* converts. "Either my work is of the Holy Spirit, or it is nothing." To this he adds, "I'm constantly aware of my dependence on the Holy Spirit."

2. *Compassion.*—Fitzpatrick maintains, "A pastor should never use his people to build his church." He goes on to state, "The people are his church." He maintains that if a pastor loves his people and ministers to them, numerical growth will be the natural result.

Therefore, he is not obsessed with numbers, as many pastors. He is often called *Pastor* rather than *Preacher,* reflecting his interest in people. Because the people have confidence in him, they call day or night for all of their problems. In every way possible, Fitzpatrick attempts to help them. His ministry is characterized by *compassion.* When asked, "Where did you get your compassion?" Fitzpatrick replied, "It is a gift from God." He indicated that preaching in the jails while at seminary in Ft. Worth gave him a compassion for people. He felt the convicts were more than just a number in the audience, so he spent time talking with them. He especially remembers one convicted murderer who responded to his friendship by rounding up the inmates and making them listen to his sermons.

Fitzpatrick deeply believes it is the will of God for him to build a large church in Riverdale, Maryland. "Every discouragement has faced me at Riverdale," answered Fitzpatrick. "I would have quit if I did not believe this is the will of God." He points to his previous pastorate, Calvary Baptist Church, Connersville, Indiana, where five

Pastor Herbert Fitzpatrick

First Baptist Church, Riverdale, Maryland

attempts had been made to organize an independent Baptist church, yet each one failed. Fitzpatrick began with a small group of 35 people on the front porch of a home the first Sunday. The following week he organized the church with 13 members. He pastored in Connersville for 17 years and left a Sunday School averaging over 1,200 and a church membership of 2,300. He indicated that he and his wife were young and many times discouraged, but always persevered. Fitzpatrick left Connersville because he felt he was "spinning his wheels" and the challenge was gone. He saw in Riverdale an unlimited field.

3. *Subdued eloquence.*—The membership was surveyed to determine why they felt the church was growing. The quiet strength of Fitzpatrick was given more than any other reason for church growth. One member commented, "He is like a tower of strength that never shows its total abilities." One teenager wrote, "The pastor is like a Cadillac; you never have to floor-board to get complete acceleration." Another commented that, even though he carries a tremendous load, he never buckles. Still another observed that Fitzpatrick manages his time. This was reflected in the comment, "Our pastor never seems busy, hurried, or frustrated; yet he is always working, making calls in homes."

Mrs. Mary Clark indicated the success of Riverdale was due to two items: first, continual visitation by the lay people and the pastor. She indicated Fitzpatrick seems to visit almost 24 hours a day. She used the phrase, "because of his personal interest in everyone." Once she brought a visitor, and a year later when the visitor returned, Fitzpatrick remembered the name. Secondly, Mrs. Clark felt the church grew because Fitzpatrick was not a hell-fire evangelist, but a gospel preacher. She observed, "He makes me want to serve God." People do not attend the church out of gimmicks, contests or promotional devices. Visitors come because they want to hear Fitzpatrick preach.

4. *A quiet way of shouting.*—Fitzpatrick spends his late evenings studying and preparing his sermons. His reason is simple: "I want to be with the people when they are available." Therefore, he spends his mornings, afternoons, and evenings with the people, and his late-night hours with his books. Fitzpatrick says, "It is proper to work and bring people in, but I must have something for them when they listen to the Word of God." Therefore, he stays fresh and seldom uses old sermons.

Fitzpatrick stated, "A pastor can't build a strong church without strong Bible preaching." Even though the unsaved are converted in each service, Fitzpatrick stated, "I preach more to Christians." Fitzpatrick's attitude is, "I preach the Bible to get it out so the Holy

Spirit can make it take effect in every life." At the same time he stated, "I don't go in for the idea of a notebook and pencil, making my preaching services a Bible conference." Fitzpatrick characterizes his Bible teaching as "knowledge with fire." But he feels that Bible knowledge alone is not enough to cause a young Christian to grow. He observes, "Babies grow by food plus exercise, so the young Christian is nurtured in Christ through feeding on the Word and winning souls."

Tony Scoglio, a student from Baptist Bible College, worked in the church during the summer and reflected, "Fitzpatrick gives more content in his preaching than other independent Baptist ministers I've heard." According to Tony, "I get tired of shallow preaching and I have been in many independent Baptist churches and have never grown." The young student observed, "I want to be a pastor, and Fitzpatrick's type of preaching has caused me to grow." He characterized this preaching as "content with enthusiasm." Scoglio, a product of the Riverdale church, indicated that when he went to the Baptist Bible College in Springfield, he knew more about the Bible than most kids from other Baptist Bible Fellowship churches.

When asked if he preaches sin, Fitzpatrick indicates, "I preach separation from sin, but don't have a hobby horse." He went on to indicate he named sins such as smoking, dancing, drinking, theater and cards. His reason for this is simple. "People won't classify sins unless you name them." He went on to say that he does not spend his time on one specific sin or emphasize questionable sins. To illustrate this point he indicated, "I have never preached against rock-and-roll music, yet was pleased when an evangelist asked kids to come forward and give up rock-and-roll." Fitzpatrick indicated, "Preaching against sin will not drive people away. People want their preacher to speak with authority—they want you to tell them what is wrong."

5. *Example.*—Youth Director Arnie Smith cites the example of Fitzpatrick as the reason for the church staff's success: "The pastor doesn't tell me what to do; he shows me by his example." Smith indicates that, because his pastor wins souls, visits the sick and counsels the unsaved, the staff is challenged to follow his pattern.

Ron Secrest, music director, states Fitzpatrick can call by name every one of the 2,000 people in church. Secrest continues, "People want to follow the pastor because they have confidence that the Holy Spirit is leading him." The music director observed, "The people have faith that the pastor knows where he is going. *They have confidence* that the pastor will do the will of God."

6. *A good wife.*—Many have said Mrs. Fitzpatrick is one of the

keys to the success of First Baptist Church. They feel that if ever a pastor had a perfect wife, Mrs. Fitzpatrick fits that image. She was superintendent of the Baptist orphanage in Ft. Worth when young Herbert met her while pastoring Calvary Baptist Church in Connersville, Ind. She is vitally interested and concerned for the ministry of the church. According to Fitzpatrick, "She is not selfish of my time but we live together for the work of Christ." Her compassion for the people is evident by the visits she makes when Fitzpatrick is sick. Each Sunday, she stands at the door with him and greets the people. When she is not there, the people ask about her. Mrs. Fitzpatrick comes to each service early and is seen going through the audience sepaking to the members and greeting visitors. According to Fitzpatrick, she takes care of problem situations before they multiply into serious problems. She counsels many women in the church who feel they cannot come see the pastor. Each Sunday, Mrs. Fitzpatrick teaches the college and career class of over 100 members. Many of those who come from her class, go into the ministry or establish Christian homes, feeling she has made one of the greatest impacts on their lives.

The Church

As visitors drive up Riverdale Road, the church comes into sight— a three-story, formidable brick building with dark blue stained glass windows. Massive paved parking lots in the front and rear of the church accommodate visitors and members. Inside the large front foyer, conducive to fellowship after the service, the visitor is impressed with a reverent attitude, rather than the typical informality found in the preaching auditoriums in the Baptist Bible Fellowship churches. The baptistry sets high above the pulpit. Red carpets reflect a royal atmosphere. Laminated beams and solid oak pews lend dignity to the auditorium. This is the third auditorium built by the congregation; the first building was a small white frame church constructed in 1928, and the second sanctuary was a two-story brick building structured in 1951. The neighborhood is settled, reflecting that the church is built on suburban homeowners. Even though this church is associated with the Baptist Bible Fellowship, it is not typical of the movement. At its location approximately three miles from the University of Maryland campus, many college students and white collar workers worship there, in contrast to the Baptist Bible Fellowship's ministry to lower classes.

In 1967, Fitzpatrick accepted John R. Rice's challenge to baptize at least 200. The church exceeded the goal, baptizing 224. Fitzpatrick indicated that reaching this goal was a big step toward ac-

The First Baptist Church of Riverdale seats 1,200 people.

celerating growth in the church. The Riverdale church is unlike the average Baptist Bible Fellowship church in that converts are not baptized immediately, but once a month. The new converts receive instruction in a young convert's class during Training Union on Sunday evening. Fitzpatrick indicated, "We would like for them to attend the class, but if they don't, we baptize them anyway." All those who come forward are visited in the home by a class member with the purpose of teaching them the Christian life and their responsibility to the church.

1. *The deacons.*—Fitzpatrick indicated he has never had a problem with lay committees in his entire ministry. He feels deeply that a deacon should not "legislate" to the pastor, but rather, serve with him to reach a community for Christ. He feels the deacons should first be dedicated to the Lord and, second, have a testimony before the congregation of a separated life. Finally, he feels a deacon should have an experience of effective Christian service. Fitzpatrick expects

his deacons to visit throughout the week, just as he does. The church holds a quarterly business meeting at which Fitzpatrick is the chairman. He also chairs the meeting of the deacons and the meeting of the trustees. He indicates, "I am not trying to assume authority, I am only exercising my leadership." Each board has a lay-chairman who will lead the meeting if Fitzpatrick cannot attend. He went on to indicate, "I have no objections for the board to meet without me, but I am usually there." Many feel that the blue-collar worker will respond to strong leadership, but middle-class church members will not. Fitzpatrick observes, "The educated men of our community respond to positive biblical leadership." To this he added, "I am not a domineering dictator; it is just that we are going to do something for God." One deacon observed, "The pastor is effective because he is always open to our suggestions."

Before Fitzpatrick came to the church, the trustees were a policy-setting board. Fitzpatrick indicated, "I never told them they couldn't set policy; I simply outlined the program for a church from the New Testament and set goals for us to accomplish. Then we rolled up our sleeves and started working."

One of the trustees remarked to Fitzpatrick early in his ministry, "Why don't you do the preaching and let us worry about the business and the money?" Fitzpatrick's answer was simple and direct. "The ministry is business and money; we cannot divorce them from God's program. There is no split in the ministry. The church has one thrust—to win souls. Every dollar will be used to win souls. Every business decision will be to win souls."

Most observers feel that Fitzpatrick's pastoral leadership turned the church into a soul-winning institution, whereas it had been a weekly Bible conference. Previously the people brought notebooks to take notes, but did very little soul winning. One observer commented, "A younger pastor would have split the church, but Fitzpatrick's love and tact won the church."

2. *The Sunday School.*—Fitzpatrick believes in expanding attendance through the Sunday School by developing a spirit of competition. Each Sunday he announces every department's attendance. "In making comments about the attendance, I keep the superintendents on their toes," observed Fitzpatrick. Even though the church has a Sunday School superintendent, Fitzpatrick gives the Sunday School leadership and purpose. The Sunday School superintendent takes care of the details. His duties are described in the statement, "A Sunday School superintendent is the extension of the pastor's ministry into the Sunday School."

There is no written job description for the superintendent or teachers. Fitzpatrick expects a teacher to visit, prepare the lesson and get the job done. He believes the outstanding teacher will have spiritual concern for his students and devote time to prayer and visitation. He feels numerical growth will result if a teacher does the above.

3. *Visitation program.*—Every Wednesday night, Fitzpatrick asks for a commitment of those who will attend visitation on the following Thursday. Usually over 50 attend, when the people are divided into teams, each group receiving six cards. However, Fitzpatrick does not realistically expect six visits each evening. "If a team of soul winners can make three good visits in an evening, I am satisfied." Even though most independent Baptist churches push soul winning, Fitzpatrick reported that his people make a variety of calls. Some visit absentees, while others go to a home with the purpose of a friendly "handshake," inviting people to the service. Also, soul-winning calls are made into the homes of lost people. Even though Fitzpatrick is concerned about reaching the lost, he stated recently to his visitors, "Don't be too pushy; don't pluck green fruit." He wants his soul winners to leave the door open for someone else to go to that home.

Conclusion

The life of Herbert Fitzpatrick is a testimony to all preachers, that any man who desires to build a large church, can do so. He is a living repudiation of the stereotyped concept of a successful pastor—i.e., he must be loud and commanding. Fitzpatrick is quiet. He has a dynamic inner strength. He reflects God's promise, "In quietness and confidence shall be your strength" (Isa. 30:15).

For those who look for the presence of the Lord in the ministry built on a leader's personality or emotional preaching, they should realize this is not the only way God works. Elijah went forth looking for God. "Behold, the Lord passed by, and a great and strong wind rent the mountains and brake in pieces the rocks before the Lord; but the Lord was not in the wind: and after the wind an earthquake; but the Lord was not in the earthquake: and after the earthquake a fire; but the Lord was not in the fire: and after the fire a still small voice." The Reverend Herbert Fitzpatrick is God's still small voice thundering the gospel throughout the Greater Washington, D. C., area.

Chapter 8

Unashamed to Reach People

Marietta Baptist Tabernacle

Marietta, Georgia

Nine years ago, the Reverend Bob Moore came from small Milford, Illinois, to become pastor of the East Marietta Premillennial Missionary Baptist Tabernacle—a large name, but a small congregation. Moore looks back and smiles at the complicated name, yet he praises God for enabling him to lead the people to change the name to Marietta Baptist Tabernacle. Even this embryonic public relations strategy move was predictive of his future ministry. There were 35 members with 47 in Sunday School when Moore came. Six attended the first prayer meeting. The growth over the years has been both steady and explosive, with an increase of approximately 100 people per year. However, the Sunday School grew by 500 in 1971.

The church was the grand award winner of the "March to Sunday School in March" sponsored by the National Sunday School Association in 1963. Two years later, the church was the divisional winner. Moore confesses, "That's when the people caught a vision of growth. In that first contest we set a goal to average 75, yet reached 113." Since December 1963, there has not been one Sunday in which a person was not saved and baptized.

There are many outstanding qualities of the Marietta Baptist Tabernacle that could be emphasized; the biblical preaching, the organized visitation program, the emphasis on teaching Bible content, the Marietta Christian Schools, the music program or the leadership of the pastor, the Reverend Bob Moore. However, since each chapter is emphasizing one or two major strengths, Sunday School contests and promotions will be highlighted in this chapter. Bob Moore has a balanced approach to promotions that can be exemplary for other churches.

Bob Moore is unashamed to reach people. His first promotion was awarding Moody Colportage paperback books to those who brought visitors to Sunday School. Even though the cost of the books was small (39 cents) the results were extraordinary to a small church: 394 first-time visitors. Moore's theory is simply "Give little things in a big way." He goes on to state, "It's not what you give, but the enthusiasm you create." This role is followed in all he does. For the following reasons Moore believes in using promotion to build a great Sunday School.

1. *Promotion is scriptural.*—To prove this point, Moore states, "I will use any idea that is not unscriptural." He points to the statement made by Paul, "I am made all things to all men, that I might by all means save some" (I Cor. 9:20). He interprets "reaching" to mean "motivating or stimulating a person to give an honest hearing to the gospel." Moore uses promotion to get people under the sound of the gospel. But he believes he has to go a step farther than getting a person in the church—biblical promotion will motivate a man to give honest *attention* to the gospel. Moore is against promotion that gets a man to church then causes him to be "turned off" by the cheapness or extremes of the promotion, so that he makes fun of the gospel.

2. *Promotion is sensible.* Moore points out that businesses prosper because people are properly motivated, and the same can be said for a church. He points to Luke 16:8, "For the children of this world are in their generation wiser than the children of light." Moore reasons, since businesses use promotion and prosper, why should a church refuse to promote the gospel?

3. *Promotion is soul winning.*—Moore points to the fact that the greatest number of people are saved and baptized in those churches which use promotion. By the same token, those churches that are against promotion usually have no vitality, their attendance is dwindling and they record few, if any, conversions. During 1971, Marietta Baptist Tabernacle recorded 3,629 public decisions for Christ. According to Moore, "I am not ashamed to use promotion to reach people for Jesus Christ."

4. *Promotion builds sound churches.* Moore facetiously said, "Empty pews cannot give a tithe, sing a hymn or offer a prayer. People are needed to have a strong church." Since Moore knows

Pastor Bob Moore

Promotion at the Church

that people become involved in the church through promotion he concludes that the more people become involved, the stronger the church becomes. Therefore, promotion builds strong churches.

Moore was further questioned about his philosophy of promotion and he simply replied, "I would rather preach to a thousand than a hundred." He was quick to add, "not to build my ego, but to further the gospel." He went on to state any soul winner can talk to one person at a time, but the pastor who can preach to thousands is both efficient and effective in his outreach. Moore uses eight basic kinds of promotion that attract people to the Marietta Baptist Tabernacle.

1. *Big days.*—On certain Sundays throughout the year, Moore expends every energy available to get many people into the church. This may be "Break the Record Sunday" or an old-fashioned Homecoming.

2. *Attendance campaigns.*—During a recent campaign in the Sunday School, one department had Space Day. The intent was to fill the space in Primary III Department, by getting as many primaries as possible to attend. Two rockets were suspended on wires above the room, and the space capsule was pulled along by the team having the most members. In one corner a large life-size poster board had pictures of the astronauts painted on it. The pupil who brought a visitor received a picture of himself and the visitor with their heads over the poster board astronaut body. In another part of the room a large rocket was constructed, and the child who had the most points got to sit in the rocket during pre-session activities.

3. *Contests.*—Last July, the church fought "the war between the states," in an attendance contest with another church, to see who could grow the largest during the month. Moore's church was losing until the last day of the contest, when he promoted an actual mock battle, re-creating the Battle of Kenesaw Mountain (Kenesaw Mountain National Park is in the suburbs of Marietta). Two hundred and fifty Civil War buffs came to fight the battle. They fired ten muzzle-loaded cannons and old muskets. The cavalry charged, and soldiers dressed in Civil War uniforms stood their ground. Those engaged in the battle were not members of the church but came because of their interest in the Civil War. The Sunday School broke all attendance records that day.

4. *Gifts for attendance on a specified day.*—In November 1970 the church advertised, "The Indians are Coming." The Klaudt Indian family came to play and sing in the morning service. Every child received an Indian headdress as a token of that day's attendance in Sunday School.

5. *Dinners, refreshments, and treats.*—Moore has promoted "Hot Dog Day." The hot dogs were cooked before the children arrived for Sunday School, and the teachers planned presession activities for the children so they could munch on hot dogs before Sunday School began. Since most adults are not interested in hot dogs, the promotion only extended to the lower grades.

6. *Special activities.*—Sunday School classes plan special trips to see the Atlanta Braves or to visit Stone Mountain. Also, attendance is stimulated by the traditional summer picnic for each class. The Sunday School used "Picture-Taking Day," in which a picture of the class was taken and a copy given to every child who returned the following week. Moore indicated everyone loves to have his picture taken, and by having all return the following week, the promotion helped to establish a pattern of regular attendance. In some departments, a student is allowed to occupy a special seat of honor, for bringing visitors.

7. *Awards for workers who excel.*—Moore believes that motivation to the pupil is important, but the staff member must also be motivated to extra effort. Therefore, Moore offered 25 trips to Florida for the workers bringing the most visitors to Sunday School.

8. *Special speakers.*—Randy Hundley, catcher for the Chicago Cubs, gave his testimony in Sunday School. All the children who came were given an 8½ x 11 glossy picture of Hundley. Many were able to get his autograph after Sunday School.

Moore will not do *everything* to reach people, he will do *anything that is biblical.* He went on to explain, "The promotion must be controlled by biblical ends." By that he meant that not every promotion will win souls. Moore believes that in order to have a biblical church you must believe the Bible, preach the Bible, practice the Bible and get biblical results—souls saved. Some criticize that "contests attract shallow people." According to Moore, Marietta Baptist Tabernacle contradicts that statement because of the way the church uses promotion; it forces people to become personal soul winners, resulting in their spiritual growth. He offered the Fireside Bible to every member who would bring 25 or more families. Twelve members received the Bible. He explained to his people, "I offered this Bible as a tool for you to use with your friends." Moore went on to explain to his people that they could tell their friends, "Come and help me win this Bible." Moore explained, "Contests only draw people; Bible teaching keeps them." In examining his growth, he indicated, "We could not keep people on gimmicks; we keep people through a solid Bible-teaching ministry."

Consistent attendance is one of the aims of the promotions and contests used at the Marietta Baptist Tabernacle. Moore indicates, "We need to bring a pupil back three or four times to make him a regular attender. By that time, he wants to come because we teach the Bible rather than because we offer him a prize."

Even though Moore uses promotion regularly, he explains, "We are not growing on gadgets, we are growing on soul winning." He states, "I teach the people *why* we have promotions. We do not give away something just to swell attendance; promotions provide a way to reach unsaved people with the gospel." Moore further explained that most Christians come to church for biblical reasons; however, outsiders come for various other reasons.

Moore advertises his promotional ideas in many ways. (1) He constantly sends letters and announcements through the mail. (2) The church uses signs, posters, and decorations depicting the promotion in the Sunday School rooms and/or bulletin boards in the halls. (3) Announcements by the pastor from the pulpit are important. Moore feels it is important for the promotion to be built around the pastor. He states, "It is good to have special speakers on occasions, but visitors want to see the pastor and listen to him preach." Therefore, he uses few outside speakers. Moore states, "It is otherwise difficult for visitors to associate the success of the day with the pastor." Moore goes on to state, "Visitors should feel the day was a blessing because of my ministry, not because of the guest." (4) Announcements made by superintendents and Sunday School teachers stir enthusiasm. (5) Image promotion is carried out constantly by advertisement via church letterhead, church brochures, newspaper and radio.

How to Promote Successfully

Moore says, "Let quality be the criterion for promotion." He indicates confidence and pride is built into the members if everything is done to the best of one's ability. They in turn become enthusiastic about the church and will carry the burden of attendance growth. He gave the following suggestions for promotion. (1) *Maintain high standards for printed and mimeographed advertising pieces.* (2) *Follow through on what has been announced.* Moore indicates that promotion is successful only when "you give the people what you have offered." He has found careful planning will avoid failures. When a pastor is unable to carry out his word, he should honestly tell the people the reasons he has failed but then carry out the promise at a later date. (3) *Do not give awards or rewards that are not earned.* Unearned rewards lessen the value of promotions in the future and will promote a bad spirit among the children. (4)

Use prizes that cannot be gained in any other way. A balloon has no appeal, but when it has the church's name on it, it is prized by the children.

(5) *Learn the best time to give out promotional items.* Moore believes that some churches let promotion get in the way of teaching the Word of God. Therefore, he usually distributes promotional items at the end of the morning service. He does this for three reasons: (a) to save time in Sunday School and morning service, (b) to avoid interruptions or noise the children sometimes cause with the articles they are given, and (c) to end the day on a happy note.

(6) *Variety is the key word in promotions.* Moore emphasizes, "Don't go to the same well too often." Therefore, he varies his promotions rather than using the same ones each year. "Yet," Moore emphasized, "we keep using a promotion as long as it will work. If you're catching rabbits as they come out of a hole, you catch them until they stop coming, then you go elsewhere."

(7) *Promotional items and special guests cost money, but they pay.* Moore cautions the young pastor, "As the church grows, increased income makes promotion pay for itself; however, money is not always the factor in promotion." Moore has learned over the years that an expensive gift without promotion has little effect, whereas the well-promoted inexpensive gift draws the crowd. However, when talking about money Moore counsels, "Do not expect your biggest attendance days to yield the biggest offerings." Moore indicates that the work of his church is faithfully supported by the tithes and offerings of the regular church family. His people feel that money invested in promotions will yield more results than any other missionary investment, dollar for dollar.

(8) *A promotion does not work; the leader has to work it.* Many churches will borrow promotional ideas from successful churches, and find they fail when used at home. Moore feels that leadership is the secret to successful promotion. He advises to begin a promotional campaign early enough so it can be advertised to all the members—then repeat, repeat, repeat. He states, "People who do not know about your church will not come."

When Moore was asked how he thinks of his ideas for promotion, he indicates they come from simple sources. (1) He gets ideas from the newspapers and bulletins of other churches that have been successful. (2) He uses suggestions of secular companies that specialize in advertising products. (3) He brainstorms with his staff to create new promotional ideas. (4) He spends a great deal of time in creative thought. According to him, "I spend my waking hours thinking of the Marietta Baptist Tabernacle." Many times he will awaken in the middle of the night with ideas to reach people for Christ.

The main criticism surrounding Marietta Baptist Tabernacle is that prizes are given to get children to come to the Sunday School. (There seems to be no criticism that the church members are shallow. This may be the result of doing a good job of teaching the Bible.) Moore does not listen to his critics, saying, "I can't work for God if I spend time answering critics." He goes on to state, "I am concerned only about the criticism of people I respect." He further concludes, "If I must offend one person to reach one thousand, I will continue to offend that one person."

Walking through one of the Beginner Departments, the visitor heard a rooster crowing; as a matter of fact, pupils heard it throughout the Sunday School. The pre-schoolers were having Pet Day and a little boy brought his rooster. A glance inside the department revealed animals of all shapes that had been brought to Sunday School that day. Another day, Tony the Tiger plastic hand puppets were given to each child in the class. As the teacher held up the puppet to tell the story, each child held up his puppet, mimicking the teacher, thus becoming involved in the story.

A favorite motto that Moore uses with promotions is, "Do it big when you are small and you'll have a chance to do it big when you are large."

New facilities of Marietta Baptist Tabernacle now under construction

Pupils at a Sunday School function

The Church

Atlanta is Moore's home. He was raised in the poorer section of the city and confesses, "I've had to overcome many obstacles in life, so I made it a lifelong practice to learn from those who know how, and then follow their example." As a result, Moore flew to the larger Sunday Schools in America to learn how they did it. He phoned ahead and asked for thirty minutes of the pastor's time. Moore had one question he phrased to each of the pastors of the largest churches: "If you had five minutes to pass your successful ministry on to me, what would you tell me?" Moore indicated, "They told me, then I left."

Moore feels that most fundamentalists have negative thinking; as a result, they do not accomplish much for God. In contrast, he feels God has designed man for success, therefore he feels he can build a successful church by following God's formula. He points to the motto of Henry Ford as a good criterion for his mental attitude toward growth, "Whether or not you think you can, you're right." Therefore, Moore believes he can build a large church.

Moore writes his own Sunday School quarterlies. He has been doing this for 9 years and feels it is an effective investment of his time. He spends fifteen minutes in the teachers' meeting, instructing them concerning the content and application of next Sunday's lesson. Moore indicates he takes a chapter-by-chapter approach to the Bible. Although the church attempts to cover one chapter each week, Moore indicates, "We take thought divisions within the chapter." After Moore has taught the lesson to the teachers, methods teachers teach them the visual aids to use in the class. The church uses the rule, "Anything that can be taught, can be visualized." When Jacob's ladder was taught, each teacher had a ladder made of pipe cleaners. When the parables were taught, a large pan of dirt was placed in each room, carrot seeds were planted and the seed envelope placed on a stick in each row. The children got a week-by-week visual lesson of growth.

In the Primary Department, blocks were used for each book of the Bible, and the children were taught to say the books of the Bible by playing with the blocks. This author noted that there were more visuals used in this church than most churches, and the church did not use any produced by Sunday School publishing houses. The teachers made excellent use of their educational atmosphere to instruct children in the Word of God.

The church has a fully organized visitation program on Monday and Tuesday nights, Thursday and Saturday mornings. Over 250 participate in visitation each week. Moore commented, "We have as many lay soul winners out visiting each week as most of the ten largest churches in America." He admonishes his workers not to drag out a home visit. He states, "Enthusiasm is the key, directness is appreciated, and faith brings results."

Moore noted that every person who receives Jesus Christ opens a new avenue for prospects. He indicates, "We do not have enough hours in the day to follow up every prospect in our files. The church has a suicide-prevention counseling ministry. The police, hospitals and doctors all know of this outreach. Anyone can phone HELP-181 and find a counselor."

A mother with a gun to the head of her baby phoned one day and told Moore, "Don't send the police car, I'll pull the trigger." Moore got her to agree to let him come to her home, where he prevented the suicide and saved the life of the woman and her child.

Enlistment of New Teachers

Moore personally enlists all new teachers. He indicated, "Standards will do more to make people confident in your Sunday School than any other program." The standards are high and the expectations are rigorous. Moore uses the following steps to bring a new teacher into the Sunday School staff. (1) He watches for people responsive to the Word of God as it is preached. (2) Prospective teachers are discussed at the staff level. (3) Prospective Sunday School teachers are selected from those who are already busy in the church activities. (4) The pastor's secretary, Mrs. Sandie Plopper, phones the potential teacher and makes an appointment for him to come to the church for an interview with the pastor. (5) Moore tells him he has a class chosen for him to teach. (6) The office of a Sunday School teacher is magnified, and the challenge of teaching is presented. (7) The age characteristics of the class are covered by the pastor and the potential teacher. (8) Moore explains what can be expected from him, the Sunday School superintendent, and fellow teachers. (9) He challenges him with the statement, "It is not what you know, it is what you *are* that makes a good teacher."

Conclusion

Even though this chapter has emphasized promotion and contests, the Marietta Baptist Tabernacle is diversified in its outreach to its neighborhood and the world. (1) Thirty-seven missionaries are supported by the church. (2) "The Challenge of the Bible," a nationwide radio ministry, is now heard on 30 outlets. (3) There is a fully equipped print shop to spread the gospel through the printed page. (4) Camp Challenge, recently acquired on 320 acres in a nearby county, extends the gospel through camping evangelism. (5) A suicide-prevention service is handled through the church. (6) Marietta Christian Schools includes kindergarten through grade nine with an enrollment of 270 students and maintains high academic standards.

Last year there were 3,629 decisions for Christ recorded in the services, 852 baptisms, and an increase in Sunday School of 497 over the previous year. The church has had a high attendance day of 2,659. The Sunday School has grown from an average of 350 just four short years ago to 1,622, becoming the 57th largest in America (Sept. 1970 to May 1971 figures).

Chapter 9

The Building Reflects Evangelism

The Bible Baptist Church

Savannah, Georgia

When Cecil Hodges was called to the Bible Baptist Church in Savannah, Georgia, a friend mentioned, "Savannah already has enough Baptist churches." Hodges gave the remark serious consideration, but with a deep sense of God's Spirit leading him, he came to Savannah. Hodges answered his friend, "Savannah has enough Baptist churches, but they are not evangelistic-oriented. My aim is to reach the entire city and Chatham County with the gospel."

The small congregation of 31 members meeting on the west side of the city appeared far from being a dynamic local church. The poor and transient lived on the west side of Savannah and the small congregation meeting in a member's home looked anemic compared to some of the Southern Baptist giants in the city.

"Balance" has been the keyword of Hodges' ministry in Savannah. The Bible Baptist Church has been balanced in its evangelistic outreach, Bible teaching ministry and follow-up, so that Christians are enlisted to become active in the local church.

Hodges led the church's growth to 750 in Sunday School with no staff except a secretary. Then he realized that he was "thrashing the waters" and not making headway. A major decision came in his life. He stated, "God had to teach me how to work through my staff."

Before going into the ministry, Hodges had a business background, managing the office of a Finance Company in Jacksonville, Florida. He spent five months at Baptist Bible College, Springfield, Mis-

Pastor Cecil Hodges

souri. A grandmother in Fernadina, Florida, he claims, taught him more about the Bible than any other one person. Hodges brought promotion and finance learned in the secular world into his church work, attempting to combine the best of the business world with the best of the Word of God.

Hodges has a great passion for stability in his ministry. He has often stated, "After I am gone, if this church goes down in attendance, I have failed in my ministry." His oft-repeated motto: "There is no success in the Lord's work, without successors." Even though he feels his Sunday School is the evangelistic arm of the church, Hodges indicated America is riding an educational crest, where everyone believes sufficient education will solve America's problems and bring happiness. Hodges believes Sunday School is the key to the educational program of the church, but education must be tempered with warm evangelistic zeal. "Education without zeal is like a head without a heart—there is no life." As a result, Hodges sees a bright future for fundamentalist Sunday Schools, that they will continue to become larger and more efficient, whereas church groups that de-emphasize evangelism will decline in Sunday School attendance.

Part of Hodges' balanced ministry is conviction that a believer must worship in spirit and in truth. The word "spirit" refers to dedication and zeal; true worship comes from the heart of man. The word "truth" refers to objective knowledge of the Word of God. Worship must be balanced between a warm spiritual heart and a clear understanding of Bible content. Hodges indicated, "A man cannot worship God and go contrary to the truth of the Bible." He makes this reference to liberal preachers. At the same time Hodges indicated, "Warm zeal is fanaticism if it is not based on Scripture." Hodges indicates that one of the first commands in Scripture is to be baptized. If a man has not obeyed the command to be baptized, he is not worshiping God in truth. Because of this, Hodges will not invite Christians to worship God at the Lord's table in his church if the Christian has not been scripturally baptized. Hodges indicated, "Since the Lord's table is worship of God, a man cannot properly worship God who is not obedient to the truth."

Hodges feels churches fold up because they are not following the principles of the New Testament. Jesus promised, "The gates of hell will not prevail against the church" (Matt. 16:18). Hodges points to general church decline and notes that lack of growth stems from disobedience to God's Word. He indicates, "Churches that follow God's principle will grow and those that ignore the truth of God's Word will not prosper."

One of the first truths for church growth emphasized by Hodges is that the minister is the chief administrator, planner and developer of the church. He is the pastor and undershepherd. The minister should lead the congregation just as the shepherd leads the sheep. The first task of the pastor-shepherd is feeding the flock (Acts 20:20). Hodges indicates he must study diligently if he is to feed his people, just as a college professor must study to teach a class. "I would be most embarrassed if I stood before my congregation with nothing to say." He feels that a New Testament church should be firmly grounded in biblical knowledge.

Hodges indicated he had falsely learned from a fellow pastor not to trust anyone to do anything in the church. As a result, as a young pastor Hodges worked himself into a state of nervous exhaustion on two or three occasions. One time, returning from a meeting, God spoke to him through the wise counsel of a fellow pastor, "The church belongs to God; He will take care of His church. You are only the servant—the pastor." From that moment on, Hodges realized God can hold his church together.

Hodges' greatest ambition is to build *men,* not an institution. To this end he claims, "I have the greatest deacons in the world." He does not have job descriptions for his staff, but he details to each man tasks and aims so that each has a clear understanding of his task. Hodges challenges the six young men on his ministerial staff to bring dignity into the pulpit along with their enthusiasm and zeal. He feels the pulpit ministry should be respected and the minister of the gospel should be a gentleman.

Stimulating church vision is another task of the pastor. He keeps the people looking to God and to the work. If the congregation does not have vision, it becomes stale and ingrown. Hodges believes that even in making announcements the pastor must create vision.

The position of leadership for the pastor is based on a godly ministry. The pastor must prove himself and "win a hearing." The pastor proves himself by godly living, knowledge of the Word, winning souls, and leading the flock of God. The pastor is the example in charity, spirituality and soul winning.

Hodges also believes the pastor is the comptroller of finances in the church. "The man that controls the money leads the church." Because of this, Hodges is the key business administrator in his church. He admonishes other young pastors, "Don't do anything in the dark." Deacons should know what the pastor is thinking, where he plans to lead the church three years from now. The deacons assist the pastor in ministering to the flock, guiding and counseling the pastor on many of his problems. Yet Hodges believes the pastor sits

Bible Baptist Church and Day School

as moderator of the deacons' meetings. He indicated, "The church and deacons have created the position of pastor, therefore he should work with them." The pastor and deacons set the salary of each new staff member, yet Hodges hires and fires and the staff is obligated to him. At the same time Hodges explains, "I would not hire someone of whom the deacons did not approve." He further elaborated, "As the undershepherd, I am charged with the obligation for the prosperity of this flock." Therefore, each staff member should be loyal to the pastor first, and the church second. If a staff member does not agree with the pastor's program, he should resign and go elsewhere. Hodges believes the pastor and deacons are a system of checks and balances to protect the church against absolute power. "In the multitude of counsellors there is wisdom" (Prov. 11:28).

The congregation approves the budget, but the pastor and Finance Committee control the spending of the money. Hodges, in the position of comptroller, delegates the actual purchasing to other members of his staff. Even though the pastor has approval from the congregation on finances, he informs the deacons of large purchases because (1) the people ask the deacons and if they don't know, both pastor and deacons are embarrassed, and (2) the congregation loses confidence in the deacons if they are not aware of business procedures. In 14 years of leadership, Hodges has never had but two negative votes because the people have confidence in his leadership.

The Buildings

As visitors approach the Bible Baptist Church, they are struck with its unusual architecture and beauty. Even in choosing the building, Hodges wanted to reflect his message of evangelism to every man in the city, whether rich or poor. Therefore, it was important that the building reflect the gospel. On each end of the building, circular walls reach out like the arms of God reaching out to embrace every man. At the entrance is a cross signifying all must come under the Cross to God.

Hodges indicated, "If God is the greatest businessman in the world, His building ought to be first-class." He went on to state that a building should represent sacrifice on the part of the people, but never become an idol. Hodges pointed to the sacrifice made by people in the Old Testament when building Solomon's Temple.

When constructing a new building, large public-school-sized rooms were built rather than small Sunday School cubicles. The architect indicated he saved over $200,000 by building large open rooms instead of small cubicles. This money was put into quality design. Hodges indicates, "The God I know is first-class and He wants His buildings to be quality construction." When reminded about the small beginning of his church, Hodges answered "It is all right to begin on sawdust—if it is the best you can do—but growth is inevitable, so eventually a church should plan for an outstanding building."

The Bible Baptist Church at Savannah is a family church. The observer will notice a number of families getting out of cars, walking to Sunday School together. Once inside the spacious hallways (the entire building and auditorium are carpeted) visitors are impressed with the efficient classrooms and friendly receptionists at each door. Adequate lighting, ventilation, and a spirit of excitement add up to a positive environment for Bible teaching. The modern pastel-colored chairs and equipment in each classroom reflect an attitude of quality education.

Hodges believes that a church should build well, so that if it has to move it can sell the old property. Even though the present building has religious symbols, it could be converted into an office building if need be.

When faced with the need for moving, the Bible Baptist Church got a survey of its old neighborhood. The survey indicated the rapid deterioration of the neighborhood and predicted "institutional blight" in a transient neighborhood. When the vote came to move some five miles away, not one member voted against the proposal. Since the Bible Baptist Church is committed to reaching the city of

Savannah, it is not the typical neighborhood geographical parish church. Even though they moved five miles, not a family was lost. The move was made exciting to all members. Hodges began five months before the move to point out that things would be different in the new building. "The worst thing to happen in a new building is for people to *wish* they were back at the old auditorium." On dedication day, the first words Hodges said to the congregation were, "I guess this will do for a temporary auditorium, until God gives us something better." The audience broke into applause. Hodges said he made this statement, beginning to get the people ready for the next move into the next building. The second statement Hodges made was, "If somebody here could give us $3 million we could build our next church. We plan to have 3,500 in Sunday School and then 5,000." The "Amen!" followed like a clap of thunder from the congregation.

The New Building Reflects Team Teaching

The new building exhibits quality construction, designed to give quality instruction. The old building featured the traditional small class cubicle rooms for 10 pupils each. Hodges was faced with several problems. First, he realized that to relocate his church, which then averaged 800 in attendance, would take $1.5 million for the 1,200 students he projected. (Hodges had seen a sister church in Savannah relocate and spend $1.5 million on small Sunday School rooms.) But Hodges only had $500,000 for relocation. Also, Hodges wanted to build his new facilities for a Christian grade school, and the traditional Sunday School cubicle was not adaptable for that purpose. Two years before the move, Hodges began rethinking his approach to Sunday School teaching. The pastor continued, "First, I wanted rooms that would be flexible; we wanted to be good stewards of the money God had given to us. Therefore, I wanted the space to be used more than thirty minutes on Sunday morning. I realized that the public schools didn't divide into small groups of 10." Hodges asked himself, "If public schools have 30 to 40 pupils in a class, why can't Sunday Schools?"

Hodges visited some public schools to see how classes were being conducted and received a third impression. "The public school has excellent environment for teaching, but most Sunday Schools do not have an educational environment. Since God is up to date, the Sunday School should be modern in building, yet old-fashioned in message." A schoolroom should say *think* when a child enters; most Sunday School rooms say *clutter,* and that is poor educational environment.

When Hodges saw public school teachers adequately leading classes of 30 to 40 pupils, he realized, "The gifted teacher with university training can lead a large class; the poorly trained Sunday School teachers usually cannot handle even small groups of students." Hodges concluded that the "gifted-trained teacher in Sunday School ought to lead a large class." He was intrigued by the ability of the gifted teacher. He had some outstanding teachers in his Sunday School, but not enough for each small class. He thought, "Why not use the gifted teachers with the large classes, and have the other teachers support their ministry?" His next question was, "Is this a scriptural approach?"

Hodges restudied the Word of God, especially noting the emphasis on great men. He concluded, "The greater the man of God, the greater the power of God working through him." Hodges then evaluated the teachers in Scripture—Moses, Paul, and, finally, Christ. He concluded these teachers instructed both the large groups and small gatherings.

His next problem was to convince the congregation that a modified team teaching approach would allow the best teachers to influence the widest sphere of students, yet allow the beginning teacher to use his gifts and serve God, thereby growing into a great teacher.

The Sunday School teachers discussed team teaching, and they were willing to try it when they realized that this plan was being used in some of the largest Sunday Schools in America: Canton (Ohio) Baptist Temple; Indianapolis (Indiana) Baptist Temple; Landmark Baptist Temple, Cincinnati, Ohio; Akron (Ohio) Baptist Temple.

Hodges refers to his master teachers as "head teachers," and they are responsible for leading the class by teaching content and accomplishing the total aims of the Sunday School. The head teacher has a team of assistants, each using a special talent in the classroom: i.e., leading singing, telling stories, teaching memory verses, making motivating announcements or acting as a secretary. In the younger age-group classes, the large group is divided into smaller groups of 5 to 10 pupils for table work after the main lesson is taught. Here the teacher follows a conversational discussion where they review the lesson, give Scripture verses, and do expressional handwork.

Hodges indicates he does not use the pure team teaching approach as suggested in public schools, defined as the co-planning and the co-gathering of aims, lesson plans, learning experiences, and the co-evaluation of results. In pure team teaching, the pupils are considered a part of the team who taught each other under the guidance of the master teacher. Hodges indicated, "Pupils come to our Sunday

School to learn the Word of God. We do not have committee-led classes." He went on to state that decisions made by committees are not always the best. Man (head teacher) can sacrifice, pray and exercise faith. God speaks directly to man. Hodges has a suspicion that a committee (a pure team of teachers) does not have the quickness to respond in obedience to God.

The entire class is under the direction of the head teacher, although the teacher receives suggestions or assistance from the helpers. Hodges indicated that pure team teaching depends upon an activity approach, whereas his Sunday School stresses content. He indicated, "The Bible is a revelation from God and our pupils must know its message to make the proper response."

There are advantages to team teaching. The *first* is that the master teacher is freed from details, to give attention to instruction. Every class at the Savannah church has a secretary at the front door to receive the offering and take attendance. Even adults and high school students check in at a table in the foyer of their classroom, conserving teaching time.

A *second* advantage of modified team teaching is that the church is able to grow without adding to the teaching staff. Upon relocation, the Sunday School has grown from 800 to a spring average of 1,585 in 1971. However, Hodges now realizes he needs 150 teachers to lift his average attendance to 2,000.

A *third* advantage of team teaching is greater, rather than less, evangelistic zeal in the classrooms. "Many of the teachers in the small classrooms would not take advantage of opportunities to lead pupils to Christ," the pastor indicated. "Now we program evangelism into the large group and are having more results. The head teacher gives the invitation, while the other teachers counsel with those who respond."

An apprenticeship program for training of new teachers is a *fourth* advantage the church has realized from team teaching. "The greatest preparation for young teachers is the power of example," the pastor answered. The untrained teacher will naturally absorb teaching skills as he watches the master teacher in operation.

Team teaching has a *fifth* advantage. An individual is responsible for one assignment. The head teacher is the most qualified teacher, promoter and leader. Hodges proclaims, "The master teacher will produce growth. We don't have a lot of discouraged teachers, because the assistant looks to the qualified leader." He went on to amplify that in the small-class concept, many teachers are discouraged because their class does not grow. But when many teachers are responsible for a large class and it grows, all are encouraged. "Our morale is much better since we went to team teaching." The Bible Baptist Church has twenty-two head teachers instead of 120 small-classroom teachers. Hodges spent 45 hours interviewing his teachers to determine which would make his best head teachers. He maintained, "There is no need to get more students if you can't keep those you have." The Bible Baptist Church maintains that it keeps 85 percent of the students it attracts.

After the church went to team teaching, one teacher complained, "I feel backslidden because I am not studying each week." Hodges points out that one of the advantages of team teaching is that less responsibility should bring about more time for quality ministry. He went on to observe, "If prevention of backsliding is the only reason some teachers study their Sunday School lesson, that is a poor motive."

The Bible Baptist Church observes special days in which attendance drives are emphasized. Recently, the attendance jumped from an average of 1,200 to 1,923 when the church had a Sunday School Parade to Sunday School. In the average church with small-cubicle classrooms, many small classes would have been necessary for expansion. However, modified team teaching allowed for the advantage of expandability of attendance without adding small classes.

Some might criticize team teaching, indicating that less absentee follow-up and visitation would result, the reason being when all teachers are responsible for the class, no one teacher feels the burden of relating to the individual students. However, Hodges has indicated that the number of visits per teacher has gone up rather than decreased. "Because they share a common concern and pray together, they naturally work harder to follow up those who are converted and to reach new pupils," indicated the pastor.

A final advantage of team teaching was the discipline factor. "We have fewer discipline problems in the large room than in the smaller rooms," answered Eddy Daring, head teacher of the sixth grade boys. "Pupils naturally become mischievous' in classes with poor teaching, but when a master teacher is getting better attention and pupil involvement, the result is fewer discipline problems."

Sunday School materials from Baptist publications are used throughout every department. Hodges observed, "Their excellent audio-aids are perfect for large-class teaching. The handwork and learning activities also are perfect for the small-group discussion." Hodges went on to observe, "I have come to trust Baptist Publications; they are true to the Bible and historic Baptist traditions. I don't have to worry about the literature leading my people astray."

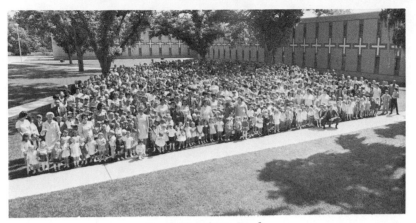

Special-Emphasis Sunday

Opening Exercise

The church does not believe in opening exercises as traditionally used. Hodges maintains, "We don't waste time on useless activities." The pupils go immediately to study the Word of God." Also, Hodges does not allow his teachers to rob time from teaching the Bible with prolonged promotion campaigns. "Sunday School enthusiasm without Bible instruction is foolishness." Also, he does not want his teachers preaching in the Sunday School. Sunday School is a time of sowing the Word, and the morning church service is the harvest, where the invitation for salvation is given.

Children's Church

There are seven extended services every Sunday morning, from cradle roll through the third grade. This is not babysitting, according to Hodges, but a ministry of the Word. Forty-nine ladies are involved with a weekly attendance of over 250 children. These extended services attract families to the church, according to Hodges, not so much because of convenience, but because children love to attend and they beg their parents to come.

Christian Achievement Programs (CAP)

Each Sunday evening at 6 P.M. classes are conducted on a Bible Institute level to train members in spirituality and leadership. The full-time staff members teach classes in soul winning, teaching methodology, child psychology, Bible survey, teen problems, and church responsibility. The sequence of courses is offered every thirteen weeks so that all members may take all courses. Hodges stresses, "We can't build the church with untempered mortar or untrained people." He went on to indicate that if the people are not well taught in Scripture, there will be an inevitable decline in attendance. A person must attend the Bible Institute classes to take part in the visitation program. "We don't plead for people to come to visitation. They must be trained to represent our church officially," stated Hodges. He indicated that a lady went out four years ago, telling people, "We don't believe in chewing, dipping or dancing." Hodges was disgusted. "She ran off more than she attracted." As a result, most visitation is done by teachers, deacons, staff members and trained workers. Hodges believes that the best training is through a supervised internship. First, a potential worker is used in the children's church (extended services); next the teacher is promoted to be an associate teacher on a team; then, if the teacher is faithful, he is promoted to a larger responsibility. Finally, after training and a seasoned internship, a teacher is given a class. "These are our best evangelistic visitors," stated Hodges. "They know *what* to say, *what not* to say, and how to attract the lost."

Christian School

Hodges began the Christian Day School not so much to expand his member outreach but to give quality education in a Christian environment for the children of his members. Today the Christian grade school has over 800 students, grades k-10, with 30 certified teachers under the direction of Dr. Pharis Scoggins, Ph.D., principal. The grade school has a waiting list and is considered one of the finest private schools in southern Georgia. "We expect to graduate 500 people in the next ten years and hope that 100 of them will be preachers." Hodges pointed to the following chart:

105,000 hours in the child's life
97,000 hours spent in the home
7,000 hours spent in school
1,000 hours spent in church

"School is making a great impact on our children, so let's increase the volume and make education a Christian impact."

Follow-Up

When a new person is voted into church membership or is immersed, Hodges believes it is biblical to inform him of his responsibility. A staff member phones for an appointment, goes to the home and teaches the new member his duties to the church. These pastors carry brief cases and study guides for a one-hour interview. In this one-hour interview, the pastor covers church history, the articles of faith, the church covenant, church government, and, finally, financial responsibility. At this time the new member is given envelopes and he is instructed how to tithe. Hodges maintains that his members know more about the Bible Baptist Church of Savannah, Georgia, than the one they have attended for the last 20 years.

At this interview, individuals are instructed to tithe and, above this, to make a pledge to foreign missions. In the church 72 percent of the family heads tithe. As the minister leaves, he tells the people to phone the church office in case of illness, death or accident. Members are told they will not receive the "annual pastoral visit." The duty of the church members is to assist the pastor in reaching the lost rather than exhibit self-centered, constant demands on the pastor's time.

The women of Bible Baptist Church have set up an information bureau in the church offices. Each family is informed of activities for the whole church. It is the duty of this office to get all the members active in church activities. Hodges maintains that the church ministers to the body, mind and soul of each individual. "We want to do more than get them in the baptismal waters; we want to get them into the entire body of Christ— the Church." Speaking of discipleship, Hodges uses a farmer's illustration: "To win 100 people to Christ and lose 75 is to sow corn on a concrete highway."

Growth

The growth of the Bible Baptist Church in Savannah has never been spectacular, just consistent. Hodges indicates attendance usually reaches the goals set for the members. The present motto: "We shall average 1501 before we are done with 1971." He introduced the motto to the workers conference and had the teachers repeat the slogan several times.

If the church continues with its balanced ministry, quality instruction and consistent growth, it will be a model to many young struggling churches searching for answers to the problem of growing in both quality and quantity.

Chapter 10

The Torch Is Passed
Kansas City Baptist Temple

Kansas City, Missouri

The Kansas City Baptist Temple is included in this book to illustrate how a church successfully passes from first-generation leadership to a second-generation pastor. The present pastor, the Reverend Truman Dollar, was only six years old when the church was organized. Dr. Wendell Zimmerman founded the church in 1943 and remained as minister in the church for 25 years. He came to Kansas City as a radio evangelist, beginning the church with 23 people who, less than two years later, entered a year-long revival meeting. Zimmerman's sacrifice and dedication over 25 years gave him the reputation of being one of the outstanding Bible expositors in America. He built the attendance in Sunday School to an average of 900 (without Glenwood Chapel) and had the reputation of being one of the outstanding Christian leaders in America. Zimmerman is presently the pastor of the Jacksonville (Florida) Baptist Temple. The thrust of this chapter will not examine the primary growth under Zimmerman who was the founder and built the church upon his powerful leadership (Chapter 12 on charismatic leadership). This chapter focuses attention on the problems of leadership when the first-generation leader leaves the church and the second-generation leader arrives. Since the Kansas City Baptist Temple is experiencing growth under Dollar, it is an example of how other soul-winning churches can "pass the torch of leadership" on to a younger man who exercises a different type of leadership and still experiences growth. Truman Dollar exercises a structured leadership, even

132

The crowd on "Friend Day"

though he has a charisma of his own. Young Dollar came to Kansas City at age 19 and worked for Wendell Zimmerman for seven years, three and a half years in the main church and three and a half years pastoring Glenwood Baptist Temple, a branch work of Kansas City Baptist Temple. Even though Truman Dollar was pastor of the Glenwood Baptist Temple, he was still considered an employee of the Kansas City Baptist Temple from which he drew his salary, and Wendell Zimmerman was his superior. Dollar maintains that the influence Zimmerman had upon his ministry is invaluable.

Zimmerman resigned Sunday morning July 12, 1968, and the deacons met that afternoon. One deacon, acting as spokesman, said, "Pastor, we've never had another pastor. Whom should we call?" Zimmerman recommended Truman Dollar and the deacons unanimously recommended him to the church. Truman Dollar was pastor of the Ambassador Baptist Church, Allen Park, Michigan, at the time. That evening, Zimmerman announced that Truman Dollar would preach the following Sunday. Dollar, a young man 30 years of age, preached July 19, 1968, and immediately after the sermon, left the auditorium. The congregations at the Temple and Glenwood both voted secretly at the same time, and all but nine votes were affirmative for Dollar. One family left the church because they thought Zimmerman had railroaded young Truman into the pastorate. However, they have come back into the church and are now superintendents in children's divisions. This church after 29 years has never had a Sunday without a pastor. To this day, there is a great love between the two men. Zimmerman entrusted young Truman with his congregation, and, in response, Dollar has great respect for his father in the ministry and is intense in his defense of the 25 years Zimmerman spent at the Kansas City Baptist Temple. The two traveled together to Israel during the summer of 1971. Two events helped mold the future direction of the Kansas City Baptist Temple.

The Monday after the election, Dr. Noel Smith, editor, *Baptist Bible Tribune,* talked with Dollar long distance and, in his characteristic manner, said, "Don't hit a lick of work until you have read a book, *The First Baptist Church,* the story of a Dallas church." Smith got a promise out of the newly-elected pastor that he would immediately phone Zondervan Publishing House in Grand Rapids, Michigan, and have the book sent to him air mail, special delivery. The problems that young Dollar would face were similar to those faced by Dr. W. A. Criswell when he became pastor of the First Baptist Church, Dallas, Texas. The book told the story of the great pulpiteer, Dr. George Truett, who was in the First Baptist Church for 47 years, followed by a young unknown, Dr. W. A. Criswell, who was at that time 34 years of age. Criswell had to deal with Truett's wife who remained in the church, while Dollar would have Zimmerman's mother in the church and a brother, Fred Zimmerman, who remained on staff in the church. Not only this, Noel Smith thought Criswell and Dollar looked alike. Dollar learned an important

New facilities now under construction

lesson from the pages of the book: specifically, that he would have to rely on his own judgment and his own program—he was not Wendell Zimmerman.

A second event that shaped the Kansas City Baptist Temple was the way Dollar related to his lay workers. He was keenly aware of his youth and knew that the job would require his best. He scheduled a 30-minute appointment with every worker in the church. This took him two weeks. Some even brought their sandwich at lunch time and shared their ideas of the future of the church. Young Dollar listened patiently, especially to needs. A deep conviction grew out of these interviews, that the lack of a comprehensive youth program was the church's greatest and most immediate need. Dollar states, "I was convinced I needed to hire the best youth director in the country." This led to the call of the Reverend Roscoe Brewer as youth minister, who eventually became associate pastor in the church.

Growth by Overcoming Obstacles

Since July, 1968, when Truman Dollar became pastor, Kansas City Baptist Temple has grown. This increase in numbers has not come easy. In the early days of Wendell Zimmerman, the church experienced phenomenal growth, but toward the end of his ministry, attendance leveled off, and finally experienced a small decline at the principle location. This was, perhaps, one of the reasons for the move to Jacksonville, Florida. Truman Dollar was faced with the problem of mobilizing the work force and inspiring the people to continued growth, therefore, this section is entitled, "Growth by Overcoming Obstacles."

1. *The church is located in a deteriorating neighborhood.*—The first major obstacle Dollar had to overcome was the institutional blight within the neighborhood surrounding the church, which has the highest crime rate in Kansas City. Dollar realized that he needed to move the church because of its location, but could not, because of finances. Zimmerman said before leaving the congregation, "This congregation can't grow until it moves." When Dollar was visiting Cincinnati, Dr. John Rawlings, pastor of Landmark Baptist Temple showed him the old location and the new location. Rawlings then showed the difference in numerical growth after the move. Dollar came home with the conviction that the church must move.

A survey was made, indicating the church members were spread in a large triangle between three areas: Independence, Raytown, and the general area of the church. Dollar, after much prayer began looking for a new tract of ground within the area of the triangle. Returning from visitation one afternoon with an assistant, E. L. Calton, he saw twelve acres located on 55th Street and Blue Ridge cutoff, only 3/4 mile from the new $73 million Kansas City Chief-Royals stadium. A small sign gave only a phone number. Dollar phoned and learned that Frank Vandergrift, owner of Hudson Oil Company, owned the property. The 71-year-old owner and Dollar went to lunch at Holiday Inn the next day. Dollar confesses embarrassedly that he forgot to take money with him, and Vandergrift got stuck with the check. The church had no money even for a deposit on the land. After one hour of negotiating the price of the land, Dollar flatly asked, "Why don't you just *give* us this land?" The young pastor explained that not only would the oil man be assisting the Lord's work, but that he would also receive a charitable deduction. Much to Dollar's surprise, Vandergrift quickly agreed. It was later determined that the wealthy businessman was entitled to a charitable deduction of $102,000.

The Kansas City Baptist Temple owns Paraclete Manor, a senior citizens' home, across the street from its present location. A new senior citizens' project was proposed to be operated adjacent to the new church. Two acres out of the proposed expansion were sold to a new corporation for $68,000 to build the second home, helping to solve some of the financial problems involved in changing locations of the church.

Today, the stadium project is complete and a four-lane highway with curbs runs immediately past the future location of Kansas City Baptist Temple. When the land was acquired, the property was unimproved. The church has now realized the appreciation of the land value with the economic influence of the massive new twin-stadium complex. The remaining ten acres have been recently appraised at $203,000, even though the church sold two acres to the New Temple Heights Corporation. The providential hand of God in the selection of a site helped to encourage the congregation and showed that God was going to work out the problems of the church.

2. *The present building was an obstacle to growth.*—First, the present building was not large enough for expansion of Sunday School attendance past 1,100. The auditorium could seat 1,400 for church services, but the basement and few rooms at the front were used for Sunday School, in addition to an old house in the area. The entire property at the Swope Parkway location totals less than three acres, leaving only a small area for off-street parking. Cars overflow into the surrounding neighborhood each week.

Dollar announced to the congregation, "We are not going to let obstacles keep us from reaching the city for Christ." He challenged his people at a Sunday School clinic, "We are not going to make excuses about our bad location. I don't want to hear this excuse again. We will grow in spite of our building." Dollar insisted that the church in the book of Acts multiplied without material advantages.

In January 1971 two Sunday schools were organized in the limited facilities. Sunday School "A" met at 10:00 A.M. and Sunday School "B" met at 11:10. The Sunday school buses went out at 8:00 and brought in the first load, then went after the second load. When they returned at 11:00, they began transporting the children from Sunday School "A" back home. At first many of the bus drivers began at 8:30 and worked until 1:30 in the afternoon.

Sunday School "B" and Junior church meet at the same time. At the beginning of the program, some teachers taught twice. Others had to be trained to help out in the program. Sunday School "A" has 160 workers; Sunday School "B" has 65 workers.

Sunday School "B" only averages 250, not a large average, but this represented 250 reached for Christ. In addition, Sunday School "B" gave confidence to the people that they could overcome obstacles. Dollar indicated, "Sunday School 'B' is not ideal, but it's the only thing we can do." He recommends it to other Sunday Schools only when all other alternatives are exhausted.

Last year, seven cars were stolen off the church parking lot during the Sunday evening service. Members have been victimized by burglaries, glasses have been broken during muggings and on two occasions visiting ministers have had clothes stolen out of their cars (members know better than to leave clothes in sight on the church parking lot). The doors have been stripped off the church safe. At one time, the church buses were regularly victimized until a German Shepherd named Rex was hired to guard the buses. An armed guard now patrols the parking area at all night services. The Methodists have rented the building next door for their ministry to the unfortunate of the inner-city area. The church has been growing in spite of poor facilities, giving Dollar confidence that the attendance will continue to expand when the new building is occupied.

3. *Counting a chapel in total Sunday School attendance.*—When Dollar first came to Kansas City Baptist Temple, the Glenwood Baptist Temple attendance was counted with the mother church. This weekly average of 175 in Sunday School made the mother church look larger than it actually was. Some have accused those churches which include chapel attendance in with the mother church of misrepresenting the facts. The criticism was really no issue to the young pastor. Truman Dollar wanted the chapel to become completely indigenous, thus reflecting his Baptist convictions and also his experience at the chapel where he pastored for three years. Dollar believed that for Glenwood to become truly strong, it must assume financial responsibility for its own program. The mother church did all of the printing, programming, planning of the youth camp, and secretarial work for the chapel. Dollar believed the help was actually detrimental to the spiritual maturity of the chapel.

Beginning in January 1970 Dollar took a very courageous move, by organizing the branch church into an independent church. This move eliminated Glenwood from the Sunday School statistics, which most believed would cause a decline at the mother church for the year. However, the Kansas City Baptist Temple still grew, overcoming the deficit, and averaged 1,202 in 1970, in spite of the fact they had never averaged over 1,200 *including* Glenwood. The following year, attendance leaped to 1,506, (average for 1971) qualifying it as one of the fastest growing Sunday Schools in America. The growth was balanced, showing a healthy increase of adults. Dollar still operates the same number of buses as when he became pastor.

During the spring drive, 1971, the Sunday School averaged 1,911 for ten weeks, breaking an all-time record. In October of 1971 the church had 3,266 on its annual "Friend Day." The Kansas City Baptist Temple baptized nearly 500 in 1971. The Glenwood church has maintained the same attendance since it became independent, but its offerings have doubled.

4. *The young age of Truman Dollar.*—Another obstacle to overcome in church growth, was the relatively young age of Truman Dollar. Zimmerman was a mature and strong leader with years of experience. He also had a national reputation. To counteract any hint of criticism about his age, Dollar watches his conduct and refuses to engage in excessive humor in public and never wears youthful styles. Rather, he dresses conservatively. When with his members, he always maintains an attitude of seriousness. Dollar indicated, "During my whole ministry, age has been a factor." He conducted his first revival at age 15, when he was considered by many too young and unprepared.

The success Dollar has had in raising money helped solve the problem of his youthful appearance. The very fact he stabilized church giving, liquidated indebtedness, and moved forward toward the new building has given him stature in the eyes of his people. The offerings have increased by $200,000 annually in only three years.

Another factor to offset Dollar's youthfulness was the immediate psychological victory of breaking the all-time attendance record. When Dollar came to Kansas City Baptist Temple, he actively promoted what has become an annual Friend Day, the third Sunday of October; 1,883 were present on his first Friend Day, breaking every previous attainment. Roscoe Brewer indicated, "This proved to the people that Pastor Dollar was their leader." Friend Day continues to be traditional in the church.

Pastor Dollar has attempted to surround himself with the best

Pastor Truman Dollar

help possible. This applied to all ministries that service the church. When Dollar came to the church, the Paraclete Manor for senior citizens was involved in a tax case. The county was suing for $75,000 in disputed taxes. Dollar was convinced, as was Zimmerman, that the home was tax exempt. After examining the history of the tax case being aired in the court, Dollar determined to get the best law firm in the city and hired Morris, Foust, Moudy, and Beckett. Although the case was eventually lost in the Missouri Supreme Court, the disputed money was awarded the senior citizens' home.

Recently, the church applied for an $825,000 bond issue. Many churches in the state have had difficulty getting approval for a bond issue from the state, some taking as long as eight to ten months to get approval. The Kansas City Baptist Temple received permission within eight days, and sold $500,000 worth of bonds within the first week. Truman Dollar personally sold $150,000.

Dollar has majored on personal soul-winning, believing it to be the key to any growing church program. "Most of our converts are saved in the home. The church has developed scores of lay soul-winners through its thirteen week soul-winning class." The soul-winning program called "won by one" was developed by Dollar and the staff. During 1971 over 300 adults went through the course.

The church also emphasizes baptisms, not just professions. Dollar believes it discourages soul-winning to report hundreds of converts whom the church never sees. The church also seeks to direct its soul-winning efforts primarily at adults. The heavy emphasis on bus children conversions is dangerous, Dollar believes.

Every member of the staff is required to personally win people to Christ. We cannot expect lay people to win the unsaved if we don't," the young pastor explained. In 1968 there were only 200 public professions, but that increased to 489 in 1971.

Second-Generation Leadership

Dollar stated recently, "Although I am considered a second-generation leader, I am in complete sympathy with the goals and priorities of those who founded the Baptist Bible Fellowship. I am fearful of the problems of the sociological cycle of church growth, yet I do exercise a different kind of leadership. My intention is not to change any of the theological or evangelistic purposes of the Baptist Bible Fellowship. I want to confirm and extend their spirit intact to the next generation." Dollar went on to state, "What Wendell Zimmerman set out to do was right—to build a large, local New Testament Church."

Dollar's only goal in life is to build a great church. "I find it harder each year to generate enthusiasm about the work of the Fellowship. I love my church. I believe they love me. I have no ambitions outside of the Kansas City Baptist Temple. The Fellowship is a tool through which my church does its mission work and trains its preachers but is not an end in itself."

Zimmerman organized his church to reach 900. Now we have to shift gears if we are to reach a larger group of people." Dollar believes that the Baptist Bible Fellowship must pass from personality leadership (charisma) to structured leadership. "In the future," he has stated, "growth will come through the leadership of gifted men, but leaders must reproduce themselves in men to help carry out a larger ministry." Dollar further believes the gifted leader must build people and programs because ministry is carried out in programs. Dollar stated, "I don't intend to run a sloppy program, because the Episcopalians are efficient." The Kansas City Baptist Temple has a highly organized program with clearly defined systems of responsibility for each leader. There are 15 on the staff. Dollar, a student of leadership, refers to Sorensen's book on Kennedy and Townsend's book on corporate management and explains why he refuses to have an administrative assistant. Dollar says, "I don't want any of my staff to come to me through someone else; I want every man to be responsible to me personally." This is done because administrative assistants unconsciously color reports or fail to give the leader all of the truth. Every program in the Kansas City Baptist Temple depends upon the man in charge of the program. The key to this church is not committee activities but the ability of each man to lead his division of responsibility. Dollar demands results, not excuses from his staff. When results are not produced, he does not hesitate to make personnel changes.

Structured Leadership

The essential ingredients of structured leadership are long-range planning and collective involvement of key staff members in the program. Two and one-half years ago Dollar instituted a unique annual staff retreat. The basic staff of the Baptist Temple is taken to a secluded meeting place, normally a motel with conference rooms available. All the expense of the two-day retreat is borne by the church. A comprehensive agenda is prepared and distributed to each staff member before the retreat begins. There is no free time allowed. The staff all agrees that the 12-hours-a-day sessions are hard work.

During this retreat each major area of the church is re-evaluated for the purpose of upgrading the entire church program. Staff members are expected to make preparation for the meeting and contribute their ideas during the sessions. Out of this collective brainstorming, the entire organization is upgraded each year. Dollar believes the sessions contribute greatly to staff morale and help to develop a sense of belonging to the team.

During these sessions Dollar encourages every staff member to be frank and open in his assessment and criticisms of the various ministries under discussion, a practice not seen in true charismatic leadership. The agenda is followed systematically. Although freedom of criticism is encouraged, the pastor maintains complete control of the meeting at all times and reserves the right to veto any suggestion. All the ground rules are laid down in the opening session. Dollar stated with quiet confidence, "I don't apologize about being the boss."

It is during these sessions that the leadership projects an entire year's program. Each staff member is apprised of the total church effort for the coming year. The ministries and efforts are coordinated and duplication of effort is greatly reduced. Dollar analyzed the annual affair: "There is no program that I have ever undertaken as a leader that has contributed more to the success of our total church effort than these staff retreats."

Throughout the year Dollar also operates with weekly staff meetings and an executive staff committee, where major programs and efforts are planned and coordinated. They begin on their knees in prayer. The two chief assistants to Dollar are Roscoe Brewer and Elmer Calton. These two men do not have supervisory powers over other staff members except where specifically designated. Supervisory power extends only to the clerical and janitorial staff, responsibility which has been specifically assigned.

The Reverend Truman Dollar believes continual growth of a church should be healthy, balanced and biblical. By this he implies that the church which stops growing is not carrying out either the New Testament command or the book of Acts example.

Dollar observes that there are churches which reach a certain level of growth and proceed no further. Although these levels of growth are not numerically precise, there appears to be some similarities between the organizational structure of the churches which develop this problem. Characteristically, a church will reach the 500 or 1,000 mark and then level off permanently unless some major structural changes occur.

Dollar stated, "Frequently when growth stops, it will be attributed to external circumstances that relate to that particular church. The blame may be laid to the location of the congregation, the current economic situation in the area, inadequate facilities, or some other reason." Dollar continued, "The answer in my judgment lies with the type of leadership, not with the circumstances, except in very rare cases." He believes that when a church is first organized, its simple organizational structure is created to meet the needs of a church that runs from 100 to 500 in Sunday School. When the attendance reaches the upper level of the pattern, the leadership does not reorganize or restructure the program, therefore future growth is retarded. If the 500 barrier is broken, the same thing frequently happens at the 1,000 mark. If a church desires to grow to an attendance of 2,000 the organization must be structured in such a way that it can meet the organizational requirements of a large church. From his vantage point Dollar believes the rare exception to this pattern is an organization headed by a charismatic leader.

Dollar stated, "Frequently young pastors reach these levels of growth while at the same time their own capacity for leadership is also growing and they are able, in time, to make the transition. If the transition is not made, one of two things will occur: the attendance of the church will level off or the pastor will resign and a new man with a greater capacity for structuring the organization will replace him." Dollar further stated, "Two years ago we reorganized our entire staff responsibility in order that we could operate like a church of 2,000. We have been growing ever since."

Dollar considers the chief asset of the Kansas City Baptist Temple its talented and qualified staff of full-time workers. Upon this staff of qualified people the whole organizational structure rests. In the business world there is great competition for personnel because much of the success of businesses depends upon the quality of its people. It is clear that the continued growth and success of any church rests upon the quality of staff it is able to assemble.

Dollar remarked, "I have observed that the success of every program and ministry of my church rests primarily upon the leadership in that division. My goal as pastor has been to surround myself with the most able, talented, and spiritual men and women to head up every division of our work. We have yet to hire an outstanding leader but what he was able to produce sufficient revenue by his contribution to the ministry of the church to pay his salary." An insecure leader will have extreme difficulty working with a highly competent staff, because he will interpret their successes as a challenge to his leadership. This will again limit the growth and success of any program. Dollar feels each of the members of his staff is far more qualified in some area than he is. He states, "I accept their excellence and feel that they multiply my ministry rather than detract from it. The greater their success, the more growth there will be in the church. So long as I am able to lead a group of talented spiritual people who know how to produce results, my church will continue to appreciate me and to look upon my staff as a complement to my leadership."

The acquisition and retention of a good staff requires attention to their personal achievement and financial needs. Dollar believes a man of great talent must be able to have a sense of fulfillment and achievement in his work, if his stay at the church is permanent. Also, certain freedom for initiative must be allowed and encouraged for responsible staff members. Then they must be able to publicly share in the victories. They must be given credit for their contributions and ideas; in short, each staff member must feel a part of the team or discouragement will soon overcome him. He cannot simply succeed vicariously in the victories of the pastor. Dollar concluded, "Scores of good staff members have been lost to the ministry because of the failure of pastors to understand this need. This sense of belonging is far more important than financial gain."

The staff member must also know he can develop some financial and job security in his position. The Bible does not compel a staff member to a poverty subsistence level of living because he has committed his life full-time to God's service. Although there will always be some limitations financially for a staff member, his needs must be taken into consideration. No staff member can operate at maximum efficiency when he is continually plagued by financial distresses at home. In the last three years, the average salary for the staff member of the Kansas City Baptist Temple has risen by 35 percent to 40 percent. A group hospitalization plan is maintained. A year and a half ago a retirement plan was instituted. The church also pays its portion of Social Security as required by Federal law. The purpose of all these fringe benefits is to help create a sense of financial stability for members of the staff. Dollar insists on hiring the best people available and wants each of these to be permanent in the organization.

Dollar stated that the difference between his structural leadership and charismatic leadership is highlighted by these issues. A charismatic leader has the magnetism to compel a following so that he becomes the initiator of new programs and much of the success depends largely upon his personal leadership. Dollar noted that normally, under a charismatic leader, even minor decisions are made by him personally. There is little disclosure of financial decisions and frequently the work deteriorates rapidly and abruptly when that individual is suddenly removed.

The young pastor stated, "One of the problems among fundamentalists that contributes to restriction of growth is the tendency to look inward. We have become the victims of our own self-esteem. Although the Kansas City Baptist Temple is in a continual state of growth, we are forever looking for new ideas and strive for flexibility in our structure. It is because of this that each year I send a number of my staff members to visit the largest and most successful churches in America, to learn what they are doing that we are not." Dollar urges his staff to read every new book on the subject in their area of responsibility.

An organization can continue to grow only as strong leadership is developed within the organization that can assume responsibility, according to Dollar. The base of leadership must be broadened. This relates both to the development of a strong staff as well as strong lay leadership. A single pastor can meet the needs of only a small organization until such time as he learns to multiply his efforts by delegating substantive responsibility to subordinates and co-laborers. There is a basic staff of 9 people upon which the Kansas City Baptist Temple organization relies. The total staff includes 15 people. The basic staff all have major responsibilities, overseeing some vital area of the work, and are personally answerable to Dollar. He feels it is a serious error to consider these men and women as simply employees. He stated, "These people, just as surely as pastors and missionaries, have a divine call." Dollar characterizes his co-laborers: "Roscoe Brewer, my associate pastor, preaches with great ability and power. Elmer Calton, my Sunday School administrator and business manager is a perceptive leader and a shrewd businessman. Harold Champion is perhaps the most effective minister to the deaf in America. Jeff Adams, our youth pastor, has the most comprehensive knowledge of the Bible of any young man I know in the ministry. Glada DeVore knows more about the bus ministry than those who have written the current wave of books on the subject. Fred Zimmerman is one of the most competent and versatile senior citizens' managers in America. Although Harold Massey is blind, he oversees the hospital ministry with a spiritual sensitivity that is unparalleled."

Dollar believes the most inefficiently administered office in any city is the local fundamental Baptist church. The business community, through trial, error and research, has developed systematic procedures. For some reason churches have been the last to make application of proven and time-tested procedures to the administration of its own business affairs. He believes the initiation of standard procedures and clear job definitions will allow staff members to work more effectively and encourage vastly improved production.

Dollar criticizes churches for operating with a single secretary of limited training and experience, often some lay person hastily chosen out of the congregation. He acknowledges that a secretary or any full-time staff worker must have certain basic moral and spiritual requirements even before the technical skills are considered. He insists, however, that the two qualifications should not be mutually exclusive.

Dollar approaches church administration much like the business community which has learned how to apply certain technical and mechanical tools to the administration of its affairs. Cost accounting is a primary lack in most churches, according to Dollar. An annual audit and a monthly statement of cash receipts and disbursements have a value to the chief administrator that goes beyond financial disclosure to interested parties. Just as it is absolutely essential for any successful businessman to know at all times the manner in which funds are being disbursed, just so the pastor must control the funds of his church. A quick glance at a summary of cash receipts and disbursements will reveal dozens of things about the quality of management and will provide solid data for future projections. The young pastor stated that Dr. G. B. Vick, pastor of the Temple Baptist Church of Detroit, greatly influenced his attitude toward church money management. He stated that, "The great Detroit pastor spent some three hours outlining his own program to me when I was only 26 years old."

Businesses also rely heavily upon a balance sheet to communicate to the business community its current financial status. Dollar realizes banks rarely make sizeable loans to churches. Although banks frequently tell churches they are not granting loans for fear of having to foreclose, often the real reason is that the financial records of churches are so poorly kept that no clear picture of its financial condition can be assessed. "We must meet or exceed the business standards of our community," he stated with fervor.

Most churches also fail to rely upon professionals for economic reasons, when in fact it is shortsighted not to do so. Dollar believes every church should employ the best attorney in the city and sign no documents or contracts without his specific approval. Although the Kansas City Baptist Temple is fortunate to have a CPA as a treasurer, Dollar still insists upon an independent, annual audit of the entire financial records. He stated, "The fact that I have some training in theology does not qualify me to practice law or accurately prepare a balance sheet. I file a monthly statement of cash receipts and disbursements with our banker and regularly seek his counsel on major financial decisions. It is because of this practice that our borrowing power is without equal in the community."

But a structured control of finances is only half of the picture. Dollar believes in a structured approach to raising finances (second generation) along with taking advantage of proper appeals from the pulpit (first-generation leadership). When Dollar first came to Kansas City Baptist Temple, he faced financial problems as faced in most churches. The long-term solution for Kansas City Baptist Temple was an organized stewardship campaign. Most Independent Baptist churches will not receive commitments from members for financial projections. But during December 1968 Dollar preached on stewardship. On the last Sunday of a month-long campaign, when he planned to receive commitments, a massive snowstorm blanketed Kansas City and only 550 people attended, the smallest attendance during his 3 years as pastor. Young Dollar took financial commitments and only got half of his goal. "I went home and felt defeated," replied Dollar, not realizing that most financial campaigns only aim to get commitments equal to half of their budget. The next Sunday the offering jumped $1,000 per week and remained that high for the next year. This campaign was so successful that the offerings increased by $50,000 in his first year. The following year, Dollar planned a Friday night banquet. Every church member was urged to be present, at which time they made a financial commitment to the work of the church. In 1971 the theme was *Soul Winning '71— $300,000*. Dr. D. A. Cavin was the speaker, and Doug Oldham sang. The projected budget for 1972 is $500,000. The offering for 1971 exceeded $321,000.

Dollar offers the following suggestions to a young preacher concerning raising finances. (1) Make a budget and present it to the congregation, so each member will realize the needs and proposed expenditures before the church year begins. According to Dollar, a

The "Master Teacher Plan" in the Youth Department.

budget should reflect what a church expects to accomplish spiritually for God in the coming year. (2) Orientate all leaders concerning the need for financial stability. Dollar believes that the church should begin with its inner circle to discuss financial policy. He brings the Reverend Roscoe Brewer and the Reverend Elmer Calton into his confidence and they begin making financial plans for the church year. (3) Next, the finance committee works on the budget, and (4) the total church staff is brought in for consultation. As the circle gets larger, deacons are brought into the pastor's confidence, next the Sunday School teachers, and finally, at the stewardship banquet, (5) the total church membership is presented with the budget for the church year. According to Dollar, the secret of leadership is to bring each level of lay leaders with each enlarging circle of influence. He feels if the inner circle is fully convinced of the total program, that group will help involve the next larger circle.

Dollar believes the average church is usually the last to use modern business technology. He says, "Church offices are notorious for crippling along with ancient typewriters, obsolete mimeograph machines, outdated mailing systems." The addition of modern office technology in the Kansas City Baptist Temple has not eliminated personnel but has greatly upgraded the production.

Dollar also stated, church offices are also notorious for being poorly managed. Even when the business community has established certain basic systems in office management, most church offices continue without efficient, disciplined and organized management. The Kansas City Baptist Temple restructured its entire office procedure almost two years ago and at the same time hired an office manager, Mrs. Clarissa Loper. Mrs. Loper's background includes accounting, purchasing, and record systems. Systems were developed to handle the work load of the nine key staff members. Dictaphones were purchased, a new addressing system was installed, a postage meter was purchased, a money counter was employed, a copy machine was purchased, and a printing press was added. The whole system was completely reorganized to meet the demands of the burgeoning work-load. Much thought and planning is being devoted to the office area of the new 60,000-square-foot building complex. The work production has at least doubled since this reorganization.

The Kansas City Baptist Temple also employs the use of an annual budget which includes all the advantages of double-entry bookkeeping. Every ministry of the church has a weekly budget. Newly instituted budget controls allow each individual staff member to make financial decisions within his own area and yet at the same time allows the pastor to control spending. Two years ago a business manager was appointed, whose responsibility includes budget control, weekly summary of budget expenditures, and execution of business transactions, within guidelines established by Dollar.

The Kansas City Baptist Temple has developed its own print shop. Although the day-to-day inter-office reproduction is handled with typewriters, duplicators, and copy machines, there is available to the varied ministries of the church a complete print shop for major printing of promotional materials. Dollar believes there is hardly a print shop in Kansas City that can turn out higher quality multicolored work than that produced at Kansas City Baptist Temple. It was recently called to Dollar's attention by one of the major printing supply houses in Kansas City that his church did more printing than any other church office that they serviced in the metropolitan Kansas City area. The printing budget, excluding salaries of personnel and inter-office duplication, will exceed $7,000 in 1972.

Pastors need to apprise themselves of basic business and managerial procedures that are commonplace to the business community, according to Dollar. The application of these simple procedures would greatly expand the ministry of churches and enlarge their influence in the community. It is high time that pastors recognize the financial shortsightedness of having a highly qualified staff member do clerical and janitorial work.

Conclusion

Dollar realizes charismatic leaders normally have a deep pioneer spirit and are generally a part of the first generation of a new movement. He has a minor in sociology from the University of Missouri. He recognizes his leadership is more structured, the kind normally produced by the second generation in any religious movement. Dollar is keenly aware that this kind of leadership has both advantages and disadvantages. Structured leadership tends to bring about increased efficiency, control and a stable approach to administration. But a structured leader can, however, be a step toward stagnation or fossilization within his own generation or, more likely, by his successors. Dollar has maintained that many second-generation pastors in a religious movement attempt to build an organization, resulting in a church more concerned about structure and perpetuation of the structure rather than the biblically compelling goal of winning the lost to Christ. Dollar said, "What I am saying is that the institution of structured leadership, if not carefully guarded, can lead to deterioration. Scores of examples of this can be found in the denominational churches."

Dollar believes structured leadership can also stifle initiative by producing powerful committee systems. He said, "I personally operate with a Finance Committee and a Board of Deacons, who are fully informed of the business affairs of the church. These men, however, are spiritual and intelligent men. I administer the affairs of the church on a day-to-day basis, operating within predetermined guidelines." The aggressive pastor believes some pastors with dead committees are hamstrung and unduly restricted. There is a tendency for committee control to increase with each change of pastoral leadership. No business or church can be effectively run by a series of committees.

Dollar concluded, "My personal leadership is fervently devoted to sustaining the primary goals of the local church; that is, to win the lost and reach the masses for the Saviour. I am seeking to employ a more structured organization than the average fundamental Baptist church. We are hopeful to achieve a combination of efficiency, intelligent planning, and results. At this point each of my staff understands that the structure is secondary and that spiritual results are primary. I am not, however, unaware that upon my removal, I may have created certain problems for the future of my church. There is little chance that it will dissolve or fall apart abruptly, as so oftentimes happens with charismatic leadership. The danger for my church is that my successor will not maintain the same priorities and use the structure effectively to win the lost to Christ. The structure can control the next pastor if he is a weak leader. Whenever the maintenance of the structure becomes the chief goal, the organization is suddenly moved toward deterioration and stagnation. The pastor has become simply a corporate administrator who mechanically carries out the functions of the organization." Dollar feels this is the chief problem faced by Southern Baptist pastors in this generation. They have produced a whole generation of new young, powerless administrator-pastors who are well-structured "keepers of the aquarium rather than fishers of men." These young ecclesiastical bureaucrat administrators will eventually bring down the whole Southern Baptist movement to their own level of spiritual poverty and will denounce conviction and principle as roadblocks to efficiency.

Chapter 11

The Sociological Cycle
of Church Growth

Parable of the Life-Saving Station

On a dangerous seacoast where shipwrecks often occur there was once a crude little lifesaving station. The building was just a hut, and there was only one boat, but the few devoted members kept a constant watch over the sea, and with no thought for themselves they went out day or night tirelessly searching for the lost. Many lives were saved by this wonderful little station, so that it became famous. Some of those who were saved, and various others in the surrounding area, wanted to associate and give their time and money. New boats were brought and new crews were trained. The little lifesaving station grew.

Some of the new members of the lifesaving station were unhappy that the building was so crude and so poorly equipped. They felt that a more comfortable place should be provided at the first refuge of those saved from the sea. So they replaced the emergency cots with beds and put better furniture in an enlarged building. Now the lifesaving station became a popular gathering place for its members, and they redecorated it beautifully and furnished it exquisitely. Fewer members were now interested in going on lifesaving missions, so they hired lifeboat crews. The lifesaving motif still prevailed in the club decoration and there was a liturgical lifesaving boat in the meeting room. About this time, a large ship was wrecked off the coast, and the hired crews brought in boatloads of cold, wet and half-drowned people. They were dirty and sick and some of them had yellow skin. The beautiful new club was considerably messed up. So the property committee immediately had a shower house built outside the club where victims of shipwreck could be cleaned up before coming inside.

At the next meeting, there was a split in the club membership. Most of the members wanted to stop the club's lifesaving activities as being unpleasant and a hindrance to the normal social life of the club. Some members insisted upon lifesaving as their primary purpose and pointed out that they were still called a lifesaving station. But they were finally voted down and told that if they wanted to save lives of all the various kinds of people who were shipwrecked in those waters, they could begin their own lifesaving station down the coast. They did.

As the years went by, the new station experienced the same changes that had occurred in the old. It evolved into a club, and yet another lifesaving station was founded. History continued to repeat itself, and today you will find a number of exclusive clubs along that shore. Shipwrecks are still frequent in those waters, but most of the people drown!

Rev. T. O. Wedel, Warden, College of Preachers
Washington Cathedral, Washington, D.C.

Parable of Church Growth

On a dangerous dark side street near the steel mill located between two taverns was a crude little storefront church building. Wooden folding chairs were set up, a crude pulpit constructed, and a few devoted members prayed constantly for the salvation of transient millworkers. With no thought for self or pleasure, the members went out visiting continually in every home, speaking to reach lost people for Jesus Christ. Many were converted and when a notorious gambler was converted, the little mission became famous. Christians from surrounding areas commuted to the church, giving their time, money, and effort. New pews were bought and ushers were trained. The little mission purchased the shop next door and doubled its auditorium size.

Some of the new members were unhappy with the crude building and poor equipment. It was said in a congregational meeting, "A man can better worship God in a comfortable pew in an air-conditioned auditorium." Matching chancel furniture was donated when new pews were installed. The members redecorated with tinted glass windows, adding Christian education facilities and a parking lot. The members lost interest in visitation, so they hired young zealous preachers to do their work. A revival was held and a man of God preached repentance. Perspiring mill hands were led to the Lord and when high school greasers started attending regularly, the deacons complained, not wanting their daughters to be contaminated. Small kids brought by Sunday School buses did not have shoes or clean clothes. The Women's Missionary Union immediately installed a "millworkers' closet" so the needy could put on proper clothes. But the women were critical when the immaculately clean floors were muddied.

At the next congregational meeting some members wanted the pastor to quit evangelistic preaching, wanting a more dignified, reverent worship service. Other members insisted soul winning was the primary purpose of the church. They were finally voted down and told to go elsewhere. "After all, millworkers like sensationalism," remarked a bank vice-president. They rented a store building across the street and began services with only crude folding chairs and a small pulpit. As the years went by the new mission experienced the same changes that had occurred in the old. It evolved into a religious club and yet another soul winning station was founded. History continued to repeat itself, and if you visit the mill section today you will find a number of exclusive sophisticated churches. Because of the neighborhood, none of those who attend the exclusive churches live there, but have moved to the better parts of the town. It was determined that not one of the millworkers in the neighborhood attends a single church in the area.

Why Churches Grow . . . And Decline

How does a lifesaving station, dedicated to the saving of drowning seamen, slowly erode into a social club? The answer is not simple, but any organization changes when the members change. How does a fundamentalist church, dedicated to preaching the gospel to individuals bound in the slavery, slowly erode into a liberal-dead church? Obviously, church buildings or organizations do not depart from the faith. When people change the church changes.

The ten churches in this book grow because of an inner strength, not organization or techniques.* They reflect the growth dynamic that is found at the beginning stage of the religious movement known as the sociological cycle of church growth. Most of these churches were founded by the present pastor or he came when the church was small. These ten churches should grow in the future because they have overcome expansion barriers. Each one is now a flaming witness for God, but sometime in the distant future, even these ten churches will deteriorate. However, their drop in attendance will probably not come with the present pastor or the next. These churches will erode into liberal edifices in the next 100 or 200 years. The present pastors will be grieved with the prospect and their members will vehemently deny that their church will grow liberal. Yet, death is as inevitable to a church as to every newborn baby. The purpose of this chapter is to examine those factors that cause churches first to grow and then to deteriorate. The most dynamic growth comes at the beginning of the cycle (where these ten churches are found). America is witnessing general church decline, yet here are ten churches that register monthly growth. Unsaved people come to hear the sermons, many of them walking down the aisle to receive Jesus Christ. Drunkards are sobered by the power of the gospel and broken homes are restored. These converts remain in the church, causing an attendance growth. Then they join in the task of evangelizing others and the church continues to grow. With time, churches change and shift in purpose, causing progress around the cycle. Natural growth based on religious factors becomes more difficult. This chapter is more concerned with positive attendance growth factors, but negative deterrents to growth will be noted.

A minister of a declining Baptist church in Chicago recently said, "Fifteen years ago, our church had a fishermen's club and we had

---

*I am convinced that numerical growth does not come because of organization, techniques or methods. Even though many authorities believe that proper administration causes church expansion, I disagree. The intangible factors that cause church growth will be examined in Chapter 11 and 12.

ten men who went on the streets to win souls and preach in street meetings. We were concerned about men going to hell." The minister sighed, "Our flaming witnesses are gone, these same men are now respectable property owners." What happened?

Another minister replied, "No one calls Christians 'fanatics' any more." The church of Jesus Christ is in the midst of radical changes, and most of them are not for the better. Harvard University was once the citadel of Conservative Christianity, training men for the gospel ministry. There was no doubt about its theological position. However, Harvard has long since slipped from its original purpose, becoming a liberal school.

Not only do churches and colleges shift to a more liberal institution, the Christian family goes through a process of deterioration. Richard Niebuhr, a sociologist, set forth the rags-to-riches-to-rags cycle that takes place in religious families. According to him:

> Children born into families of first-generation sect members begin to change the sect into a church even before they reach adulthood. With their coming, the sect must become an educational and disciplinary institution in order to make the new generation conform to its ideas and customs. The second generation holds its convictions less fervently than pioneers of the sects, whose convictions were formed in the heat of conflict and sometimes at the threat of martyrdom. With each succeeding generation, isolation from the world becomes more difficult.[1]

The process of degeneration from a high revival peak to a low valley of sin is often noted in Scripture. When God finds His people in the mire of sin, He raises up a man who can lead the people back to a high point of spiritual devotion. God's working is limited to men—they are His channel. The more abilities a man has, the greater God is able to work through him. The pastors of the ten churches in this book are godly men and they accomplish much because of their abilities (see Chapter 12 on charisma). The cycle evident in Scripture, shows that when the godly man died, the people eventually fell into sin.

> And the people served the Lord all the days of Joshua, and all the days of the elders that outlived Joshua, who had seen all the great works of the Lord, that he did for Israel. And Joshua the son of Nun, the servant of the Lord, died being an hundred and ten years

[1]H. Richard Niebuhr, *The Social Sources of Denominationalism* (Hamden, Connecticut: Shoe String Press, 1954), pp. 19-21.

old . . . And also that generation were gathered unto their fathers: and there arose another generation after them, which knew not the Lord, nor yet the works he had done for Israel. And the children of Israel did evil in the sight of the Lord, and served Baalim (Judges 2:8-11).

Critics claim the Sunday School is dying. Thirteen years ago, Wesley Schrader suggested in *Life* magazine that Sunday School was the "most wasted hour of the week." Attendance in mainline denominational Sunday Schools is markedly going downhill. These are substantiated facts. However, at the same time there is a growth in most Sunday Schools among the evangelicals and fundamentalists.

After studying the ten largest Sunday Schools in America, this author maintained that those churches were the largest in America because they had sectarian-type characteristics or were closely identified with characteristics of fundamentalism. Ernst Troeltsch, the German philosopher-sociologist wrote that churches grow from a sect status to *ecclesia* or a denominational stage.[2] The following cycle is an elaboration of Troeltsch's position to show the church's sociological cycle. A church begins as a sect and moves to the second stage on the cycle, an institution. The third stage on the cycle is a fully organized denomination, and the final stage is deterioration. In this chapter the sect will be associated with the theological position called *fundamentalism*. The second stage of the cycle called the *institution* will be identified with evangelicalism.[3] *Denominationalism* will be associated with the mainline denominations and/or the position of theological liberalism.[4]

Sociological Cycle

The thesis of this chapter is that Sunday School numerical growth reflects the theological and sociological posture of the church's posi-

---

[2]Ernst Troeltsch, *The Social Teaching of the Christian Churches,* trans. by Olive Wyan (London: George Allen and Unwin, 1931), 2 Vols. An outstanding analysis of the factors that cause deterioration in churches.

[3]The term "evangelical" is generally synonymous with neo-evangelical.

[4]I have often been asked to evaluate and place the Southern Baptist Convention on the sociological cycle. I find Southern Baptist churches at each stage of sociological development. In reference to the sociological cycle, Southern Baptists do not usually classify themselves by the label *fundamentalist* and *evangelical*. Rather they tend to use the label *conservative* and *liberal*, leaving out the mid-point designation of evangelicalism or institutionalizationism.

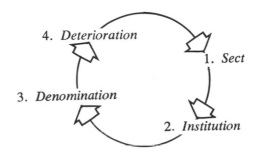

tion on the sociological cycle. (1) Fundamentalist churches have the capacity for the fastest numerical growth, although not all fundamentalist churches are growing. The ten churches of this book are found at this stage of the cycle. (2) Evangelical churches have a capacity for growth, although not as fast as fundamentalism. Also, all evangelical churches are not growing. (3) Liberalism or mainline denominationalism does not have the religious dynamic to naturally attract individuals. When the attendance at denominational-type churches climbs, it does so for extraneous reasons of an external nature. Most denominational-type churches do not grow because they apply no external pressure for growth or their spiritual life is void, hence they have no internal dynamic for growth.

David Moberg, the church sociologist from Marquette University, has designed the cycle as "a process by which cults originate, develop into sects, and then change into denominations, perhaps finally to emerge from the process as churches."[5] Harvey Cox in his controversial book, *The Secular City,* explains the development of churches in relationship to the socio-economic factors of society. He sees the cycle as: (1) the tribe, (2) the town, (3) metropolis, and (4) megalopolis.[6] His cycle has many parallel factors to Moberg's and Troeltsch's cycles.

---

[5]David O. Moberg, *The Church or a Social Institution,* (Englewood Cliffs, N.J.: Prentice-Hall, Inc., 1962), p. 100.

[6]Harvey Cox, *The Secular City,* (New York: The MacMillian Co., 1965), pp. 1-13. When Cox sees the bankruptcy of American denominations he suggests we advance to a religionless society, where God is dead, as an answer. When I see the same bankruptcy, I maintain we must return to the origination, the sect/fundamentalist church.

An Examination of Sects/Fundamentalism

Webster defines the sect as "A class, order, or kind of men; a group having in common a leader or a distinctive doctrine; a following; a school, as of philosophy; a group holding similar views; a party. In religion: (a) a party dissenting from an established or parent church; a body of sectaries, (b) one of the organized bodies of Christians."[7] The sects have theological beliefs that fall within the context of historic Christianity.

The evangelical and/or fundamentalist movement, arising in this country since the turn of the century took its name from the magazine, *The Fundamentals,* which was a rallying point for theologically conservative individuals. However, the term *fundamentalist* that once reflected a conservative enlightened position no longer has that connotation in the perspective of others. In the mind of many the term fundamentalist today implies a negative connotation. But those who are fundamentalist are proud to wear this label.

Carl F. H. Henry, past editor of *Christianity Today,* is a severe critic of fundamentalism, indicating that it is more than a doctrinal position, that fundamentalism has a life-style or methodology all its own. "Historically fundamentalism was a theological position; only gradually did the movement come to signify a mood and disposition as well."[8] Later Henry went on to describe fundamentalism both theologically and methodologically:

> Fundamentalism is considered a summary term for theological pugnaciousness, ecumenic disruptiveness, also unprogressiveness, scientific obliviousness, and/or anti-intellectual inexcusableness. By others, fundamentalism is equated with extreme dispensationalism, pulpit sensationalism, accepted emotionalism, social withdrawal, and bawdy church music.[9]

Fundamentalists and sects have similar characteristics and these will be developed in this chapter. Some fundamentalists may resent being called a sect. However, Christianity was a sect in its beginning

---

[7]*Webster's Third New International Dictionary,* (Springfield, Mass., 1963).

[8]Carl F.H. Henry, "Dare We Renew the Controversy?", *Christianity Today,* June 24, 1957, pp. 23f.

[9]Carl F.H. Henry, "What is Fundamentalism?", *United Evangelical Action,* July 16, 1966, p. 303.

I find Henry's evaluation of fundamentalism as example of an uneducated name-calling bias, without documentation. He has the same weakness he criticizes in the fundamentalists.

(Acts 4:5, 28:22), as was the Pharisees (Acts 5:17, 15:5, 26:5). Hence, the title *sect* in the Scriptures is a religious title.

Arnold Hearn, writing in the *Christian Century,* 1958, in an article entitled, "Fundamentalist Renaissance" describes a "revival" (his term) going on among fundamentalists concerning scholarship and scientific investigation.[10] (We are not sure whether Hearn was referring to fundamentalist or evangelicals as a group; he probably was referring to all church groups to the theological right of the neo-orthodox position.)

William Hordern recognizes a division in the right wing of the theological world in a chapter entitled, "The New Face of Conservatism," written for *New Directions in Theology Today,* claiming many in the church thought:

> Fundamentalism was pronounced dead, and it was assumed that it would soon disappear from its sanctuaries in the hinterlands. To those who were writing the obituaries of fundamentalism, there were disturbing signs.[11]

Hordern indicates the strength of fundamentalism is growth in church attendance, higher per capita giving than liberal congregations, and the fact that these fundamentalists were providing far more than their share of candidates for the ministry.[12] These facts are reflected in a survey of the 100 largest Sunday Schools in America. Hordern was teaching at Garrett Theological Seminary, Evanston, Illinois, where he observed the conservative churches of Chicago changing in nature from the fundamentalist to the evangelical camp. He characterizes these changes:

> During the fifties, however, a group of young scholars arose from the fundamentalist circles to forge a new theology. These scholars rejected the term "fundamentalist" because they felt that it had become a term of abuse and not a meaningful description of a theological position. Furthermore, they were conscious of the shortcomings of their theological fathers and wished to remold the tradition. They were as concerned as the liberals of an earlier day were to make Christianity relevant to the modern age, but they were determined not to repeat what they saw as the errors of liberalism.

---

[10]Arnold Hearn, "Fundamentalist Renaissance," *Christian Century,* April 30, 1958, p. 528.

[11]William Hordern, *New Directions in Theology Today, Vol. I., Introduction,* (Philadelphia: The Westminster Press, 1966), p. 75.

[12]*Ibid.*

Although most of these young men came from fundamentalist seminaries and colleges, they began taking graduate degrees at nonfundamentalist institutions. They returned to their denominations and seminaries to revitalize the theology that had hardened during the fundamentalist-modernist controversy. There is no agreed name . . . They prefer the name "evangelical" or "new evangelical."[13]

The categories for a sect that was developed by Troeltsch are perhaps the best outline to use in this chapter to describe fundamentalism.[14]

1. *Sects/fundamentalism is comparatively small.*—Troeltsch lived in Lutheran Germany where the state church encompassed most of the inhabitants. Sects, according to his observation, were small. However, in Protestant America sect-type churches are rapidly growing and are numbered among large denominations. This author indicated in the book *The Ten Largest Sunday Schools* that these churches were sectarian in nature. (He has preached in 71 of the 100 largest churches in America and feels that most of the large churches are sectarian in nature.)

2. *Sects/fundamentalism tend to avoid state and society.*—Most fundamentalists have a deep desire to be separated from secular influences that would contaminate their life. Some fundamentalist denominations, such as the General Association of Regular Baptists and the Independent Fundamental Churches of America, seem to place personal purity as the first priority for the Christian. By doing this they make personal separation an *end,* rather than a *means.* The churches of this book feel that evangelism is the main priority of the church. However, personal holiness is not neglected, for these churches preach separation from sinful practices. These churches feel separation is a means to gain spiritual power so that a Christian may be an effective soul winner. However, most fundamentalists, whatever the purpose, feel separation is a vital aspect of living the Christian life.

Some fundamentalists feel ecclesiastical separation from doctrinal heresies also is a criterion of the Christian church. For this reason, Bob Jones University will not fellowship with Billy Graham, not because they disagree with the content of his preaching, but because Billy Graham fellowships with liberals who cooperate in his evangelistic endeavors.

---

[13]*Hordern, op. cit.,* p. 76

[14]*Troeltsch, op. cit.,* The following discussion is based on a summary of Vol. I, pp. 331-81, Vol. II, pp. 993-1013. This summary was made by David Moberg, *The Church or a Social Institution,* pp. 74-75.

Elizabeth Nottingham indicates there are several types of sects.[15] Some are *withdrawing* sects who take on the characteristics of the medieval monastic orders. These might be Plymouth Brethren or Old Amish Mennonites. Others are *militant* sects who are aggressive in their outreach. Nottingham indicates that many of the present denominations at one time were sects, such as the Methodists and Southern Baptists, but have made their peace with the world. These groups no longer practice personal separation based on biblical commands.

3. *Sects/fundamentalism is connected with lower socio-economic classes.*—When visiting these ten churches a vast number of lower-class (Socio-economic) people are observed in the congregation although there is an evidence of both middle-class and upper-class members. When Dr. Jack Hyles, pastor, First Baptist Church, Hammond, Indiana, was asked what class his people were, he replied, "All my people are upper class." By this he meant his respect for each person, but on many occasions he indicates his love for the common man. Some high-church ministers tend to criticize lower-class churches, equating them with naivete and/or ignorance. The strength of sectarianism/fundamentalism is in its identification with the common man. Jesus indicated a rich man had as much difficulty entering into heaven as a camel passing through the eye of a needle (Mark 10:25). Also there are a number of Scriptures that criticize the rich (Matt. 13:22, James 5:1-4) and commend the poor (James 2:1-4). Perhaps the poor are more aware of the harshness of life: lack of food, adequate shelter, financial security, and recreational pleasures. The poor, during the New Testament as well as today, find in Jesus Christ the answer to many pressures of life. Money can give a false sense of security to the affluent. The rich suburbanite insulates himself from the ultimate issues and lives in a plastic world created by his own wealth. Money usually produces self-sufficiency and a man who has little material need, does not turn to God as readily as the poor. Perhaps the poor, as the fundamentalist, reflects a constant need for the presence of God in his life.

4. *Sects/fundamentalists oppose the established culture.*—When most sociologists examine the content of sermons preached by fundamentalist preachers, they find a heavy emphasis on the Second Coming of Christ and the judgment of this world. Since fundamentalists believe this present culture will eventually be destroyed, they put little stock in its present enjoyment. Also, since man is sinful in

[15]Elizabeth K. Nottingham, *Religion and Society,* (Garden City, N.Y.: Doubleday and Co., 1954), pp. 62-67.

his design and nature, the culture that he creates is a product of that sinful nature.

When a man is converted in a fundamentalist church, he usually has a great desire to spend time working in his church. A truck driver was led to the Lord at the Thomas Road Baptist Church and he immediately began driving a Sunday School bus, spending 6 to 8 hours each Saturday visiting in homes to reach others for Christ. Because he loves Christ and the church, he totally involved himself in its ministry. His former friends feel he was missing the pleasures of life; however, he no longer enjoyed drinking with his friends. He had found new pleasures for this life and enjoyed serving in the church.

5. *Sects/fundamentalists have voluntary membership based upon a new birth for entrance.*—Many mainline denominational churches accept a person for membership based on a verbal agreement with the church doctrinal statement. However, sectarian/fundamentalist churches emphasize the new birth experience and many of their members are brought into the church through conversion, rather than by transfer of church membership. One of the signs that a church is beginning to move around the sociological cycle is when most of the new members transfer in from other churches rather than being converted in the church. The number of conversions in these ten churches indicate that they are alive. Their growth is reflected in the weekly baptismal service where new Christians are immersed in water.

6. *Sects/fundamentalists emphasize enthusiasm as a sincere expression of their dedication.*—Preaching at fundamentalist churches is sometimes interrupted with shouts of "Amen!" Zeal is a criterion for spiritual service. Pastors spend time making announcements to motivate Christians to soul winning and Christian service. Outward enthusiasm is an obvious characteristic of fundamentalist churches. New members are judged by this zeal and emotional vitality.[16]

The critics of fundamentalism accuse them of being emotional, hence shallow. The morning service in a fundamentalist church is not characterized with liturgy, ritualism expressed in printed programs, robed choirs, anthems and threefold amens. The churches in this book emphasize informality and warmth of fellowship. Dr. Jerry

---

[16]I feel one of the basic differences between a fundamentalist and an evangelical is the emphasis stressed on either the emotional or the rational nature of Christianity. The fundamentalist tends to "feel" his Christianity deeply. He then makes feeling the criterion for "finding the will of God" and other personal needs. The evangelical tends to be rational in his approach to the Christian life, requiring a logical understanding for actions and attitudes.

Falwell, pastor, Thomas Road Baptist Church, said to Doug Oldham, soloist, "Sing another solo; they are not ready to listen to the Scripture." Oldham sang a song with "happy enthusiasm." When Oldham had finished, Falwell felt the congregation was ready to receive the preached message.

Fundamentalists point to Christianity in the New Testament. They indicate there were no formal cathedrals or sanctuaries; rather, congregations worshiped God in simple houses, fields or street meetings. The preaching of the gospel and the teaching of the Word of God was the catalyst that drew people together. Dr. Jerry Falwell indicated a blueprint for building a church auditorium: "Preach the gospel and put walls around it."

Fundamentalists still emphasize the rededication service, whereby individuals are asked to stand or come to the altar as an outward profession of an inner act of dedicating oneself to God. Many evangelicals who have moved in the cycle, do not appreciate a rededication service. A minister in the Evangelical Free Church stated recently, "If a man is dedicated to God, it's a fact; he doesn't have to keep reminding God." The fundamentalist answers this charge by rebuttal that all men are sinners by nature and have a tendency to slip into sin. The biblical principle of leaven, that sin can permeate the whole of man, forces the fundamentalist to constantly preach rededication.

7. *Sects/ fundamentalism emphasize conversion experience.*—The fundamentalist believes that the conversion experience prepares a man for heaven. The term *experience* is the core of understanding what happens to a man when he is born again. First of all the conversion experience is based on *knowledge* of the Word of God. A man must know he is a sinner and that "the wages of sin is death" (Rom. 6:23). This knowledge includes the fact that Jesus died for sin and that man must believe the fundamental facts of the gospel to become a Christian. However, this knowledge does not qualify a man for heaven. A person must have an experience based on that knowledge. *Emotions* are the second step involved in this conversion experience. A man's total being is affected; as a result he may hate sin or love God—both are emotions. The emotion of love is as strong as the nature of man and a man must love, to be converted (Matt. 22:37-39). Third, the *will* of man is involved in a conversion experience. The man must want to be saved. His will must respond to God and he "must receive Jesus Christ" (John 1:12). These three aspects make up a conversion experience. Fundamentalists stress this conversion experience, that is usually emotional in nature. Evangelicals usually stress an academic conversion. One of the signs

that indicate a church is drifting into liberalism is when "mental-belief" or agreement with the doctrinal statement is substituted for a conversion experience. A church begins to drift into liberalism when it no longer stresses conversion experiences, but rather only emphasizes rational understanding of Christianity.

8. *Sects/fundamentalists emphasize lay leadership at the pastoral level.*—One of the amazing phenomena found in these ten Sunday Schools was that a number of full-time staff members had never attended Bible college and/or theological seminary. They were laymen who were promoted to full-time staff status as a result of their successful ministry in the church. Reverend Roscoe Brewer, youth minister, Kansas City Baptist Temple, is one of the most influential youth directors in America. In the past few years, he has been responsible for preparing over ten laymen who have not had formal training for the positions of youth ministers. These men are now in full-time Christian work. This author would judge that approximately one-third of the staff members of these churches have never attended a Bible college or theological seminary. They have learned how to build a church by working in a local church under a successful pastor. One visitation pastor commented, "I attended the school of hard knocks."

The use of laymen in full-time positions brings zeal into the leadership of local churches which usually produces results. But some of these lay leaders also bring theological shallowness. Most of these lay pastors have only a lay knowledge of the Bible and doctrine, learned from their pastors. One visitation minister (not from these 10 churches) told me, in all seriousness, "My course in the power of positive thinking by Dale Carnegie is excellent theology. It's all a young man needs to go into full-time Christian service." This naivete scares me.

9. *Sects/fundamentalists emphasize a mystical religious relationship to God.*—Troeltsch said a mystical relationship to God is characterized as communicating with God apart from the five senses: i.e., sight, taste, hearing, smell and touch. The fundamentalist believes he has a relationship with God through a sixth sense, "the Spirit bears witness with our spirit that we are the children of God" (Rom. 8:16). Ask the fundamentalist who arises from his knees if he talked to God. His reply, "God spoke to me—I know it in my heart." Because of mystical inclination, many fundamentalists rely much on feelings rather than the rational teachings of the Word of God.

There is nothing wrong with mysticism; all true Christians have Jesus Christ in their hearts, which results in a mystical relationship to God. "Christ lives in my heart," testifies the believer. Paul witnessed, "I am crucified with Christ, nevertheless I live, yet not I but Christ liveth in me, and the life which I now live in the flesh I live by the faith of the Son of God who loved me and gave himself for me" (Gal. 2:20). "Mystical" does not mean unreal, but refers to an unseen relationship with Christ. The basis for a mystical relationship is in the objective revelation—the Word of God. A mystical relationship with Christ cannot prove one's Christianity, but only reflects one's walk with God.

10. *Sects/fundamentalists emphasize law more than grace.*—In this designation, the manner of living by law is referred to rather than salvation by law. Fundamentalists have always emphasized salvation by grace through faith. By this is meant the complete sufficiency of the atonement of Jesus Christ applied to those who repent and call upon God. But in the Christian life, fundamentalists do apparently emphasize law. Their emphasis on the doctrinal basis of law is sometimes confused with the laws found in the New Testament for Christian living. The New Testament teaches that the Christian is to live a disciplined life. One of the fruits of the Spirit is self-control. This self-discipline is not an end in itself but a means to spiritual power for evangelistic outreach. When a Christian refuses to smoke tobacco, partake of alcoholic beverages, or indulge his sexual appetites, it appears that he is emphasizing legalism. However, his negative prohibitions are motivated by self-discipline rather than a search for merit before God.

The sect/fundamentalist is not antinomian (without law). The laws of God as seen in the Ten Commandments are reflective of the nature of God. Both the character of God and His attributes, which make up His nature, are reflected in the laws revealed in the Old Testament and the standards of the New Testament. Fundamentalists are accused of obeying laws out of religious naivete. However, the fundamentalist obeys the laws of God as a reflection of faith and love to God.

11. *Sects/fundamentalists believe in the personal bodily return of Jesus Christ, retribution of wickedness and the establishment of the millennial kingdom.*—Troeltsch observed that sectarian movements literally interpreted the Scripture, which forced them into a view that God's people expect Jesus Christ to conclude the events on this earth. Troeltsch stated that sectarians believe, "God will allow His elect to pass through tribulation and misery, but finally He will complete the work of redemption upon His return to earth and the establishment of the kingdom of God."

The fundamentalist does not believe that ecology will run its course, so that man pollutes himself to death. Neither will the population explosion cause man to populate himself out of existence. They believe that Jesus Christ shall return as judge to bring vengeance upon all unrighteousness on this earth. But this age represents a day of grace in which God's mercy and love offers to every man salvation. The fundamentalist believes it is his duty to reach every living person on this earth with the gospel, motivating the lost to receive Jesus Christ.

12. *Sects/fundamentalists believe the work of redemption was completed in the atoning death of Jesus Christ.*—Since they have a literal interpretation of Scripture, fundamentalists believe the work of Jesus Christ upon the cross was final and that nothing in man's goodness could add to personal salvation. The sinner must humbly receive the mercy granted because of the death of Jesus Christ. Christ's death was not designed as an example nor as a moral influence upon all men. The death of Christ satisfied the wrath that God had for sin—all sin. Since God's vengeance is satisfied—atoned for—God is now free to respond in mercy to those who repent and believe.

13. *Sects/fundamentalists believe in literal obedience to primitive church ideas.*—The field of Christian education becomes a dividing line between evangelicals and fundamentalists. The evangelicals believe that the church must apply the methods of education, psychology, sociology and philosophy to the Christian education process. Of course, evangelicals believe the *method* changes from generation to generation. Relevancy becomes the dividing issue. But in contrast, fundamentalists believe the *message and method* are implied in Scripture. The church should obey the scriptural methods to carry out God's work. Fundamentalists believe that the New Testament church in the book of Acts supplies the biblical method: i.e., house-to-house visitation, personal soul winning, public proclamation, private Bible study, public and private prayers. These methods allow the Holy Spirit to work through the cleansed man of God.

Fundamentalists do not believe the church must become relevant to the sinner, but the sinner must become relevant (repent) to God's plan of salvation. Therefore, coffee houses, dialog groups, Koinonia fellowships, the Jesus People, and other relevant ministries are not adopted and used by most fundamentalist organizations. Evangelicals, because of their apparent lack of faith or their desire to be relevant, have found that traditional soul-winning techniques have not been effective for numerical growth. Therefore, they turn to other methods as a viable option, which is in fact a turning away from Scripture.

14. *Sects/fundamentalists teach constant renewal and revival.*—
The theological basis for the continual need of renewal and revival is
found in the doctrine of sin. The old nature is not eradicated once a
man becomes a Christian, but a new nature (the power of the Holy
Spirit and the presence of Jesus Christ) is added to the man's nature.
The old and new natures constantly strive for supremacy. Hence, the
Christian needs to be constantly reminded to place Jesus Christ on
the throne of his life. Since the sinful nature allows the old man to
occupy the throne, the Christian needs to constantly return and
place Christ at the center of his life. This is repentance or rededication, where the Christian returns to the first principles of Christianity
to renew his walk with God. Evangelicals seldom have rededication
services and altar calls for adults and high school students to yield
their life to God. Many times the rededication service is looked
down on, perhaps because of a softened attitude toward sin.

15. *Sects/fundamentalists expect to transform the world solely
by the moral principles of the gospel.*—Evangelicals are fast embrac-
ing social action as an extension to the gospel ministry. So much so,
that they are in danger of losing their emphasis on evangelism. At
the same time, fundamentalists see their biblical task as presenting
Christ to unsaved people so they can be saved. Social action of the
evangelicals takes many forms, such as: the war on poverty, feeding
the poor, voter registration, and drives for racial equity. The fundamentalist is not anti-social action, but feels deeply that the transformed individual will ultimately make an impact against social and
civil ills. The fundamentalist, however, will not give primary consideration to social action but to soul winning. Dr. Jack Hyles has
often said, "We do more social action on our way to win souls than
the average liberal church does on purpose."

16. *Sects/fundamentalists differentiate between themselves and
hypocrites or heretics.*—Since fundamentalists believe in the verbal-
plenary inspiration of Scripture, those who deviate from this position
are noted as "heretics." A "hypocrite" is one who claims to live by
the standards of Scripture, yet fails to live by that standard either
by his ignorance or deceptive practices. A "heretic" is one who has
espoused the beliefs of fundamentalism and has doctrinally deviated.
Fundamentalists believe the Scriptures teach a position of doctrinal
and personal purity. Therefore they (1) note those who deviate and
(2) separate themselves from those who are heretics.

Those who dislike fundamentalists accuse them of being "fighting
fundamentalists," but misunderstand their motives. Those who attacked Bishop James Pike for his doctrinal deviations were not seeking harm to the man. Fundamentalists attack people they believe are

heretics because they want to protect the young Christian and un-taught believer from contaminating their Christian walk and witness for God. However, there are some fundamentalists who carry crusades to fight Billy Graham or liberals as a personal vindication for their ministry or other subliminal motives. These fundamentalists might be motivated out of pseudo-charismatic qualities (messiah complex). The minister constantly faces the problem of balance in his ministry, yet one doubts if God calls a man to spend his main energies and time in attacking religious deviants. God calls ministers to win souls and build churches.

Summary.—The true fundamentalist church is an aggressive band of born-again Christians who have mutually agreed that the world is going to hell and the drift of this life is governed by the lust of the flesh, the lust of the eyes, and the pride of life. Therefore, strict standards of personal purity are prized. Every man who has not ex-perienced the new birth is lost and going to hell, so the aggressive fundamentalist attempts to win him to Christ, caring nothing of the charge of proselyting. The passive fundamentalist is committed to pure doctrine, giving diligent attention to teaching children and new members the doctrine of the Scriptures. Doctrinal deviates are ostracized from fellowship.

The fundamentalist is judged by his zeal in personal service and attendance of meetings. He walks in a day-by-day communion with his Lord whom he loves, and counts his church life the center of his existence. He feels his Christianity at a "gut" level and is sure of the correct stance of his position.

Institutional—Evangelical

The term *evangelical* is sometimes broadly applied to all Bible-believing Christians, including fundamentalists, evangelicals, neo-evangelicals, or conservatives. However, this is a wrong usage of the term; most fundamentalists do not want to be called evangelicals. The broad use of the term *evangelical* is usually used by mainline denominational spokesmen.

Evangelicals prefer to think of themselves as conservative in doctrine, yet *relevant* in methodology. One thing an evangelical knows for sure, he is not a fundamentalist. There are other names which might apply to evangelicals. The term *orthodox* and *con-servative* is usually applied to both fundamentalists and evangelicals. However, the term *orthodox* and *conservative,* when applied, usually designates "that branch of Christendom which limits the ground of religious authority to the Bible."[17] As a result, the term *orthodox* and *conservative* can be applied to Christians who are either evangelical or fundamentalist.

Christian Life defined eight trends of the evangelical that distinguish him from a fundamentalist.

> These include: a friendly attitude toward science; a willingness to re-examine beliefs concerning the work of the Holy Ghost; a more tolerant attitude toward varying attitudes on eschatology; a shift away from so-called dispensationalism: an increased emphasis on scholarship; a more definite recognition of social responsibility; a reopening of the subject of Biblical inspiration; and a growing willingness on the part of the evangelical to converse with the liberal and dialectical theologians.[18]

The sect/ fundamentalist is characterized by a compelling concern to reach people by any and every means, persuading them to repent and turn to Jesus Christ. Crowds hungry for spiritual answers come to fundamentalist churches to hear the Word of God. Ministers give attention to the function of Christianity rather than to its form. Little thought is given to choir robes, printed programs, liturgy, or education of the minister (one indication that *Christian Life* shifted from serving a fundamentalist audience to an evangelical clientele is that they substituted the term *pastor* for the more sophisticated term *minister*). To the fundamentalists, evangelistic and educational function is more important than outward form. This truth might be illustrated by special music; it is more important for a soloist or choir to "speak to the heart" than to enunciate correctly or use a higher class of music (anthem). The following points reflect the institutional/ evangelical interpretation of Christianity.

1. *The evangelical/institutional Christian is interested in efficiency and coordination.*—The evangelical feels a basic point of the church is to have a pattern or organization as seen in Scripture. Whereas the fundamentalist might let his emotions guide the arrangement of the morning service, the evangelical is concerned about

---

[17]Edward John Carnell, *The Case for Orthodox Theology*, (Philadelphia: The Westminster Press, 1959), p. 13.

[18]"Is Evangelical Theology Changing?" *Christian Life*, March, 1966, pp. 16ff. There is little theological difference between the fundamentalist and the evangelical; they differ in methodology. The eight issues pointed out by *Christian Life* reflects a different approach to Christianity. Therefore, the field of Christian Education, a discipline of methodology, reveals where fundamentalists and evangelicals basically disagree.

wasted motion, wasted time and wasted energy. The fundamentalists are concerned about efficiency, but this is not a basic assumption. When the evangelicals see a growing number of agencies in their churches, they usually organize a Board of Christian Education so there will be a coordination of energy rather than an omission or over-emphasis in their ministry. The Board of Christian Education helps to coordinate and systematically plan the activities of the church. It is felt, "In the multitude of counselors there is wisdom" (Prov. 11:14). Therefore, responsibility is turned over to committees so that the work of God may prosper.

2. *The evangelical/institutional Christian is motivated by rational appeals to the intellect.*—When a person is saved from raw heathenism (he is not a member of a church family and has no church profession) he does not need a course in apologetics to prove the existence of God. His emotional experience becomes the basis of his salvation and the basis of his faith. "I know God exists because He saved me." The average first-generation fundamentalist has little difficulty with the theory of evolution or other attacks against the Bible. He might say, "I know God created the world, because He saved my soul from sin. My experience proves the existence of God to me. I know God lives because my life is changed." Because fundamentalists base their Christianity upon their experience (emotions), if their feelings change, their basis of salvation can crumble. But many keep an even keel throughout life. However, when second-generation Christians (their children) come along, there is usually not a radical change in the life-style of the children at their conversion. They do not repent from outward sins. Therefore, they cannot appeal to their emotions. These children grow up in the church. Sunday School becomes an educational experience and they usually have a rational rather than an emotional commitment to Christ. Therefore, Christianity must be reasonable to them because their faith is based upon an intellectual understanding of Christianity. The evangelical needs a clear articulation of his convictions. The son speaks to his father, "If smoking is wrong, why can't you prove it to me?" Across the generation gap, another father is perplexed, "Why can't my daughter see that dancing is wrong?" The father deeply feels (emotions) dancing is wrong, but the daughter wants reasons. The father feels that since Christ saved him from sin, his daughter should not want to sin. However, the father doesn't realize the daughter has not had the same experience. Yet the daughter, reflecting the evangelical position, loves Christ as much as the father.

3. *The evangelical/institutional Christian will cooperate with both the fundamentalist and the liberal.*—Because the evangelical wants dialogue with the mainline denominations, he will cooperate in the

local ministerial with ministers who are not of the same theological conviction. Evangelist Billy Graham has a crusade and the evangelical is happy to cooperate with mainline Presbyterian or Methodist denominations, or other groups of broad theological conviction, even though his fundamentalist friends will not. At the same time, the evangelical wants to cooperate with the fundamentalists, because they have the same theological persuasion. The evangelical minister might phone the fundamentalist church to arrange a singspiration for his teen-agers, only to be refused politely. Evangelicals are noted for their tolerance for others holding differing opinions. Fundamentalists are noted for their dogged allegiance to the tenets they feel are biblical.

4. *The evangelical/institutional is committed to relevant Christianity.*—The evangelical is concerned about social action and cooperates with community projects in drug abuse, temperance, and campaigns for civic decency. The evangelical points to the Old Testament prophets, indicating that preaching was socially oriented, aimed at changing society. Therefore, the evangelical feels he is following a biblical mandate.

Dr. Lois LeBar, professor of Christian education, Wheaton College, in her latest book, *Focus on People in Christian Education,* builds an entire philosophy of Christian education on the basis that needs become the starting point in Christian education, "ministry is meeting needs."[19] She uses the following cycle, indicating those who serve Christ must know needs before he can meet them.

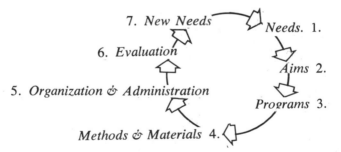

This cycle has been adopted by most evangelicals as a basis for their ministry; however, most have not analyzed its implications. A basic weakness of the chart is a definition of the term *needs.* If the ministry is "meeting the needs" of an individual, all effort could be channeled into supplying food or shelter for the poor. The ministry

---

[19]Lois LeBar, *Focus on People in Christian Education,* (Westwood, N.J.: Fleming H. Revell Co., 1968).

then is aimed at the *felt need* level. If the ministry begins with *ultimate needs,* Christian education is a biblical imperative. The Bible indicates the greatest need of man is spiritual—salvation from sin—because man is a sinner. However, when needs are interpreted as *felt needs* then the ministry is aimed at alleviating the temporary problems of man. These problems are usually physical or material. When a church gives all its energy to meeting *felt needs* it is easy to stray from the biblical imperatives of the Word of God. Both the YMCA and Salvation Army now serve with the supposition that their task is to meet needs (felt needs). At one time these organizations were known for a soul-winning ministry (ultimate needs), but have degenerated into primarily humanitarian organizations, departing from the biblical imperative of personal regeneration.[20]

The ministry in most evangelical churches is measured by its ability to meet needs; however, need is not the first step in establishing strategy for church ministry. Strategy is formulated on biblical imperatives, from which needs are viewed.

The fundamentalists believe there are truths a pupil should learn; these lessons are not primarily practical (relevant), nor do these lessons meet *felt needs.* Some doctrine does not have immediate practical application, but the child of God is commanded to know doctrine. Facts about God should be taught simply because God is the source of Christianity. Therefore, the fundamentalist does not accept the presupposition of relevancy to guide his curriculum construction. However, he feels that the Word of God when properly learned will change his life, making the student relevant to God. The fundamentalists would go a step farther. The sinner should be made relevant to Scriptures, and not vice versa.

5. *The evangelical/institutional church emphasizes the positive Christian life.*—Many evangelicals feel fundamentalists are not motivated by guilt feelings in their separation from worldly amusements. The evangelical points to the positive aspects of the Scriptures and interprets verses about happiness to teach that God has given many good things in life to enjoy.

The evangelical teaches that separation is turning *to* God *from* sin (1 Thess. 1:9). Whereas, the fundamentalist emphasizes the opposite. The evangelical tends to emphasize turning to God, or the positive. Whereas the fundamentalist emphasizes repentance or turning from

---

[20]I feel many liberal churches have followed the pattern of the Salvation Army and the YMCA, simply because they have departed from allegiance to biblical authority. I fear that many churches in the evangelical camp will follow the same course.

sin, many evangelicals would permit dancing, movies, and social drinking, if done in moderation. A teen-ager arrives home from high school, and argues, "But, Mother, the daughter of the minister of the First Baptist Church is going to the prom. Why can't I go?" As a result, fundamentalist parents are caught in tension; either they give in to their convictions or give in to their children. Neither is satisfactory to the fundamentalist.

6. *The evangelical/institutional church is held together by organization.*—When a religious movement is in its primitive state, growth is realized through dedication, zeal and active involvement by the entire membership. Many times growth comes through charismatic leadership. As the church becomes more institutionalized, leadership changes into the traditional mold. Authority is decentralized and the staff of specialists assume more responsibilities. Full-time ministers of music, recreational directors, ministers of education and business managers are employed to carry on the work of the church. The organizational *form* becomes more important than the church's *function*. It is not clear whether specialists are employed because laymen no longer have the zeal to carry on the ministry, or lay members no longer feel needed because full-time workers are employed. However, they have less zeal to carry on the work of the ministry. With the shift of leadership from laymen to the professional, efficiency becomes a standard of operation. The professional guides the church, with the laymen widely involved in the actual work. Only later as the church approaches denominational status do the laymen seem to lose their interest and involvement in church affairs. At that time "institutional blight" affects the church.

The sectarian/fundamentalist places high emphasis upon zeal and dedication, which is reflected in emotionalism, at the same time deemphasizing educational qualifications of the ministry. Many fundamentalist ministers will publicly criticize higher education, which is synonymous with college education, seminary training or intelligencia, yet at the same time they deeply respect the intellectual they personally meet. Academic excellence is equated with liberalism and is placed in an opposing position against zeal and fundamentalism. When the church grows into an institutional state, a growing desire to articulate convictions is felt, whereas previously the congregation is held together by a deep emotional level of commitment. One might theorize that the fundamentalist puts faith (a term that might mean emotional commitment) over reason. The slow evolvement to institutionalism sees rational Christianity slowly replacing emotional Christianity. Generally, solving the problems of higher criticism (i.e., inerrancy of Scripture, the deity of Christ, the existence of God, and evolution) seem to be the topics of conversation among evangelicals rather than fundamentalists.

The pastors of fundamentalist churches assume a laymen's mentality, even though many of them have graduated from Bible college or a fundamentalist seminary. These schools give the pastor knowledge of theology, Bible, Christian education and training in pastoral duties, but do not provide a liberal arts education. The liberal arts graduate is broadened, i.e., made a man of the world. Because of this lay mentality and desire for charismatic leadership, most true sectarian pastors rarely leave their first pastorate because they feel called by God to reach a neighborhood. Reverend Larry Chappell, United Baptist Church, San Jose, California, has often said, "I plan to make my life's ministry in San Jose." Hence, pastors from sectarian churches have longer tenure than evangelicals. The pastors of the ten largest churches in America have an average tenure of 24 years, two months. The evangelical pastor has a more professional attitude to the ministry, and at the same time a less provincial outlook, resulting in a lessened identification with any one neighborhood. Hence, the evangelicals tend to change pastorates much more frequently than do fundamentalists. Many pastors attempt to climb the totem pole to success by changing churches every three to five years. As a result, they do not build large churches because they do not invest enough time to establish their ministry and build momentum which might result in attendance growth. Any minister who changes pulpits too often, seeking greener pastures, is guilty of "green grass, low-fence mentality."

7. *The evangelical/institutional Christian bases separation from worldly amusement on a rational basis.*—Since many evangelicals are second-generation Christians, they seldom have the emotional/guilt motivations for separating from sinful practices that were characteristic of their parents. The first-generation Christian is saved from the damaging effect of sin upon the life; his conversion centers around repentance from the polluting effects of sin. The factory worker knows that drinking beer, dancing all night in a night club or carousing in a tavern did not satisfy. When he received Jesus Christ he put away sin. His love to Jesus Christ motivates him to serve Jesus Christ with all his heart. He often quotes, "Therefore if any man be in Christ he is a new creature, old things are passed away, behold all things are become new" (II Cor. 5:17). Most second-generation Christians have grown up in a church and never had the opportunity to participate in outward sin. Their conversion is seldom an emotional-based experience. There is no turning from outward sin. Many second-generation Christians are converted early

in life, receiving Jesus Christ in Sunday School or at mother's knee. These second-generation Christians feel cheated, not having an opportunity to enjoy the pleasures of the world. "What's wrong with a mini-dress?" the daughter asked her mother. The daughter is given emotional arguments, but she is searching for rational arguments. Hence, she sees nothing wrong with short skirts, if the mother cannot give rational reasons.

The evangelical uses the Scripture to formulate arguments against sinful practices. But the basis of interpreting the Bible is logic and rational Christianity. The question to be answered: "Is the Christian life based on logic or feeling?" The fundamentalist and evangelical usually disagree in their answer.

8. *The evangelical/institutional position places emphasis on the man rather than on the whole.*—The evangelical has a higher commitment to the person than he does to the church. He feels man is the center of the universe and the purpose of redemption. Therefore, he builds a ministry on *sensitivity* and *respect* for individuals. Since man is made in the image of God, he argues that a ministry must be built on respect for individuals. The evangelical often accuses the fundamentalist of "playing the numbers game," which is getting people to church, only to count a large attendance. The evangelical will spend more time in counseling people with problems. The evangelical seminaries will concentrate on positive counseling courses, whereas most fundamentalist schools usually do not have any course in this area. Dr. Lee Roberson once answered the people at Highland Park Baptist Church, Chattanooga, Tennessee, "If someone has a problem, I have two minutes to spend with him; my time is reserved for reaching the lost." He went on to say, "If a Christian will take advantage of proper Bible study and the fellowship of church attendance, he will not have problems."

The fundamentalist places a high emphasis on the corporate community—the church. He believes that a strong church will produce strong Christians. Hence, the whole is important, perhaps more strategic than the parts. The fundamentalist feels that if the church is growing in attendance and quality ministry, the individual Christian will also grow. He feels the illustration of an army best reflects the church. Just as the soldier is part of the whole and loses his individuality in the army, so the Christian is a member of God's army. Irenius said in the first century, "Christians, like soldiers and slaves, ask no questions." Therefore, the fundamentalist emphasizes yieldedness to God and active service through the church. When this militancy is lost, church attendance begins to decline. Hence, evangelicals have difficulty attracting a large crowd, while fundamentalists, will have both a growing and a large attendance.

Summary.—The evangelical is committed to Jesus Christ and feels his Christian life should be a positive influence in his church and community. He does not want to be labeled a fanatic or "wooden-headed fundamentalist." He attempts to integrate his faith into every area of life, being consistent. He wants the respect of the unsaved and feels the best testimony is a positive, constructive life that attracts others to Jesus Christ.

Evangelical ministers base their preaching upon the clear explanatives of the Word of God and feel the unsaved should understand God's Word, so they will respond to the gospel. The evangelical does not resort to "buttonholing" the unsaved, persuading them into the church. They have a high regard for the personhood of each individual and feel that manipulation is wrong, even when the goal is proper. The person is more important than the local church, because the universal church is composed of individuals, each important to God and His program.

Denomination—Deterioration

The third category in the evolution of church growth is the denominational stage. Webster has defined it as "a religious organization uniting in a single legal and administrative body, a number of local congregations." However, the term "denomination" used in the sociological cycle carries a broader meaning than an organization of many small churches. A denomination represents a group of churches which allow central control to gradually centralize and decision-making power to slip from the members who founded the churches out of deep theological conviction, to clergymen who view their task through the eyes of professional competence. The term *denominational* can be applied to (1) a group of churches, (2) administered under a central organization, (3) that has been in existence long enough for the primary commitment of charter members at individual churches to slowly evolve to professional clergymen and (4) a state of institutional blight which settles throughout the social life-style of a movement. Institutional blight is the process of social decay where individuals, committees, and churches lose sight of the original goals of the founding fathers and succeeding generations unable to identify with the principles that formed the original catalyst, search for a new reason for existence. When the organization is unable to find a new *reason for existence,* the whole superstructure tends to drift with little aim. Voices within the denomination cry for a return to the original precepts, yet these prophets appear to have a hollow cry, because no one will heed them. One observer has characterized such denominations as having an *identity crisis.*

Even though the term *denomination* is used, the social process can refer to an individual church or a religious organization. The church first begins as a sect, then changes its nature and basic tenets. The church desiring more efficiency, slowly builds an organization. The denominational stage of the cycle is the natural outgrowth of organization efficiency of local churches. The denomination is an extension of local church institutional system at a "super church" level. According to David Moberg, the denominational level of the cycle takes on added sociological characteristics. He defines these as:

> Formalism saps the group's vitality. Its leadership is dominated by established bureaucracy more concerned with perpetuating its own interests that with maintaining the distinctives that helped bring the group into existence. Administration centers on boards and committees that tend to become self-perpetuating. Dominated by the small group, the organization may become like boss-ridden parties . . . the very small ones who, because of the position they hold, should be most ready and anxious to make the Christian ministry a real brotherhood, talk one thing and practice another.[21]

1. *The denomination reflects the religious life of the community.*— The denomination is tolerant of the outside world, no longer at war with society. They are accepted as a part of the community. Denominational churches are tolerant of sin and no longer prohibit the "questionable practices." Respectability becomes a motive for people joining the membership. People transfer from one "status" church to the next, often more concerned about business prospects or women's clothes styles than the actual religious commitment of the church. Activities the sect once considered worldly are now the center of interest. Ministers become members of the Kiwanis Club, and the official board feels it is important that he has a membership in the local country club, to make the right contacts. The church has a distinct image to uphold in the community, and no longer desires to be considered fanatical or "wild-eyed Baptists."

2. *The denomination is committed to a relevant ministry.*—The minister in a denominational church has a commitment to existential philosophical assumptions. Since he must find self-definition, his church also must seek an identity in a changing world. As a result, he resists any type of ministry that does not meet human need at an

---

[21]Moberg, *op. cit.,* p. 120.

individual or corporate level. As a result the individual and his needs are primary in planning programs or administering the church. When this happens the focus of the church has moved away from God-centered priorities to a human-centered authority. The authority of God over the individual is no longer important and the necessity of making programs relevant to individuals becomes the criterion for judging the success of a church.

3. *The denomination is concerned about perpetuation.*—The Sunday School superintendent in the sectarian church is primarily responsible for leading the staff in an evangelistic outreach. When the church evolves to institutional status, the Sunday School superintendent loses the evangelist's role and becomes an educator. Now, he is more concerned about educating students. Sunday School literature gives him guidance in retaining "dropouts." Usually he is more concerned with "keeping the Sunday School going" rather than aggressively reaching the neighborhood for Christ. Committees and offices that were constituted to perform a job, often enjoy status simply because they get the job done. With the passing of time, people take the job because they want the status, yet are hardly capable of functioning on the committee. Hence a Sunday School superintendent may be appointed because "nobody else wanted the job." Or a committee continues to exist without a function, "We always have DVBS in our Sunday School; if it is dropped this summer our children might go to the Presbyterian Church."

Another factor that characterizes the denominational development is the growing desire of pastors to leave the pastorate for administrative positions. The shift reflects a change of values. The pastor comes to believe that the work of the denomination is of greater importance than the local church. When pastors believe that the denomination's work is of more significance than the church for which Jesus died, decline is inevitable. Three years ago 600 Presbyterian pastors applied for two administrative openings at their denominational headquarters.

Deterioration

The final stage of deterioration in the cycle results from over-institutionalization of local churches, with the resultant disintegration of the denomination. Churches decline because the original purpose of the church changes. People lose interest because their spiritual needs are not satisfied; then attendance drops and income declines. Membership begins to fall off. Since there is no urgency in reaching the community, new candidates for the ministry are difficult to find. Churches go without pastors. Moberg describes the process of deterioration as, "diseases which show symptoms of this stage are: formalism, indifference, obsolescence, absolutism, red tape, patronage, and corruption."[22] The original spiritual vision of the founding group is gone. The impersonalization of people sets in. Schaller calls this "institutional blight."[23] The member feels detached from the church; the denominational headquarters are not responsive to their needs. The leaders at headquarters, removed from local church economy and individual responsibility, may feel they can and should lead the church into new programs of action, whether or not the individual members respond. In the past few years several denominational officials have attempted to lead a group of churches into programs of social action, because the denominational hierarchy feels the members at the grass roots level are biased and/or ignorant. The officials of the United Presbyterian Church of America persisted in donating money to defend Angela Davis, charged with conspiracy in the death of a courtroom judge. According to an opinion poll, the church members voted against supporting Miss Davis, but the officials ignored their obligation to the clientele of the denomination. When denominational leaders no longer represent the membership, deterioration sets in when those paying the bills refuse to give and attend. Schaller observes:

> The inevitable decline of congregational economy and the accompanying socialization of the decision-making process within the hierarchy of the denomination is not necessarily a deplorable trend. While it is true that power has a corruptive influence, it is also true that independence has encouraged irresponsibility.[24]

The long evolution toward centralization of church authority usually causes a church to operate more efficiently, resulting in a stronger denomination. The sect and institutional church become stronger through organized outreach. When churches shift to a centralized authority, they reach more people. But usually in the process, the members become less responsible for church direction, hence over a period of time the movement becomes weaker. The problem is time. Those wanting a larger, stronger church are willing to delegate leadership to the paid staff. When the professional gets

[22]*Ibid.,* p. 122.
[23]Lyle Schaller, *Planning for Protestantism in Urban America,* (New York: Abingdon Press, 1965), Schaller gives an excellent summary to causes of church and denominational deterioration, especially analyzing the bankruptcy of many inner city churches.
[23]*Ibid.,* p. 209.
[24]*Ibid.,* p. 211.

results, the membership is generally satisfied. However, with the passing of time both the membership and leadership change, then the next generation of leaders alter the direction of the church, and the membership is either powerless to stop them or does not care. Schaller predicts, "It now appears that the future is almost certain to witness a further deteriorization of congregational autonomy."[25]

Kinchela, in his article, "The Behavioral Sequence of a Dying Church," notes that a congregation finally dies in one of three ways: (1) vacated by the pastor, (2) securing a part-time pastor, and (3) complete abandonment or by merging with another group.[26] Schaller gives an analytical and practical discussion of a dying church in the deterioration cycle. They can (1) merge, (2) relocate, or (3) remain and struggle with death.[27]

Many believe the present-day trends of merging denominations is simply a move by dying organizations to save the deteriorating superstructure from oblivion. Leaders feel that the consolidation of headquarters and reduction of overhead cost can eventually save the denomination. However, by alienating members at the local church level, the ecumenical movement cannot fulfill its promise.

As the church deteriorates in vitality, many people leave and seek to get their spiritual needs fulfilled elsewhere. Where do they go? Moberg indicates that people who withdraw from institutionalized or deteriorating churches withdraw "into new sects or are drifting without any formal church connection."[28] Many of the sectarian churches have received members from mainline denominations. Some new members (those already converted) usually bring their church memberships with them and serve God out of renewed dedication. Other individuals become converted, throwing over empty church membership for vital union with Jesus Christ. They find a spiritual rapport with other members and serve God with renewed zeal.

The sociological cycle indicates that a fundamentalist sectarian church is founded upon warm fervor to God and ends up in a cold liberal denominational church on the brink of deterioration.

---

[25]*Ibid.*

[26]Kinchela, "Behavioral Sequence of a Dying Church," *Religious Education,* Vol. 24, pp. 329-45.

[27]Schaller, *op. cit.,* pp. 15-46.

[28]Moberg, op. cit., p. 122. Moberg cites a footnote at this point, "Insofar as sects result from weaknesses and failure of churches, the proliferation of sects is a judgment on the churches." (Editorial, "The Judge and the Judgment," *Christian Century,* 74 [May 1, 1957], pp. 551-52). Whereas Moberg deplores the founding of sectarian churches, I rejoice when they fulfill the biblical imperative.

Principles of Church Growth Drawn from the Sociological Cycle

1. *Churches can move through the cycle sociologically, and not theologically.*—A small fundamentalist sectarian church may grow because of an inner dynamic. However, without realizing the subtle shift in emphasis, the church changes its methodology. Even though the sect-church does not change its message or beliefs, it changes its methodology. Most denominations become cold, from making the organization the goal of existence, rather than fulfilling a biblical purpose. Dead churches cannot produce life. Dr. Jerry Falwell places some dead fundamentalist churches in the same category as liberal churches. "Whether a church has dead orthodoxy or dead liberalism, makes no difference—to be dead is dead." A church can be orthodox in doctrine, but not biblical in purpose. A living church is correct in doctrine and purpose. One of the dangers of dead conservatism is degenerating into a single desire for doctrinal purity. This emphasis is only half correct—which makes it half wrong. A church must have correct message and correct methodology. The General Association of Regular Baptists and the Independent Fundamental Churches of America many times give the appearance of being more concerned about purity of doctrine than aggressive, warm, evangelistic outreach. Not all, but some of these churches are dead. Even though they call themselves fundamentalists, their organizational structure and lack of evangelistic outreach place them in the denominational stage of the cycle, making them similar to liberal churches. Of course, not all of their churches are characteristic of this generalization.

2. *Churches tend to reflect more than one phase of the cycle at a given time.*—It is possible that small sectarian churches have some of the organizational characteristics of institutional churches. A fundamentalist church may have the appearance of a denomination. The Baptist Bible Fellowship, which is a sect, has large churches which are beginning to organize for efficiency. However, having some marks of denominationalism does not mean every characteristic is found in a cycle stage. The controlling characteristic places a church on the cycle. Moberg makes the following observation, "The five stages in the church's life cycle overlap."[29]

3. *The cycle is inevitable.*—Most fundamentalists believe that their church or Bible college will never go liberal. This is a naive observation. The cycle is inevitable because of the sinful nature of man, the principle of leaven within the individual, and natural

---

[29]Moberg, *op. cit.,* p. 122.

desire for perpetuation. Most ministers in the Baptist Bible Fellowship deeply believe that their movement will never go liberal. However, every church, Christian school and movement has inevitably deteriorated into liberalism and/or an institutionalization.

Dr. Noel Smith, editor of *The Baptist Bible Tribune,* often writes editorials against the control by the headquarters of the Southern Baptist Convention over cooperating churches. He has pointed out that local churches which support the cooperative program are giving to liberal colleges and seminaries. Smith apparently believes that pointing out the sins of the Southern Baptist Convention will keep the Baptist Bible Fellowship from following in its steps.

Many concerned Christians ask, "What can be done to save our church from slipping?" The first answer is simply, place emphasis on reaching people according to the biblical mandate, rather than organizing the church for efficiency. People gather together, organize themselves into a church for the purpose of meeting their spiritual needs and winning others to Jesus Christ. Institutionalization sets in when people begin overemphasizing their organization and/or buildings. These improvements are not wrong when emphasis is placed on ministry to individuals. But when improvements become an end rather than a means of ministering to people, deterioration sets in. If the local church keeps its eyes on original purposes i.e., evangelism, building churches, and Christian education, then the process will be stopped.

The cycle is inevitable, but at least not for two or three generations. The lesson from the kings of Israel teach that God's people serve the Lord for approximately two generations after a revival. Joshua served the Lord, and the elders that outlived him; but in the third generation, Israel sought other gods and worshipped Baalim (Judges 2:8-11).

The Baptist Bible Fellowship
The Fastest Growing Religious Body in the U.S.

The Baptist Bible Fellowship will become the largest denomination in the United States.[30] The ministers of the Baptist Bible Fellowship

---

[30]The Baptist Bible Fellowship is chosen for examination for two reasons; first its fast growth. Beginning with 13 churches in 1950, the 1971 *Directory* lists 1,756 churches. The author first examined the Baptist Bible Fellowship in an article, "The Fastest Growing Sunday Schools in the U.S." *Christian Life,* September, 1968. Second, because the Baptist Bible Fellowship reflects a movement at the beginning stages of the sociological cycle. A study of Baptist Bible Fellowship will help the reader to understand the drift of American churches and perhaps help some to stop the drift in their life and church. The popular accepted use of initials BBF will be used to refer to the Baptist Bible Fellowship.

will immediately reject this statement, because the word *denomination* is used. They feel the Fellowship is a movement rather than a denomination. At present the Baptist Bible Fellowship is a movement; however, within the next 30 years the Fellowship may take on the organizational characteristics of, and appear similar to, other denominations. At present the BBF is a movement made up of churches of similar emphasis and description.

What Is the Baptist Bible Fellowship?

1. *The Baptist Bible Fellowship is a movement describing itself as a fellowship, and not a denomination.*—At present there is no hierarchy nor centralization of authority. Each church is independent and responsible only to the members, as are all true Baptist churches. The BBF is a dynamic movement because of the internal growth. The churches are characterized by soul winning, where sinners are transformed from a life of sin to a life of godliness. Also, life-giving quality is seen in the churches. In the 1971 yearbook, 376 new churches were listed. Many of these were begun by individuals in the fellowship; of course some were churches that admired the BBF and joined the movement.

The term *movement* reflects life and action. Whether one agrees with what action is found in the BBF churches, one cannot deny their vitality. Money is being raised, crowds are growing in attendance, numerical growth is registered each year, and people are excited about Christianity.

2. *The BBF is a movement of methodology, not doctrine.*—Even though BBF churches are conservative or fundamental in doctrine, theology does not hold the BBF together as in other similar conservative denominations. Most BBF churches believe the orthodox position expressed in the footnotes of the Scofield Bible, and their pastors carry King James Bibles; yet theology is not the primary catalyst. The BBF is a movement of methodology best expressed as evangelism. The principles of their methodology are not yet written for outsiders to study. Most of their churches are similarly organized, their Sunday School classes are similar in administrative techniques, and their pastors lead their churches as though all are instructed by the same teacher. The methodology of BBF churches is more "caught" than learned in the classroom. When this author first realized so many pastors of growing churches were trained at the Baptist Bible College, Springfield, Missouri, he examined carefully the curriculum and life-style of the Spingfield school to determine its success. Here he found the spirit of early Americanhood prevails the campus. Pastors of large churches speak in chapel

and young men desire to imitate their success. Dr. G. Beauchamp Vick, pastor of Temple Baptist Church, Detroit, Michigan, a pastor of 4,000 people, and Dr. John Rawlings of Landmark Baptist Temple, the pastor of 5,000 people, are president and vice-president, respectively. Young men have little aspiration to climb ecclesiastical ladders to success. Upon graduation from the three-year course of study, they pack their car on the following morning, drive to a town God has laid upon their hearts, and begin knocking on doors, inviting people to a rented building. They have a vision of beginning one of the largest Sunday Schools in that area. The young men who graduate from the school have "caught" the movement and they are singleminded in their purpose to build a Sunday School. These young men are not highly trained in theology, sophisticated in pastoral techniques, nor are they eloquent in the English language. They simply know the Bible, know how to lead people to Christ, and have the passion to build a great church. Young pastors admit that they remember more of the challenge from great men than the classroom material.

3. *The BBF is a movement of pastors.*—Most denominations are an organization of local churches, similar in doctrinal conviction and lifestyle. Most congregations can vote themselves in or out of the denomination. However, the Baptist Bible Fellowship is a movement of pastors. The pastor can determine if he will join or not. This may seem unusual to the average churchman, expecting a local church to be governed by the deacons. The churches in the BBF are not committee-controlled, nor do the deacons exercise delegated responsibilities or authority. The churches are pastor-led, and the success of a local church is measured by the pastor's success in guiding the congregation, even to becoming a member of the Baptist Bible Fellowship. The movement believes that the pastor is shepherd of the flock and leads the flock. Dr. Vick pointed out, "You never saw a flock leading a shepherd." When asked if he believed in democracy in his church he indicated, "Yes, and I'm the biggest democrat of all." By that he did not imply dictatorship but aggressive leadership. The pastor has executive power to administer the church and he looks to his deacons for counsel. The congregation is the legislative branch of the church, making decisions such as approval of annual budget, purchase of equipment, or beginning of new programs. The pastors believe that the congregation is the seat of authority. Most of them boast, "The congregation has never voted me down on one point." The Reverend Cecil Hodges came to his church when it was a small infant group meeting in the living room of a member on the west side of Savannah, Georgia, considered the poor section of the

city. The church progressed rapidly and, after a couple of years, some men presented a list of demands to the pastor, in essence charging that he had too much responsibility. Hodges had been away on a series of meetings and when he came back, he met with his men for approximately six hours. Two of the men brought a list of demands and read them to Pastor Hodges. The first dealt with his having too much authority and leadership. Hodges discussed the item with the men for approximately an hour, searching the Scriptures for the place of biblical leadership. At the end of the hour, the men agreed that the pastor was the leader of the flock, and was responsible for preaching, oversight, rebuke of sin and false doctrine, leading an aggressive program of evangelism, and building up the people in the nurture and the admonition of the Lord. The second question dealt with Pastor Hodges having control of the finances. Hodges spent the second hour showing the relationship between money and the work of God in a local church. It was determined, "The man that controls the money, controls the leadership of the church." Of course Hodges had never signed a check or actually counted the money, but had acted as comptroller and purchasing agent for the church. At the end of the second hour the men agreed that he should remain the leader in financial affairs. The third criticism had to do with Hodges' appointment of staff and leaders in the church. Hodges pointed out that the workman is loyal to the boss who hires and fires. He said, "If I have no control over my staff, they will never work for me." Hodges pointed out to the men the built-in problems of a staff member whose loyalty was to the men, yet alleged responsibility to the pastor. At present, Hodges does not hire staff members nor appoint lay leaders in the church without the knowledge of the deacons, but in the final analysis he makes the decisions, with the blessing and support of the deacons. Should he choose, he can go directly to the congregation for a vote on staff members.

Dr. Wendell Zimmerman, former pastor, Kansas City Baptist Temple, was criticized for 25 years for being a dictator. Yet his dynamic leadership was required to build a church through the first stage of growth. Reverend Truman Dollar works more closely with his lay leadership, yet is insistent that he be the leader if he is the pastor.

Dr. J. Frank Norris, pastor of the First Baptist Church, Fort worth, Texas, at one time was the titular head of the BBF movement before it broke from the World Baptist Fellowship. Norris said on many occasions, "The statue of a pastor casts a long shadow over the congregation." The congregation becomes the spiritual extension or reflection of the pastor. His preaching, example and leadership is usually reflected in the lives of his members. Inasmuch as the BBF is a movement of pastors, it becomes a movement of like-minded men. Since most of the pastors are soul winners, the lay leaders and core members of their congregations also are soul winners. Since the Baptist Bible Fellowship is a movement of like-minded pastors, it is a movement of like-minded congregations, because the people reflect their pastors.

Churches do not vote to become a part of the BBF, rather pastors make the decisions. Therefore, a pastor who desires to fellowship with the BBF may begin fellowshipping and have the name of his church listed in the directory of the Baptist Bible Fellowship. There is no commitment on the part of the pastor or congregation to the policies of the BBF; there is no vote to determine agreement with doctrine, support of program, or turning over physical assets to headquarters. Traditionally, a church has been listed in the directory if it made a financial contribution to the college in Springfield or to one of the approved missionaries going to the foreign field.

Dr. John Rawlings has often said, "You don't join us, you just start having fellowship with us." By that he meant any pastor that attends the pastors' monthly fellowship meeting was a part of the BBF. These monthy meetings usually have several inspirational sermons preached on one day, centered on the theme of evangelism and rededication of pastors to the work of Christ. The movement is not concerned about minor doctrinal deviations in pastors who might want to fellowship. The commitment is to evangelism, not purity of doctrine. However, if doctrinal deviation is so severe that it is not compatible with evangelism, the pastor usually stops attending the monthly pastors' fellowship; hence is out of the BBF. Dr. John Rawlings also mentioned, "You don't vote to un-join us, you simply stop fellowshipping." Because no vote is taken to join there is no vote to disassociate. Hence, the BBF is a movement of like-minded churches rather than a confederation or organization of churches with similar beliefs and/or practices.

Some pastors in the BBF have basic disagreements with other pastors, but fellowship together because the commitment is to local church evangelism. The pastor who is revered is the one who is having evangelistic success—which usually means growing numerically. Academic success is usually not revered, nor is monetary success. Rev. Roscoe Brewer, associate pastor, Kansas City Baptist Temple, once said, "If any man in our fellowship has an earned doctor's degree, I don't know it. He probably has a church of less than 100."

Why the BBF Can Become the
Largest Religious Body in the U.S.

The following reasons have been gleaned from observation of the movement over the past six years. The reasons may not be complete. I take full responsibility for the observations.

1. *A cautious desire to organize without losing the esprit de corps movement.*—The Baptist Bible Fellowship is slowly drifting around the sociological cycle, taking on some of the characteristics of the institutional stage. The printing ministry was consolidated into fellowship publications from a decentralized ministry of three agencies. The *Baptist Bible Tribune,* the *Crescendo Press* under the college, and *Christian Youth Today* magazine in Kansas City Baptist Temple, were consolidated into Fellowship Publications. This move was suspect in the minds of some BBF pastors, while most felt it was a positive step forward.

The board of directors, made up of thirteen pastors, each elected by his fellow pastors, represents a geographical district. The directors have been given more power to direct the movement.

Local churches are using more organization and pastors are getting more education. As of yet, most of them have not switched from a Bible-preaching, evangelistic ministry to a relevant-oriented ministry. Evangelism still controls the local church. However, the desire for efficiency of organization is seen throughout the movement. Of course the purpose remains evangelism, which indicates numerical growth in the future.

2. *The isolation of churches and insulation of Christians.*—The Baptist Bible Fellowship still preaches separation from the world. Also, the churches separate themselves from neo-evangelical influence. As a result, their members do not accept the life-style of Christianity presented in interdenominationalism, i.e., the National Association of Evangelicals. Pastors have kept their people isolated from the type of Christianity reflected in groups outside the BBF, simply because they do not cooperate with other church groups. They have preached against neo-evangelicals, not allowing the influence of neo-evangelicals or the NAE in their church. Pastors also continue this insulation by writing their own Sunday School literature. Hence, they have protected the corporate body of believers from the influence of evangelicalism and individual believers are isolated to the Word of God for their religious stimulation. Cecil Hodges stood before his people and held a *Christian Life* Magazine up, "I don't believe most of what's in here, but you should buy it and read what Elmer Towns says."

3. *Ecclesiastical leadership is centered in growing churches rather than large churches.*—The Southern Baptist Convention has several large churches and the man who assumes the pastorate of these congregations automatically becomes one of the leaders in the Convention. However, the Baptist Bible Fellowship has not followed this example. Several large churches have been vacated, but the man who assumed the pastorate did not become a leader in the Fellowship simply because he pastored the church, nor did he receive admiration of other pastors because of that position. Rev. Wendell Zimmerman spent 25 years in the Kansas City Baptist Temple building up the Sunday School. When he left, Truman Dollar took over the pastorate as a young man, basically unproven. Even though Dollar should have been congratulated for being called to such a large church, one of his friends said, "Just because you are pastor of a large church does not mean you have made it. Remember, you never built a church yet." The criticism stung, but Truman understood its implications. He had to build a great work of God to receive the respect of his peers. Also in Kansas City was the Blue Ridge Baptist Temple, begun in 1957 by Rev. Parker Daley. Daley had built this congregation from a small handful of people to over 1,200 in Sunday School. He received the approval of the Baptist Bible Fellowship, becoming its president.

In the coming years, the leadership and control of the Baptist Bible Fellowship will continue to rest with pastors who are building large churches. The men who are building churches will not change pulpits to get a better church or more influence. Most will remain in one place and build one church. These men will not gravitate to the large churches that have already been built, after the present pastor dies. Rather, men without the pioneer spirit or men who are not able to build churches will tend to climb up the totem pole to these large churches. However the previous influence of these churches will not transfer to the second-generation pastors. Influence in the BBF will transfer to first-generation pastors, pastors of large existing churches who have proved themselves in the role of evangelism, these will have a great influence in the movement. The leadership of the entire movement will continue to reside with first-generation Christians, hence controlling the whole movement and making for continual growth.

4. *The BBF is anti-interdenominational.*—The interdenominational movement in America has seen unparalleled growth since the Second World War. These movements are reflected in such organizations as the Gideons, Youth for Christ, Christian Servicemen's Centers, interdenominational mission boards, and a number of other

organizations, each created to meet a specific need of a segment of Christianity. The basic premise of most interdenominational agencies is, "Since the church has failed, we have been raised up to meet this need." Youth for Christ speakers often preface their remarks with the assumption that the local church has not met the needs of high school students; therefore God has raised up Youth for Christ to evangelize the high schools with the gospel. Also Youth for Christ assumes the responsibility of providing education and nurture for Christians who are in the high schools. Most BBF pastors look upon this as unbiblical, quoting the statement by Christ, "I will build my church and the gates of hell will not prevail against it" (Matt. 16:18). Truman Dollar listened to a Youth for Christ speaker and said after the service, "He is accusing Christ of being a liar, since Christ predicted His church will never fail." Therefore, with invincible faith and boundless energy, the BBF pastors go about building local churches.

A second assumption of interdenominationalism is the universal church, the mystical body of Christ. Most evangelical Christian organizations teach the twofold interpretation of the church; i.e., the church is a local organization and the church is a mystical body; therefore, every Christian is a member of the mystical body which is reflected in interdenominationalization. However, most pastors in the Baptist Bible Fellowship reject the universal church as taught in Scripture. They believe every reference to the word "church" in the New Testament should be interpreted according to its Greek connotation, assembly (*ecclesia*). Since they believe the church is an assembly of believers, there is no mystical union—ruling out the existence of interdenominationalism. Therefore, the Baptist Bible Fellowship teaches every organization of Christians should be in a local church. Pastors do not dissipate their energy by encouraging their Christians to participate in interdenominational activities. Instead, they teach that loyalty to Jesus Christ is measured by loyalty to the local church, the only organization taught in Scripture. The Baptist Bible Fellowship is strong on loyalty to the local church as an institution. Since serving Christ is building a local New Testament church, the Baptist Bible Fellowship will pour its energies into building churches, another factor that can cause it to be the largest denomination in America.

According to a survey of the Baptist Bible Fellowship churches in 1970, the average Baptist Bible Fellowship church has 427 members, with an average attendance of 357 in Sunday School. They are growing at a 4.7 percent annual rate over the previous year's base.

5. *A desire to build large churches rather than dividing into small neighborhood geographical parishes.*—At present there seems to be no desire on the part of pastors in the Baptist Bible Fellowship to send out missionary teams from a local church to start other New Testament churches in the immediate vicinity. In contrast, there is an extreme desire to build a large testimony, if not the largest church in the city in which they are located. This desire to build a great church will result in growing numbers and enlarged membership, causing the Baptist Bible Fellowship to expand. This desire for large testimonies does not rule out a desire to start mission churches. Dedicated laymen or young students from Bible college are given assistance in going into new areas to start churches. However, colony teams (as 20 families sent to start a branch Sunday School) are not encouraged among the BBF.

The desire for large churches seems to have proper motivation, rather than the alleged wrong motives attributed to BBF pastors: "They are building an edifice to their ego or for self-gratification." Their desire to build large churches can be summarized in the following seven reasons. (The results of a large church are given by Dr. Greg Dixon, Chapter 4.)

(1) A large church is biblical and reflects the numerical growth in the book of Acts. (Acts 1:21; Acts 2:41; Acts 4:4; Acts 5:14, 28,42, Acts 6:1,7.) The emphasis on large numbers in the book of Acts allows for a local church to be large.

(2) The large church is able to evangelize the entire metropolitan area. BBF pastors feel the day of the local neighborhood parish church is dead, and that they must raise up an evangelistic testimony to reach the entire area. The author previously wrote, "The ten largest churches were large in the heart of the pastor long before they were large on the street corner."

(3) The large church provides all of the spiritual gifts to the total local church. This argument simply allows for specialists to minister to each area of need in a local church. A spiritual gift is a capacity or ability given by God to a man to perform a spiritual task. Large churches have a staff of many gifted men with many different abilities so that the corporate needs of a local church can be met.

(4) The large church can be a conscience to the community. Small churches do not influence the community by their stand against sin or social evils. However, the large church can speak out against the social evils in the community, and has the ear of the population simply because of its size and access to mass media.

(5) The large church replaces the necessity for a denomination.

There are four basic services that a denomination gives to a small local church. First, it provides fellowship for the pastor and Christians; second, it provides counsel and planned program of outreach so that the small church does not have to plan the total church program; third, it provides finances for loans, purchasing and other corporate buying; and fourth, it services the denomination with literature, advertisement and other helps to carry out a small church function. The large church can provide all of these four services within its local church organization, hence ruling out the need for a denomination. Dr. W. A. Criswell, pastor of First Baptist Church, Dallas, Texas, stated, "The Southern Baptist Convention needs us more than we need them." By that he meant many small churches would follow his example. But in the final analysis, a church as large as First Baptist Church in Dallas is self-sufficient and does not need the Southern Baptist Convention for services, fellowship or counsel.

Dangers in the Baptist Bible Fellowship

Even though the Baptist Bible Fellowship has the possibility of becoming one of the largest denominations in America, there are implied dangers in the movement that could stop its growth. First, there could be a split into several smaller movements. This split could arise from personalities. A strong pastor up North could gather many young pastors around him, while a similarly strong pastor from the South with a different organization might gather young men around him. A second split could come in the Fellowship over geography. Churches on the West Coast sometimes feel isolated from those on the East Coast, thus precipitating a split. Also, there could come a split around schools. The Baptist Bible College in Springfield is the only officially recognized school. However, several pastors in local churches have started a Bible college. There could be a natural cleavage to these schools with the movement pulling away from itself, rather than becoming organized for efficiency.

A split could happen when the founding leaders of the movement at the Baptist Bible College, Springfield, Missouri, die. The greatest challenge to the BBF is the problem of succession. The tendency toward schism among fundamentalists has always occurred at the point when the first generation leadership died.

Another split could occur over doctrine. Many of the Baptist Bible Fellowship churches in Florida believe in a "Baptist bride" position: i.e., when Christ returns with His bride, it will be those who have been most obedient, that is Baptists who have been immersed and associated with local churches. Those who attend the marriage supper are saved and in heaven, yet not in a place of prominence of

God's blessing. These will be other believers, but not members of Baptist churches. A layman's guess indicates that 25 percent of the Baptist Bible Fellowship support the "Baptist bride" position. If the Fellowship loses its allegiance to evangelism as its catalyst and espouses pure doctrine as its aim, a split could occur, keeping it from becoming the largest denomination in America.

Another reason to keep the Baptist Bible Fellowship from growing would be a change of emphasis. At present its Sunday School is an evangelistic, reaching institution. The original Southern Baptist purpose of the Sunday School is the guideline for the average BBF Sunday School, which is: (1) to reach, (2) to teach, (3) to win, and (4) to train. However, when their Sunday Schools become educational institutions, turning away from evangelism, this shift could curtail their outreach and hurt their growth. Also, if the second generation of the BBF allows deacons to control their churches rather than remaining pastor-led, the movement could be curtailed in growth, especially in evangelistic outreach. Literature will have to be forthcoming, explaining to their churches the built-in detriment of deacon-controlled churches. If deacons, who are the continuing leadership symbol in a local church, can pass leadership from one pastor to the next, their churches can continue growing in numerical outreach.

The leaders of the BBF use Biblical charisma. Charismatic leadership usually refuses to allow young leadership to develop. It is then always difficult to extend the spirit of the movement into the second generation. A "crisis of leadership" frequently develops. This could either split the movement or a second generation leader of different persuasion could detour the fellowship from its original purpose.

Finally, if the Baptist Bible Fellowship does not progress too rapidly around the cycle, becoming first institutionalized in local church government and finally denominationalized in the movement, the Baptist Bible Fellowship will continue to grow numerically. Remember, movement around the cycle is inevitable, and the Baptist Bible Fellowship is slowly moving toward becoming a large denomination. If the entire movement will realize the dangers implied in becoming a denomination and will slow the growth, the BBF can enjoy the dynamic expansion of sectarian movement. If not, the efficiency they desire may be the albatros that ultimately drags them to deterioration. But if the Baptist Bible Fellowship can keep the zeal and growth of its sectarian movement, and incorporate the efficiency of growth of institutionalization without being hurt in its zeal and dedication, the Baptist Bible Fellowship should become the largest religious force for God in America.

Chapter 12

Charismatic Leadership*

Some pastors seem to have an "extra power," so that the masses are moved by their sermons; their requests are unquestionably obeyed by followers, people seem to empty their pocketbooks into the offering plate, and sinners almost run down the aisle at their invitation.

These few unique pastors go forth and preach the gospel, as most pastors, yet their results are startling. They turn communities upside-down, and some even capture whole cities for God. They revive dead churches, restore broken homes, and see alcoholics released from bondage under their ministry. Their results are much greater than the average pastor.

How can Jack Hyles build a church from 700 to 5,000 with over 50 adult professions each Sunday, yet a few miles away several fundamental pastors struggle with mediocrity? Those struggling pastors serve the same God, have access to the same spiritual reserves and follow the same principles, yet one seemingly fails and another is eminently successful. The difference between a growing church and a stagnant one is pastoral leadership. Gifted men build great churches and average men build average churches. Obviously, the pastors of the ten fastest growing churches are gifted men with a unique type of leadership. Dr. G. Beauchamp Vick, pastor of Temple Baptist Church, Detroit, has said, "Some are 200 men, 1,500 men

---

*The term *charisma* does not refer to the pentecostal manifestation of tongues, miracles or other phenomena surrounding the alleged "second blessing." The term is used by sociologists to designate personal magnetism used by leaders to accomplish a predetermined goal in their organization or movement.

193

or 3,000." By this Dr. Vick implied that some pastors could build a church of 200; others 1,500; and still others 3,000. Whether these predictions are true is not the issue; Vick could see in certain young men an intangible quality of leadership that could enable the potential preacher to build a church, if the circumstances were equal in all cases.

"Mystical leadership" is the theme of this chapter. The author is convinced a pastor will not become a great leader by reading this analysis; he will receive some insight into what motivates these pastors. A pastor can become a great leader by direct influence of a great pastor. Among the ten largest Sunday Schools, three pastors (Vick, Rawlings, Henninger) served on the staff under J. Frank Norris, a man who definitely had this mystical leadership. Two pastors in this book served on his staff. The author believes charismatic leadership can be learned, even though many believe it is an inborn quality. This chapter is dedicated to examining the nature of leadership found in large churches and fast-growing churches.

After making the study of *The Ten Largest Sunday School and What Made Them Grow,* the author sensed a type of leadership in the pastors of these churches never before personally experienced, even though this dynamic attraction is seen in historical literature. The term *charisma* kept poking its head into conversations. "Jack Hyles has charisma," said one observer. Webster defines "charisma" as, "an extraordinary power (personal magic of leadership arousing special popular loyalty or enthusiasm) given a Christian by the Holy Spirit for the good of the church."[1] This chapter will attempt to answer several questions. What is charisma? How does a pastor develop charimatic leadership? Can a pastor use charisma to accomplish New Testament aims?

Charisma comes from the word *chàris,* "a gift of grace." The word *charisma* usually refers to gifted individuals. A study of doctoral dissertations on the topic indicate that leadership charisma is usually found in political, military, and religious circles. Some refer to charisma as "a personality cult," while Freud referred to men who apparently had charisma as having a "messiah complex." A popular magazine article referred to the charisma of John Kennedy as sex appeal. These generalizations attempting to reduce charismatic leadership to such simple formulas cannot be accepted.

---

[1]*Webster's Seventh New Collegiate Dictionary,* (Springfield, Mass.: G. & C. Merriam Company, 1969), p. 140.

Max Weber, the German sociologist, was the first to define the term charisma as "a certain quality of an individual personality, by virtue of which he is set apart from ordinary men and treated with supernatural, superhuman, or at least specifically exceptional powers or qualities which are regarded as of divine origin or exemplary."[2] This definition describes the personality of a leader but does not include the results of his ministry.

Apparently the word *charisma* first entered popular journalism in 1949 through the pen of Daniel Bell, former Columbia University professor. Used in *Fortune* magazine as a caption to a cartoon describing the qualities of John L. Lewis, an editor blue-penciled the word *charisma* out of Bell's article accompanying the cartoon because the word was obscure. The word *charismatic* was inserted beneath the picture of Lewis at the last minute because an eleven-letter word was needed to fill out the line.

When examining leadership, Weber suggests three broad categories by which society is governed and to which an ultimate appeal of authority is made by the leader when leading his group. (1) *Traditional:* leadership based on rigid societal forms of antiquity. The monocracy or rule by a tribal chief falls under this category. A person (usually a king) becomes a leader because he was born into the office or the process of history evolves him into that capacity. (2) *Legal-rational:* leadership based on adherence to laws established by democratic process. A leader depends on being elected to the position for his authority. (3) *Charismatic:* leadership based on personal magnetism of one man. This area is also termed *revolutionary* leadership, because an individual leader usually is elevated to his office because of social needs by the masses; those needs are expressed by the populace or perceived by the leader. Weber felt charisma had been too dominant in the past to ignore it as a type of government. Most new revolutionary governments are established upon charisma but ultimately pass to legal-rational and eventually to traditional.[3]

Charismatic leadership in this chapter has nothing to do with the charismatic gifts in pentecostal-type churches. Some pentecostal pastors may have charismatic leadership, but the basis of his success is not speaking in tongues, healings, etc. The reason the two may be confused is because of similarity of the term charisma (root-

---

[2]Max Weber, *The Theory of Social and Economic Organization*, trans. by A. M. Henderson and ed. by Talcolf Parsons (New York: Oxford University Press, 1947), p. 358.

[3]*Ibid.*, p. 65.

meaning, "gift of grace"). The extensive use of the term *charismatic leadership* by sociologists should have eliminated confusion, but it has not. Some Baptist ministers are insulted when the author implied they have charismatic leadership. However, an explanation usually solves the problem.

Charismatic leadership is a natural gift. In this chapter the gift of charismatic leadership will be attributed to the ten godly men of these churches. But anti-Christian leaders have charismatic leadership, such as Napoleon, Hitler, Mussolini and Fidel Castro. The gift is an ability that a man can dedicate to the glory of God or to the destruction of society. The ten pastors have yielded their leadership gifts to God, and have been used to build a local church. Since charisma is a natural gift, we can examine it to understand its workings. The quotations from sociological studies will reflect the operation of charismatic leadership in political and military circles. Insight from these churches will be reflected in religious circles.

The following outline will analyze charisma.[4] (1) Charismatic leadership arises during unstable social milieu. (2) The charismatic leader devises a special formula for deliverance. (3) The charismatic leader has a basis on which to guarantee success. (4) The degree of charismatic leadership is measured by the allegiance of the followers. (5) Transcendental/divine-like qualities are attributed to or claimed by the charismatic leader.

Charismatic Leadership Arises During Unstable Times

Two of the main characteristics of charismatic leadership are (1) an awareness of the dilemma of the populace and (2) a determination to do something about it. These two qualities alone do not make a man a charismatic leader, but they are necessary ingredients. Some past political leaders with potential charisma have attacked the establishment, but the masses were not ready to revolt and embrace his leadership. Even though a crisis did exist, neither the economic, social or political scenes was severe enough to cause the populace to lose confidence in the traditional leadership. Barry Goldwater, presidential candidate in 1964, emerged with potential charismatic

---

[4]James Davis, "Charisma in the 1952 Campaign," *American Political Science Review,* XLVIII, (December, 1954), p. 1085. Davis argues that the social conditions make a political-charismatic leader. He set forth five postulates that determine charisma: (1) Appealing leaders, (2) Despondent followers, (3) Weakness of inhibiting political tradition and institutions that hinder the supermanpolitican, (4) A degree of political instability (so people will turn to the leader rather than elsewhere for solutions), and (5) Existence of a crisis. These criteria are found in the pastors with charismatic leadership.

qualities, attacked the establishment, suggested new remedies and promised the government would undergo profound structural changes. However, aside from 24 million faithful Republicans, he could not attract a mass following. Since charismatic leaders rarely provoke indifference or neutrality, Goldwater was attacked as a demogogue and dictator, and hence defeated. Some Bible-preaching pastors attempt to begin a church, yet the results reflect failure. The pastor did not establish a "need" in those he attempted to reach. He could have created a "spiritual need" by preaching on sin. Some charismatic leaders use the unsettled social conditions to create a "need," hence gather a following.

Max Weber indicates there must be a crisis, turmoil and psychic strain where people begin looking for a political messiah. He feels that pressurized social conditions alone do not necessarily produce charismatic leaders; times of stress only afford opportunities for the charismatic leader to become visible.[5]

The successful charismatic pastor stands against the established church society of tradition and ritualism. He sees a dead Methodist or Baptist church as a tool in Satan's hand; therefore, he attacks the traditional churches and maintains his church is correct because it is founded on the Bible. He attacks hypocrisy, just as the Old Testament prophet preaches against sin. He attacks the evils in government, the secularization of public schools and the permissive society. Dr. Jack Hudson received popular support from the TV and newspapers of Charlotte, North Carolina, when he opposed topless and bottomless dancing in the city, striking out against nudity. The common man who feels helpless identifies with the charismatic leader who voices his "beefs" against the establishment.

Fundamentalist preachers who have a deep belief in total depravity (doctrine of sin) are convinced that sin is the disruptive force that keeps society in a constant state of turmoil. They preach that a return to God and repentance from sins will solve the issue at hand. Some fundamentalist preachers mistakenly preach that America should return to the "good ole days." Those citizens who are afraid of the future or find security in the past identify with this preaching. The author's experience with the pastors in the ten fastest growing Sunday Schools did not seem to be a yen for past America, rather a return to the biblical principles of the New Testament.

Some charismatic leaders attempt to establish a church in a neighborhood that is conducive to their ministry. When the populace

---

[5]*Ibid.*, p. 72.

to which they appeal are alienated from established society, these people will respond to preaching that attacks society. Most charismatic leadership is found among the poor in the slums or in housing projects. Many large fundamentalist churches in the North are built on transplanted Southerners who feel isolated among the surrounding "Yankees." This social phenomenon does not take away from the integrity of these churches. God is working through a person's sociological environment to motivate him to get saved. The strong churches founded by The Evangelical Free Church in Northern cities were built on foreign-speaking Scandinavians who were alienated because of their language or life-style.

In contrast, some charismatic leader will have difficulty building a church in a middle-class suburban development, simply because the populace has a degree of financial security and feels a general acceptance in community life.

When we view the members of the churches in this book, we see the fur-clad drivers of Cadillacs, middle-class families in Ford station wagons, and the poor of the community on buses. Can these people be called the disenfranchised Americans? No, at least not economically and geographically. However, there is a negative feeling against organized religion among these Christians, because they are "fed up" with fakery in traditional churches, emptiness of life, and futility of social contacts without Jesus Christ. More and more, Americans are disillusioned with the emptiness of money. All these factors produce a spiritual restlessness, that drives individuals to churches with charismatic pastors.

Richard Fagen writes in the *Western Political Quarterly* concerning the charismatic authority of Fidel Castro, stating that one base of Castro's success was the unstable times in Cuba, which he either created or took advantage of.[6] This unstable condition is reflective of the French Revolution that gave rise to Napoleon or a similar panic in England that led to the collapse of Prime Minister Chamberlain in 1939, propelling Winston Churchill into the leadership of Parliament. Later in life Churchill, the writer-historian, gained

---

[6]Richard Fagen, "Charismatic Authority and the Leadership of Fidel Castro," *Western Political Quarterly*, XVIII, (January, 1965), p. 275. Fagen made a firsthand study of the Cuban Revolution under Fidel Castro, examining five hypotheses concerning charismatic leadership: (1) The charismatic leader is always the creation of his followers, (2) There are no universal charismatics, (3) The leader regards himself as elected from above to fulfill a mission, (4) The emergent leader is anti-bureaucratic, and (5) Charismatic authority is unstable in nature. Fagen found all five of these principles were true in Castro's leadership.

prestige for producing his multi-volumes of history, in which he holds the philosophy "Man makes history." Churchill projects charisma-like qualifications back on many past political and military leaders, without which, according to Churchill, the free world would have been consumed by the tide of oppression. Interestingly, Churchill who so definitely had charismatic leadership, projects it to others of bygone days . . . or did Churchill so identify with leaders of the past that when Hitler threw all of the strategy of his military machine at the almost defenseless island of England, Churchill had to act out the hero of his dreams? Churchill's grit and charismatic leadership through his speeches, turned the tide against Hitler: "We will fight on the beaches, in the fields, and in the streets."

The Charismatic Leader Devises a Special Formula for Deliverance

When a charismatic leader begins his climb to leadership, he initially states a doctrine or formula which is easily understood by the people. This formula is an answer to the dilemma of the populace. The charismatic leader is usually known for his great oratory and persuasive abilities. The people believe in him and his message. He correctly analyzes the dilemma of the masses, hence giving the leader acceptance because of his insight into the problem of the community. The formula, because it is easily understood by the populace, becomes a basis of hope. The people believe the leader because they believe that the answer to their problems found in his message will lead them out of their dilemma.

Since charismatic leadership is revolutionary in nature, the leader depends upon the people wanting to be delivered and reciprocates by promising a new day. Fagen suggested Castro was a charismatic leader created by his followers, though Fidel himself claimed to be elected from above, "transcendent" to fulfill the mission of freeing Cuba.[7]

The charismatic leader usually express his ideas in nostalgic or historionic speech. In many cases, the newly emerged deliverer is a mouthpiece for sentiments that exist at the subliminal level of the masses. Many charismatic pastors use country or western phrases in their sermons, especially to appeal to members of the congregation who come from rural backgrounds.

America was built on the Protestant value system: i.e., the value of

---

[7] *Ibid.*

the future, hard work to gain rewards, purity of sex, retribution for evil, honesty of one's word, pride in accomplishment, planning for the future, cleanliness of the body and home, and success; Americans admire success. Most journalists today criticize the Protestant ethic and have generally succeeded in creating a bad image so that anyone who practices the Protestant ethic is "out of it." Perhaps journalists are just products of the American educational system which has repudiated the Protestant ethic. However, sociologists maintain that the Protestant ethic was a powerful influence in the founding of America. They also maintain that the Protestant ethic grows out of preaching based on a literal interpretation of the Scriptures.

When charismatic preachers offer a formula, they do more than "rant and rave in the pulpit." Since charisma demands a formula to lead people out of the dilemma, the pastor who correctly uses charisma must: (1) offer a formula to individuals to change their life; and (2) offer a formula to cause a dying or lethargic church to grow rapidly and succeed. Bound up in the formula of the charismatic leader are changed lives of individuals, numerical growth in the church, financial success, continued building programs, and continual enlargement of the ministry.

In preparing the book *The Christian Hall of Fame,* the author read seven or eight sermons from each of the 80 outstanding ministers or heroes of the faith who are enshrinees of The Christian Hall of Fame located in Canton (Ohio) Baptist Temple.[8] One fact arose from reading these great sermons: the great preachers of the past not only preached the *message* of God (the content of revelations) but preached *methods* whereby the work of God could be accomplished. Hence, they preached a formula for deliverance of the people.

The ministers of the ten fastest growing Sunday Schools have not created a formula for the deliverance of the people nor have these preachers manufactured it out of their thinking. They deeply believe that the only answer to man's dilemma is found in the Word of God. Jesus Christ transforms individuals; a drunkard can become a Sunday School teacher, a prostitute can be cleaned up and work in child evangelism, and Americans with meaningless lives can become avid soul-winners. Also, the pastors in this book understand the method of building a great church.

Two years ago, a study revealed that 23 pastors of the 75 largest Sunday Schools in America graduated from the Baptist Bible College,

---

[8]Elmer L. Towns, *The Christian Hall of Fame,* (Grand Rapids: Baker Book House, 1971).

Springfield, Missouri.[9] This author studied carefully the curriculum at the Springfield school, trying to determine what made the college such an effective preacher factory. The college curriculum was no different than most other Bible colleges, yet no other school had such outstanding results among its alumni. The successful ministers in the Baptist Bible Fellowship understand "how" to build a Sunday School. They learned the methods from the pastor who led them to Christ. These methods are not learned by studying class notes, but were learned by coming in contact with great pastors who were building growing churches. Great preachers are brought to the chapel periods at the Baptist Bible College to inspire future preachers to go out and begin churches. Young men leave the college to found New Testament churches, beginning with nothing but the vision of building the largest church in town.

The Charismatic Leader Has a Basis on Which to Guarantee Success

The charismatic leader must have a basis for the success of his formula or the clientele will not follow him. His mystic influence over people is difficult to describe. Usually, the charismatic leader influences people both individually and en masse. The degree of success of his leadership is measured by the allegiance of his followers. Usually, past successes of the leader become the basis on which the people believe he can produce results in the future. The young pastor who can win one alcoholic to Christ is assured of a place of "specialness" in the eyes of his congregation. When he personally leads several "down-and-outs" to Christ, the congregation is wiling to give him greater allegiance. He becomes greater than the average preacher in the eyes of his people. A young pastor may attack city council and defeat a liquor ordinance. Since he has shown the "boys at city hall," the average man will follow his direction. They know he can get results, so when he asks for tithes and offerings, the people are not reluctant to give. The congregation of Thomas Road Baptist Church gives a higher financial ratio than the national average because each week over 50 adults profess Christ during the invitation. They know their money is used to win souls.

Carl Friendrich, in his study of charisma, *Journal of Politics,* indicates that there are usually four appeals to authority by the charismatic leader: (1) appeal to absolutes, (2) appeal to tradition,

---

[9]Elmer L. Towns, "The 75 Largest Sunday Schools in America," *Christian Life,* (August, 1970). pp. 15ff.

(3) appeal to experts, and (4) appeal to the will of governed.[10] The fundamentalist preacher first appeals to the absolutes of the Word of God. In the early days, Billy Graham often repeated his appeal to authority, "The Bible says . . ." Also, many fundamentalist preachers appeal to tradition. He reasons that what God has done in the past, He can do in the future and is willing to do. Experts are quoted by the charismatic leader in his appeal to the congregation. Bob Moore reflects his charismatic leadership by the will of his people, "My congregation has never voted against a recommendation of mine."

The Madison Avenue public relations executive cannot create a charismatic leader. Advertising cannot make a great leader, although some have tried it. Publicity may enhance leadership of the traditional pastor or can be used by the charismatic leader once he has gained his following, but the charismatic leader must have a previous basis for his leadership before a public relations man polishes his image.

Since the image of the leader may be manipulated by effective propaganda campaigns, the type of relationship of the pastor and people before he gains the office and after his ascension to office must be examined. The pre-office charismatic leader is socially accepted by the group he leads and is so judged by the intensity of personal devotion given to him. Political charismatic leaders use two devices to gain power: unity and factualism. The politician appeals for unity, aiming his argument to the fringe groups of the society (educationally disadvantaged, geographically disadvantaged, and economically disadvantaged). In each, he will attempt to convince the group that their dilemma is blamed on the status quo. Deliverance is promised through his program. Usually the charismatic leader reinforces his claims by appealing to the nostalgic history of the disenfranchised. He appeals to their hero and will probably adhere to their traditions. Cultural symbols that give him strength and courage are emulated, such as speech, temperament, style of action, ideas expressed, or identifying oneself with the legendary heroes of the past. The many comparisons of John F. Kennedy to Abraham Lincoln after Kennedy's assassination only validated his earlier charisma, and later perhaps enhanced the rising charisma of Robert Kennedy before he was assassinated. The many biblical allusions used by Franklin D. Roosevelt to captivate his audience gave him acceptance by the biblically-oriented American society.

---

[10]Carl Friendrich, "Political Leadership and the Problem of Charismatic Power," *Journal of Politics,* XXIII, (February, 1961), p. 26.

The Degree of Charismatic Leadership Is Measured
By the Allegiance of the Followers

The charismatic leader is socially validated by his followers and so evaluated for success by the intensity of the personal devotion they give him. The charismatic leader needs to communicate to his followers a sense of continuity between himself and his mission. Weber says there is no universal gift of charisma, but it is identified with a culture. The charismatic leader can only influence another society or culture to the extent that he shares common histories or value systems. Hence, the minister who grew up in a housing project or on the wrong side of the tracks can be a great leader of the poor. This leadership is more than a "hometown boy makes good" but certainly his success contributes to his leadership.

Why do people follow the charismatic leader? Many people follow the charismatic pastor, not for rational reasons, but because the odds are against him and, in fact, appear insurmountable. The charismatic leader appeals to the deep feelings of the populace and they hope he can somehow "pull it off." Since the leader claims to have transcendental/divine-like characteristics, his sense of mission seems to make him omniscient and omnipotent in the eyes of the people. Many people said of J. Frank Norris, "If he wanted to charge hell with a water pistol, I would follow."

Tucker suggests another reason why charismatic leaders are successful: the populace response is not necessarily absolute obedience toward their leader, but simply that by virtue of extraordinary qualities, he exercises a kind of domination over the followers. Tucker also suggests, "The personal characteristics of the leader are promoted and copied by a large segment of the group."[11] Hitler, Mussolini and Napoleon had charismatic leadership and their insight into problems supported their mystical leadership. Even though their insight proved wrong, the populace believed them for a while. Bierstadt goes on to say, "Charismatic leadership depends on belief by the people, that the person designated is fully able to receive destiny in a way that no ordinary man can fathom."[12] Becker indicates that the followers of the charismatic leader realize that for society to remain integrated (orientated towards acceptance) one

---

[11]Robert Tucker, "The Theory of Charismatic Leadership," *Daedalus,* XCVIII, No. 3, (Summer, 1968), p. 747. Tucker advances the "personality cult" concept of charismatic leadership. In this book this is referred to as the pseudo-charismatic leader.

[12]Robert Bierstadt, *Modern Social Sciences,* (New York: McGraw-Hill, 1964), pp. 269-70.

functional prerequisite was the continuance of the past inheritance and the central value system. The charismatic leader promised that, therefore, the people needed him.[13]

Transcendental/Divine-like Qualities are Attributed to/Claimed by the Charismatic Leader

Many charismatic leaders possess traits that would distinguish them from ordinary leaders. Two facts are prominent from the sociology literatures: (1) Some charismatic leaders claim divine qualities (this is perhaps a pseudo-charismatic leader), while others (2) have divine-like characteristics thrust upon them by the followers.

The charismatic pastors who follow the New Testament pattern of church growth do not claim divine characteristics nor are these qualities attributed to them by their followers. These are regular men who have appropriated the spiritual assets available to them for the Christian life and service. These men have incorporated into their lives the spiritual power available to all believers. But they have been chosen by God to lead a church. God has worked through them to a greater degree than He has worked through average pastors, hence the congregation has attributed to their pastor a high degree of loyalty. These pastors win more people to Christ, get answers to prayer, attack sin in the community and win.

Because of the eruption of a volcano when Bobby Kennedy visited South America, he was attributed with divine characteristics. Also, a charismatic leader can associate with divine authority without making divine claims, and enhance his leadership: "The Lord led me to establish this church." Not all pastors with great accomplishments have charismatic leadership. Some pastors never claim to be great, nor will they accept credit for their greatness, yet their accomplishments point to their greatness. These pastors will not let their congregation think of them as special. Other pastors boast of great accomplishments, yet their disillusioned followers do not ascribe loyalty to their pastor. Perhaps the boasting is without basis. If a charismatic leader can get his followers to believe his boastings, he may get loyalty from his followers until they learn the truth.

John Markus argues that transcendence is one of the dominant themes of charismatic leadership, reflected in various forms as union with God, a breakthrough of the walls of suffering (Ghandi), with-

---

[13]Howard Becker, *Modern Sociological Theory*, (New York: Dryden Press, 1959), p. 20ff.

drawal into fantasy toward the fulfillment of aesthetic experience, and an historical consciousness leading to some teleology of history.[14]

Charismatic Personality

The true charismatic leader believes he will not, cannot fail. During the Second World War, Dallas Billington, pastor, Akron Baptist Temple, found out an embargo was placed on his Sunday School buses. He appealed directly to President Franklin D. Roosevelt and got the embargo lifted, hence elevating the pastor's esteem in the eyes of his congregation.

Some might accuse charismatic leaders of having a great confidence in themselves. This might be true, as they are usually correct in their judgment, even about their own ability. They usually have greater knowledge about human personality than those about them. Sometimes charismatic pastors appear to be egotistical. The pseudo-charismatic leader is usually egotistical, but those used by God usually do what they do for the Lord's glory. Some average pastors might criticize a pastor of a large church for driving a Buick and living in an air-conditioned home. However, the charismatic pastor-leader might reply, "The large car and the air-conditioned house save my strength so I can preach more sermons and win more to Christ." This statement leads to the conclusion that the charismatic leader has great ego strength. The pastor with "false humility" can never be a great leader of a congregation, because his personality will not allow it.

Some pastors do not grow in their leadership ability because they are unwilling to risk, to extend themselves. The charismatic leader never takes the safe route, but is willing to risk himself many times. Just as there are no victories without a fight, there are no successes in the Lord's work without attempting great things for God. (A pastor who is afraid of failure will not build a great church.) At the same time, the charismatic pastor has never had a great defeat, at least outwardly. This author has observed some men who have been growing in their leadership ability, but a severe setback scarred their personality and hindered their personal growth so that they never reached their full potential. The charismatic pastor usually explains away his failure. Thomas Road Baptist Church advertised a goal of 12,000 in Sunday School. The goal was not reached and Jerry Falwell said, "This is the first time I've ever apologized for 9,172 in Sunday School."

---

[14]John Marcus, "Transcendence and Charisma," *Western Political Quarterly,* XIV, (March, 1961), pp. 236-237.

The most interesting question to be raised is, "How is the charismatic personality formed?" Ann and Dorothy Willner in *Political Leadership* list multiple causal factors[15] which influence development of the charismatic leader: (1) heterogeneity rather than homogeneity of family background in one or more dimensions, (2) mobility and/or instability of family during the childhood of the leader, (3) mobility of the leader and consequent exposure to varied social and geographical environments in his youth. This observation basically means that the pastor who would lead a great work must be able to live in more than one social environment. Plato stated, "He who would preach in the marketplace must know more than the marketplace;" so the pastor who would preach to a congregation of blue-collar workers must know more than the blue-collar world, yet identify and be identified with that world. This varied background is obtained by travel, education, and many types of employment and experiences.

Charismatic leadership is one-generation long, and it cannot be passed to its followers. After the charismatic leader dies or passes off the scene, the next leader tends to have traditional and rational leadership. Hence, Abernathy will not succeed Martin Luther King, Jr., and hold the same esteem and loyalty in the eyes of his followers. An article in the *Chicago Daily News* indicates Abernathy understands this and is moving toward a traditional-democratic-type leadership.[16] Weber indicates, "The charismatic leader being the source of legitimate authority, (1) is a revolutionary force, tending to upset stability of institutionalization and order, and (2) it cannot itself become the basis of a stabilized order without undergoing profound structural changes."[17] Most researchers feel that the charismatic leader cannot undergo that change. Castro will never give Cuba the

---

[15]Ann and Dorothy Willner, "The Rise and Role of Charismatic Leaders," *Annals of the American Academy of Political and Social Science*, No. 358, (March, 1965), pp. 61-69. Although many in social research have examined charismatic leadership, only the Willners have been brave enough to attempt a personality profile. After having close fellowship with many of the pastors in the largest churches of America (those most likely to have charisma), I am convinced there is a distinct personality pattern in charismatic leaders. The Willners have given us great insight, but I think more study needs to be done in this area as we have not gained full understanding of the charismatic personality.

[16]L. F. Palmer, Jr., "Jesse Furor Points to New Black Leadership," *The Chicago Daily News*, (April 20, 1971), p. 13.

[17]Weber, *op. cit.*, p. 66.

stable government, but after his death the next leader can if another revolution does not happen.

It is an observable phenomenon that the sons of charismatic leaders are better educated, more sophisticated, better organized, but alas, infinitely less effective. Charismatic leaders have inevitably experienced great hardship which helped mould their capacity for leadership. Their sons almost never have this opportunity and share in the financial benefits of the success of their fathers.

Weber wrote, "Charisma can only be awakened and tested: it cannot be learned."[18] He went on to summarize that when leadership is channeled through routine strategy, its charismatic character is altered. Leadership is no longer dependent under the personality of the leader, but upon the forms of the newly established institution. Hence, the charismatic pastor is not in favor of a board of Christian education, job descriptions, or normal channels of authority. He is concerned with the *function* of a church, not its *forms*.

Ann and Dorothy Willner were the only authors brave enough to suggest a personality trait list of charismatic leaders.[19] They have suggested the following list: (1) *A high level of energy or extraordinary vitality.*—The charismatic leader can give long campaigning hours or can exist on little sleep while keeping a heavy schedule, such as when Winston Churchill was prime minister of England in the Second World War. (2) *Unusual presence of mind under conditions of stress and challenge.*—The charismatic leader has the ability to think on his feet. This gives him the "edge" on both his followers and those who disagree. He usually has a wide vocabulary and can use it appropriately. (3) *The charismatic leader is strong-willed and firm in decision-making processes.*—His resoluteness is a source of strength to his followers. He usually appears unmoved, stubborn, and, once he has made a decision, will not change from his point of view. Sometimes, this quick ability to make decisions is called naivete. He is accused of refusing to analyze the issues. His stubbornness gains admiration from his followers, because he will not buckle. Also, his stubbornness might grow out of naivete with a simplistic view to politics either in Washington or in denominational headquarters. (4) *The charismatic leader has unusual mental attainment.*—The Willners believe the charismatic leader does not always have high intellect, but he usually has the ability to seize upon information from many sources and by an excellent memory give the

---

[18]*Ibid.,* p. 367.
[19]Willner, *op. cit.,* pp. 61-69. See footnote 15.

impression of being widely read, hence knowledgable.[20] Dr. Jerry Falwell has a photographic memory and in high school was defeated in a state spelling test. During the following year he read the complete dictionary, knowing that once he saw a word he could spell it, and the following year won the state spelling contest. (5) *The charismatic leader has a flair for originality and a capacity for innovation in his own behavior.*—Creativity may be reflected in his speech, ideas, even to the extent of his being a phrase-maker. Catchy slogans will gain attention and keep interest in a sermon. Creativity may be expressed by his unique solution to the unstable social problems of the masses. Or, creativity may be a new technique he uses to attract more people to Sunday School. (6) *The charismatic leader usually has a lack of understanding of economic or financial matters.*—He may be naïve in offering simple financial solutions to complex problems. Also, the Willners suggest possibly an indifference or impractibility with respect to personal financial affairs. At first I thought this point does not apply to great pastors, because they are usually financial businessmen and operate their churches by detailed accounting systems. But their faith in God to supply money may be a reflection of this characteristic. This is why they are called naïve. They might spend money to reach lost people, knowing that once the person is saved, he will give to the church. The average pastor will not spend money on advertisement, especially if he does not have it. Many charismatic pastors I know have led their churches to over-borrow because they believed in the future of the work. The reaction might be, "I know God will supply because He led me to begin the church." Because the money comes in, he once again is vindicated in the eyes of his people. But many average pastors follow the same role and go bankrupt. (7) *Charisma has the ability to elicit an extraordinary degree of devotion and self-sacrifice from women.*—It is noted that two women made this observation, and perhaps saw this most in churches where churchmen depend upon women for a following. However, in these large churches a high degree of members are men. (8) *Charismatic leaders have extraordinary eyes which are fierce and hypnotic in effect.*—When Billy Graham first preached in Harringay Arena, London, England, he

---

[20]Charles Wegener, "Lord Morgan or Churchill: Mastery Over Men," *Ethics*, LXXVII, (January, 1967), pp. 148-151. Most people consider Churchill a brilliant person, yet Wegener states, "Churchill was a very intuitive and creative individual with a practical bent. He possessed a burning desire for personal distinction. He was poorly educated, not well read, of unstable temperament, but had an indomitable will."

was accused by the press of coaxing people forward through his hypnotic, piercing eyes.

Traditional Leadership

Traditional leadership works under the authority of a democratic process, where the leader is elected. In the church setting, the pastor is called to a church by a popular vote, usually upon recommendation of a pulpit committee. One author described the role of the traditional pastor as: "Leadership is the activity of influencing people to cooperate toward some goal which they come to find is desirable."[21] This definition is broad and can be applied to several situations. It does not say *how* the leader influences people nor does it indicate the motives or success of the leader. Gangel uses the following definitions, "Leadership is the exercise by a member of a group of certain qualities, character and ability which at any given time will result in his changing group behavior in the direction of mutually acceptable goals."[22] He goes on to explain that leadership is an ability to work with people. Most pastors in America will follow the traditional leadership model, as they are not personally equipped to be charismatic leaders.

Biblical Charismatic Leadership

The Bible seems to teach that the success of the work of God is in direct proportion to the ability of the man of God. Hence, Moses, Abraham, Elijah, Isaiah, and Jeremiah were great leaders who used charismatically defined leadership. Also in the New Testament, Peter and Paul used charismatic-type leadership. The Bible seems to teach the "gifted man" philosophy.

Time Magazine argues that charisma, "one of the dominant cliches of the 60's, is clearly on the wane."[23] The article goes on to say that charismatic leaders are the product of a social-economic turmoil and since we have no major struggle in the United States we have no need for charismatic leaders. Of course the magazine referred to political leaders, yet was wrong in its analysis. The black street gangs of Chicago, the civil rights movement, the war in Southeast

---

[21]Ordway Tead, *The Art of Leadership,* (New York: McGraw-Hill, 1963), p. 20.

[22]Kenneth Gangel, *Leadership for Church Education,* (Chicago: Moody Press, 1970), p. 12.

[23]"What Ever Happened to Charisma?" *Time,* SCIV, (October 17, 1969), pp. 40-41.

Asia, uneasiness about crime in the streets, and inflation demand answers. "If America is not in social-economic turmoil now, what is peace?"

Many church leaders are claiming this is the decade of the common or average man. By this they mean there will be no great leaders in the future. Some are claiming that Billy Graham is the last great charismatic leader. Therefore, small Bible study groups are suggested as theological answers, rather than great preachers who speak to large audiences. Pastoral counseling has become vogue rather than life-changing soul winning. The observer wonders whether the emphasis on small groups has ruled out recognition of the great men of God or vice versa. Has the day of John Wesley, Dwight L. Moody, and Martin Luther passed? Or, does the unsettled times of the American church scene lay the groundwork for the emergence of perhaps the greatest leaders of the past 2,000 years? This author contends that some of the pastors in the large churches of America are reaching and influencing more individuals than did some of the great charismatic leaders of the past, such as Asbury, Billy Sunday, Jonathan Edwards, and John Calvin.

Charisma seems to be a personality trait that grows naturally in certain men. The trait is amoral, hence one cannot say that to use charisma leadership is good nor bad. Perhaps the answer is that the great man of God, with charismatic qualities, who is under the control of the Holy Spirit, can accomplish great works for God.

Wayne Lukens in his masters thesis on charisma maintains that charisma is used primarily to build numerical attendance, and transform or revive old religious forms.[24] He goes on to declare that the exercise of charismatic leadership will not bring about good-quality Christian education in a program.

Leadership is usually attributed to two sources: First, the leadership ability is inborn. Some men apparently have leadership from the time they are small children and the qualities that make them a great leader apparently are inherited.[25] Second, leadership can be developed. Certain leaders seem to successfully face a crisis and through that experience become greater. The question naturally follows, "Did the pastor with leadership ability inherit his gift or was

---

[24]Wayne Lukens, "A study of charismatic leadership in Christian Education," (unpublished Master's thesis, Department of Christian Education, Trinity Evangelical Divinity School, 1970).

[25]Weber, *op. cit.,* p. 367. Weber believes charismatic leadership is inborn. "Charisma may only be awakened and tested; it cannot be learned or taught." This cannot be proved and I tend to doubt its validity when applied to pastoral-charismatic leadership gifts.

it learned?" The fact that pastors of 23 of the 75 largest churches in America have been associated with or received their education from the Baptist Bible College, Springfield, Missouri, leads one to conclude that leadership can be developed. Or, those with potential charisma are sent or come to this college.

God uses a man according to his ability. It is incongruent with the nature of God to bring a person with leadership ability to salvation, then place that person on the shelf and not use his leadership ability. First, God may give leadership ability, and, second, God may guide in its further development. Charismatic leadership is a natural gift that some pastors have used to build a great church. If these men were not pastors they would be great leaders in some other area of life. There are several elements from a spiritual perspective that make up charismatic leadership.

1. *Implicit faith in God.*—The leader who is aware of the sovereignty of God and His intervention in the affairs of this life will have an inner confidence that God can guide his affairs. This inner confidence results in outer respect by the populace, making him a better leader. This psychological reason is only half the picture. The leader who has great trust in God will have great spiritual power.

2. *Yieldedness to the purpose of God.*—When the followers see the hard work and personal loyalty of their leader, they also will sacrifice for the cause. The charismatic leader is the one who emulates respect and obedience from his followers. The pseudo-charismatic pastor builds an image of dedication to God, while in reality he has no true biblical passion to reach people. He uses his leadership abilities for wrong reasons. The leader who is totally dedicated to his local church is the leader who will motivate members to greater service.

3. *Unswerving obedience to divine absolutes.*—There are many common men in life who are looking for answers. The minister who stands and thunders, "Thus saith the Lord" will gather a hearing, if he gives the people a basis for believing him. Since God has spoken, and these pastors believe the Scriptures are divinely inspired and inerrant, they believe their leadership is based upon divine authority. Even though these charismatic leaders see themselves as channels, their followers project onto them a level of "specialness" that is reserved for a select few.

4. *A belief in the devastation of sin.*—The pastors of these churches believe that a man cannot build a great New Testament church without a deep conviction in the damage and damnation that results from sin. When Truman Dollar pleads, "We're singing another verse for you to come forward and find Jesus Christ," this is

not a salesman begging for a signature on the dotted line. He is deeply convicted that men stand on the precipice of hell and eternity waits to suck them away. Dollar may sing ten stanzas of "Just As I Am" during the altar call. He stated, "I fear the wrath of God greater than the irate displeasure of a parishioner whose dinner plans are spoiled." Sin is the greatest dilemma, as far as these pastors are concerned. Their success is directly related to their ability to convince others of the effects of sin.

5. *A trust in the infinite power of God to work through the weakest human channel.*—Pastors in these fast-growing churches do not see themselves as possessing a unique holiness. They were each individually asked if at any time in their life they had an experience with God, apart from salvation, that uniquely equipped them to pastor a fast-growing church. They were specifically asked if they had an experience of the baptism of the Holy Spirit, the infilling of the Holy Spirit or a similar type of experience. Each of the men testified he had had no special experience to make him holy or that gave him power to build a fast-growing church. Herb Fitzpatrick declared, "I am an average man. Any average man can build a great church if he is willing to work hard, win souls, and be faithful to preach the Word of God." Fitzpatrick went on to indicate, "When I speak of hard work, I refer to man's part. Of course, I realize that God must work and He does so through yielded, dedicated men, but there is no spiritual secret to building a fast-growing church."

Pseudo-Charismatic Leadership

Pseudo-Charisma.—The abuses of charismatic leadership are abundant. A pastor eliminates the board of deacons, runs the church as a dictator, and finally absconds with the till, stealing thousands of dollars. A second pseudo-charismatic pastor elicits devotion to himself rather than Christ, and has a sexual affair with a woman of the church. Also, pseudo-charisma is seen in the belligerent dictator who rules his church with the iron fist, destroying people rather than helping them. When this oligarchy crumbles, the deacons get together and resolve that no pastor will ever again have absolute authority. The pendulum swings in the opposite direction, resulting in a committee-led church.

Robert Tucker in *Daedalus* indicates one of the marks of the charismatic leader is the existence of a cult personality.[26] The leader is revered, resulting in a worshipful relationship of the led to the leader. Tucker goes on to indicate that in this setting, members will

---

[26]Tucker, *op. cit.*, p. 747.

most likely imitate their leader, attempting to live the same kind of life-style as he. The pseudo-charismatic leader inflates his personal ego or builds his machine rather than matures his followers.

A pastor who builds the church on his personality rather than through his leadership, is using pseudo-charismatic leadership to build a church. True biblical leadership develops the Christians who are following the pastor. However, when the work is built on the pastor's personality, the attendance declines when the pastor leaves or dies. A pastor who is ministering according to the New Testament standards will develop mature individual Christians and a strong local church. If the church deteriorates after the charismatic pastor leaves or dies, the decline proves he has pseudo-charismatic gifts.

J. Frank Norris built the First Baptist Church, Ft. Worth, Texas, into the largest Sunday School in America. In his early life he apparently employed a biblical charisma but toward the end of his ministry in the church turned into a pseudo-charismatic leadership. In his early life his Sunday School averaged over 5,000 in attendance. After Norris' death attendance declined and today there are less than 500 in attendance.

Another form of pseudo-charismatic leader is found in the individual who desires power and maintains it through advertisement or control, but is not revered by his people. Emmet studied the pseudo-charismatic leaders of Africa, indicating they attracted large crowds, evoked interest, but did not enjoy a sense of specialness in the eyes of the populace.[27] These pseudo-charismatic leaders are usually intensely popular, enjoy close emotional bonds to the followers who make up the majority of the people, yet are narrowly elected to office, and after election use mass media and huge propaganda campaigns to keep their popularity. Emmet indicated their difficulty in collecting taxes was a reflection of the weakness of their leadership.[28]

The pseudo-charismatic leader in Christian circles may give lip service to Jesus Christ but in the final analysis his work, whether in the lives of individuals or in the corporate testimony, does not measure up to New Testament standards. Some pentecostal-type preaching tabernacles in downtown areas fall under this category. These are usually found in abandoned movie houses or similar auditoriums. The pseudo-charismatic leader claims to preach the gospel but the Spirit is lacking. He apparently "uses" the gospel to further his own aims. The New Testament warns against the false shepherd who would deceive God's sheep (John 10; Acts 20:29; James 3:1).

---

[27]Dorothy Emmet, *Function, Purpose and Powers,* (New York: MacMillan, 1958), p. 6.
[28]*Ibid.*

Succession of Charisma

Pastoral leadership has eternal implications for a local church. The pastor should have a stronger place of leadership than the average American church allows. The Scriptures show Christ as the leader of the church and the shepherd of the flock. The pastor is the under-shepherd and is responsible for leading, feeding and protecting the flock. (Acts 20:17-31). Too often, pastors have abdicated their leadership to the board of deacons, tying their hands and curtailing the work of God.

One key problem in a new church is the succession of leadership from the founder of the church to the second pastor. God uses a man to constitute a local church and this man usually becomes the first pastor. Because of his dedication and service, he has a special level of respect among the people. Usually the founding pastor's faith, vision and spiritual sacrifice provide the growth of the church. This pioneer pastor leads many adults to Christ and in the early days before an exhaustive organization, his personal leadership holds the church together. Since the founder has led most of the deacons to Christ, they never question his authority or leadership in meetings. His success gives him some charismatic reverence in the eyes of his followers. When the founder passes off the scene, either through death or by being called to another church, the problem of choosing a successor falls to the shoulders of the deacons. The deacons who have been in the role of secondary leadership suddenly shift into a primary leadership role. Since the deacons give leadership in calling the new pastor, he is responsible to them, placing him in the role of secondary leadership or a subordinate. Thus, a church passes from charismatic leadership to traditional leadership. (see chapter 10).

Lingeman wrote in *New York Times Magazine* that charisma is rarely transferred by heredity or other means.[29] Fidel Castro has charisma but cannot pass it on to his brother Raoul. However, Lingeman believes Ghandi gave it to Nehru. Reinhard Bendix suggests three ways in which the succession of charismatic leadership may take place:[30] (1) A prospective leader who resembles the former charismatic leader is found and appointed. (2) The original charismatic leader designates his own successor. William B. Riley, pastor of the First Baptist Church, Minneapolis, and president of North-western Schools, upon his deathbed pointed to Billy Graham as the

---

[29]Richard Lingeman, "The Greeks Had a Word for It—But What Does It mean?" *New York Times Magazine,* (August 4, 1968), p. 30.

[30]Reinhard Bendix, "Reflections of Charismatic Leadership," *Asian Survey,* No. 7, (June, 1967), p. 307.

successor to the presidency. (3) The disciples can appoint a new leader to take the place of the departed. Though these methods of succession may work in isolated incidents, they usually are unsatisfactory.

Problems of Charismatic Leadership

Charismatic leadership can be stable or unstable, depending upon the maturity of the leader, because direction and momentum of the movement resides in the leader. Charismatic leadership lasts throughout the tenure of the founder. The success of the ten largest churches was in the length of their tenure, 22 years and seven months (now over 25 years tenure). When the pastor is stable and has had a long tenure at the church, there is stability. However, not all pastors are stable enough to build a large church because they are not emotionally secure enough to remain at one church over a long period of time. When the educational program is built upon the unstable personality of the pastor, the program is questionable. Christian education is oriented towards equipping the individual for the work of the ministry (Eph. 4:11,12). One of the oft-repeated axioms of Christian education is that the pastor/minister of Christian education should work himself out of a job, so the laymen can carry on the work of the ministry. The very nature of charismatic leadership is that the pastor leads the church because of his ability. The pastor is the Sunday School superintendent, director of promotion, comptroller and personnel manager wrapped up in one. Christian education usually attempts to decentralize leadership into committees, involving many individuals. Charismatic leadership draws leadership to itself.

1. *The danger of authoritarian leadership.*—Since the charismatic pastor tends to consolidate power around himself, the members must look to him for guidance. Some large churches are built on the personality of the pastor, while others are built on his leadership. When the pastor realizes he is an undershepherd, receiving his authority from the Word of God, he gives an *authoritative* leadership to his church. When the pastor localizes power in his personality, he gives *authoritarian* leadership to his church. Many churches handcuff the gifted pastor and do not give him the freedom to lead the flock. The Bible recognizes the gifted man and teaches that the greater the man, the greater the results. A leader must be authoritative without becoming authoritarian. Because some pastors swing to one extreme, the lay leaders strip the next pastor of his ability to lead. This is a tragic swing to the other extreme because God still works through individuals. The greater the leadership ability of the man, the greater

the work he can accomplish on earth. A pastor with gifted leadership should be working in two directions at the same time. First, he must continually pull more leadership to himself, attempting greater things for God each year. At the same time, he must push (delegate) more authority to his laymen, making them responsible and accountable for the work of God in his church. Most Christian educators advocate the second but deny the first.

2. *Charismatic leadership may produce quantity not quality.*— Charismatic leadership may bring about superficial Christians because these pastors tend to build loyalty to themselves, rather than to Christ. Charismatic leadership tends toward centralized heirarchy, hence it may manipulate individuals. The church should be built on a solid foundation of doctrine and knowledge of the Word of God. A church should be based on quality, where each layman, using his abilities given to him by God, ministers in evangelism and edification. Wayne Lukens in his thesis advocates that charismatic leadership is most effective in producing numerical growth, but is most negligent in producing maturity in followers. However, this point is only theory and cannot be proved. Lack of quality lives may be a result of pseudo-charismatic leadership, while New Testament charisma may produce maturity among the followers.

3. *Charismatic leadership usually attracts the disenfranchised fringe area of society.*—David Moberg in *The Church As a Social Institution* argues that factors of social migration, social disorientation, social change, conflict, and socio-economic disenfranchisement contributes to the rise of new religious bodies, especially through charismatic leadership. These factors could certainly be labeled social distress, and any church built upon these factors alone would be the result of pseudo-charismatic leadership, certainly not New Testament charisma. The deeper question lies, what caused these above-mentioned unstable social conditions? If sin is the ultimate problem with the universe, then the pastor must approach social problems from the point of view of the gospel.

The Scriptures teach that the person undergoing social mobility is the greatest candidate for salvation. A man goes through mobility when he moves his home (geographical mobility) or changes his job (economic mobility), or his wife has a baby (psychological mobility), or there is a death in the family (existential mobility). A man in mobility is more concerned about ultimate questions because change brings about a threat to his existence, hence he is a candidate for the gospel. Also, the poor in housing projects or in the ghettos are not insulated from the anxieties of life nor are they isolated in the protective custody of suburbia. Since they daily face the ultimate questions and dilemmas of life, perhaps they are greater candidates for the gospel. The New Testament charismatic pastor has a great opportunity to present salvation to them because they will be responsive to his leadership.

The charismatic leader stands over against the established society and preaches a return to former values. Liturgy and ritualism is the catalyst which holds many traditional American congregations together. The members of typical middle-class congregations are likely to look to former rituals as a major support for their faith. Therefore, the pastor who religiously reacts against the general culture in the U.S. usually preaches an antiliturgical and antiformal message. Therefore, congregations of charismatic leaders are usually antiformal, which was the case in the ten largest Sunday Schools.

4. *Members are only personal disciples of the charismatic leader.*—Max Weber in *The Theory of Social and Economic Organization* describes how the charismatic leader organizes his staff. Subordinates cannot occupy leadership positions in the traditional sense of organized government. By this, Weber meant a subordinate is traditionally chosen for his ability or past competency. The staff member of the charismatic leader is usually chosen on his personal devotion to the leader. Staff members are judged by their enthusiasm for the cause, and personal loyalty to the leader, or both. The staff members of the ten largest Sunday Schools were not always chosen because of their theological training in a Bible college or a theological seminary, but were chosen because of their loyalty to the local church, and success as layman in that church.

The pastor is the undershepherd and responsible for the growth of the flock. But as the flock grows in size, the leader is limited in time, by geographical boundaries and energy to carry out all of the ministry to the flock. Therefore, he delegates responsibilities to a subordinate. In the cast of ministering to the youth of the congregation, a youth pastor is hired. The question arises, "Does the youth pastor work for the board of Christian education, the deacon board, or the pastor?" There is no question in charismatic-led churches— the youth pastor is responsible to the senior minister. The position of the youth pastor is described as, "The youth pastor is the extension of the pastoral ministry into the lives of he young people." Therefore, the youth pastor must have extreme loyalty to work both *for* and *with* the senior pastor. He must see himself as a person under authority, yet a minister of Jesus Christ; he must use all of his abilities to accomplish success in his youth department.

Conclusion

On the basis of sociological research and a study of large Sunday Schools, it has been determined that the principles of charismatic leadership contribute to the rapid growth of the Sunday School in a local church. Probably the most fertile soil for rapid growth would be the marginal and mobile groups of our society. The working class would seem more susceptible to the successful strong leader than the middle or upper class. This principle was taught and practiced by Jesus Christ.

The type of preaching that would appeal to the masses is a theology of hope in the future and expectation of the present working of the power of God. The pastor should have simple faith in God, a strong will to carry out the dictates of God, and yet be a loving, kind leader. He must be financially capable of managing large amounts of money and of inspiring people to instant action. The pastor must have evidence of a special calling of God upon his life to the ministry, qualifying him to preach the gospel. This qualification arises above all other worldly success, even academic training. Once the pastor has fufilled the spiritual expectation of a church and has given evidence of the special hand of God upon his life, he could be classified as having New Testament charisma. He would not then be able to inspire people because he has charisma *but* his ability to inspire people is evidence of his charisma. When he has such evidence, he qualifies to be "the chief administrator both in the church and Sunday School and/ or the Christian education program of the church."

Statistics
America's Fastest Growing Churches

	Calvary Heights Baptist Temple St. Louis, Mo.	Thomas Road Baptist Church Lynchburg, Va.	United Baptist Church San Jose, Calif.	Indianapolis Baptist Temple Indianapolis, Ind.	Northside Baptist Church Charlotte, N.C.
PASTOR					
Age	35	38	29	39	49
Tenure	2¼ yrs.	16 yrs.	5 yrs.	16 yrs.	17 yrs.
Education	Th.G., B.D., B.A.	Lynchburg College Baptist Bible College Honorary degrees from Bob Jones	Pillsbury Baptist College (3 yr.), Western Baptist Bible College (1 yr.), San Francisco Theol. Seminary	Baptist Bible College, Th.G.; Honorary degrees from B.B.C., 1970, Bob Jones, 1971	Tenn. Temple Th.G., D.D.
CHURCH					
Membership	300	11,000 (approx.)	1485	5547	3298
Income (last yr.)	$55,000	$2,000,000 (aprox. audit not in hand)	$176,956	$438,118.63	$414,617.65
Est. Value, bldg. and property	$1,100,000	$7,000,000	$500,000	$1,724,588	$995,400
Seating capacity	400	3200	600	3000	1450
Off-street parking spaces	140	1500	200	Not Known	750
SUNDAY SCHOOL					
Enrollment	275	6,000	3450	9610 (Approx.)	5000
Workers	29	286	70	315	100
No. of Buses	4	58	20	29	23 (run 18)
Average No. Riders	Not available	1600	731	987 (1971)	700
Pub. of Materials	David C. Cook	Write own	Baptist Publications	Write own	0-6th grade—Bap. Pub. Jr. Hi.-Adult-Write own
VISITATION Plan followed	Ladies, morning. Church & Staff, evg. Host home calling in various areas of city.	Teachers & bus. wkrs. visit 3-5 hrs. weekly. Organized bus visitation Saturday, 9:00 a.m.	All-Church & Youth, Thur. p.m. Ladies, Fri. a.m. Bus calling, Sat. Staff & S.S.—all week	Organized Visitation Thursday evening and Saturday morning.	Mon. night—Couples & Men Tues. a.m.—Ladies & any men who can Sat. afternoon—bus & S.S. teachers
No. of laymen who visit weekly	20	200	90	250	175
No. of calls by laymen weekly	40	2500 homes	1275	2500	1000
Calls by staff wkly.	50	1250	60	200	25 each
Full-time staff	3	120	10	22	13 (Church only)